Blackstone's

Student Police Officer Workbook

Blackstone's

Student Police Officer Workbook

Edited by

Dr Robin Bryant

and

Sarah Bryant

Contributors:

Dr Bryn Caless, Kevin Lawton-Barrett, Roy Murphy, Robert Underwood, and Dr Dominic Wood

OXFORD
UNIVERSITY PRESS

OXFORD
UNIVERSITY PRESS

Great Clarendon Street, Oxford OX2 6DP

Oxford University Press is a department of the University of Oxford.
It furthers the University's objective of excellence in research, scholarship,
and education by publishing worldwide in

Oxford New York

Auckland Cape Town Dar es Salaam Hong Kong Karachi
Kuala Lumpur Madrid Melbourne Mexico City Nairobi
New Delhi Shanghai Taipei Toronto

With offices in

Argentina Austria Brazil Chile Czech Republic France Greece
Guatemala Hungary Italy Japan Poland Portugal Singapore
South Korea Switzerland Thailand Turkey Ukraine Vietnam

Oxford is a registered trade mark of Oxford University Press
in the UK and in certain other countries

Published in the United States
by Oxford University Press Inc., New York

British Library Cataloguing in Publication Data

Data available

Typeset by MPS Limited, A Macmillan Company
Printed in Great Britain
on acid-free paper by
Ashford Colour Press Limited, Gosport, Hampshire

ISBN 978-0-19-957768-2

1 3 5 7 9 10 8 6 4 2

Acknowledgements

Robin and Sarah Bryant

To Paul, for reading through some of the scenarios and observing that 'It's not as good as *The Wire* is it?', before going back to the cricket.

Bryn Caless

I would like to thank Clare for her forbearance and support (as always).

Kevin Lawton-Barrett

My wife Zoe for her continued patience and training in Light Rooms, Chief Inspector Mark Harrison and the staff at Canterbury Police Station, especially Sarah Harding, for lending me their new custody area for photographs.

Roy Murphy

To Stephanie, in recognition of the tolerance and patience of a long-suffering detective's wife, who was always promised that he would find more time for 'us'—but now finds me locked away, pounding a keyboard, and with my nose in a book.

Robert (Bob) Underwood

I would like to thank my fellow contributors for their expert and complementary additions to the scenarios I wrote in this Workbook. I would also like to show my appreciation to Sarah Bryant for her contributions, as well as her painstaking and careful editing of my original material and also to Robin for his editing skills. Thanks also go to my colleague Barry Spruce for making a number of professional recommendations and, finally, my family to whom I owe a great deal of gratitude for their continued support and patience whilst I worked alone for long periods of time.

Contents

Introduction

In the last few years there has been an increase of regular public blogs written by serving police officers giving an account of their day-to-day work and particularly the bureaucratic frustrations of the job. An example is the online blog of 'inspectorgadget' (presumably a pseudonym) dated 7 July 2009, which informs the reader that:

> Here on F Division, we have taken on board the message that our prime reasons for existing in 2009 are:
> 1. To be terribly nice to everyone all of the time, especially criminals.
> 2. To help the local council pick up dog poo.
> 3. To stop children playing outside and being children.
>
> (Police Inspector Blog, 2009)

Several collections of blogs have even been published in book form, and serialized in national newspapers, notably those of 'Pc Copperfield' (aka Stuart Davidson, formerly a Pc with Staffordshire police).

An earlier 'official' report in 2001 (Home Office, 2001) found that police officers do indeed, spend almost as much time in the police station (doing 'paperwork' and processing suspects for custody and possible prosecution) as they spend on the streets. More recently, in 2008, Sir Ronnie Flanagan also found that 'risk aversion' was the cause of much unnecessary bureaucracy in police work (Flanagan, 2008). However, Flanagan also noted the change in demands on the police service in the last 30 years or so, and there can be little doubt that 'the job' is more complex and demanding than at any time in recent history. Certainly, the work of the police officer is an energy-sapping combination of tedium mixed with excitement, the routine shattered by the unexpected. These demands are particularly acute for the student police officer, who not only has (by law) to perform the duties of a Constable (after attestation, which normally occurs in the first few weeks after joining) but also to spend two years proving his or her competence.

Blackstone's Student Police Officer Workbook consists of eight chapters that describe, in narrative form, a number of the routine, and a few of the less common, police tasks. Each chapter has an introduction, a knowledge check with multiple choice questions, a scenario with questions, the answers to the scenario questions, and a concluding puzzle as a review.

The material covered in this book will certainly be of value to those preparing for a career in the police and students undertaking further and higher education courses in police studies, forensic investigation (or forensic science), and criminology. The content might also be of interest to a more general readership interested in the work of the police officer in England and Wales in 2010. No doubt some readers will be surprised by the complexities involved in even the most straightforward-looking police task. It is no longer, and perhaps never was, simply a case of 'You're nicked!'

The scenarios reflect some of the realities of policing for the student police officer and, taken together, cover many of the situations (both routine and non-routine) that the student police officer is likely to encounter during their two years of training. In many scenarios the student police officer is accompanied by a qualified and more experienced colleague and the student might play only a part in the early stages of an enquiry or response. This reflects the reality of training, particularly at the stage before a student police officer is permitted to undertake Independent Patrol.

We have attempted to make the scenarios as realistic as possible: indeed, the skills and practices portrayed (although anonymized) are derived from the authors' operational experience of policing. This means that not all information will be available to you at the outset, the situations are often confusing, apparently contradictory or unclear, and the answers to questions are not always clear cut. It also means that the police officers are also portrayed as human beings, and hence make the odd mistake, are sometimes frustrated, and, by and large, use ordinary language when speaking (when not using police jargon!).

Taken together the eight scenarios cover the following themes:

- Risk assessment and heath and safety.
- Communication skills.
- Upholding human rights.
- Forensic awareness.
- Use of criminal intelligence.
- Arrest and detention.
- Reporting and record keeping.
- Working with other agencies (eg the CPS).
- Competence and assessment (eg the relevant Skills for Justice NOS elements).

Whilst every one of the eight scenarios at least touches on all of the themes listed above, there are particular emphases in each, and these are listed in the table below. (A tick indicates that the theme is a major aspect of the scenario.)

	Risk assessment and heath and safety	Communication skills	Upholding human rights	Forensic awareness	Use of criminal intelligence	Arrest and detention	Reporting and record keeping	Working with other agencies (eg the CPS)	Competence and assessment
The Handy Store	✓	✓	✓	✓	✓		✓		
The Burcher's		✓		✓	✓		✓	✓	✓
Dovestone Road	✓	✓			✓	✓	✓	✓	
The Stella Estate	✓	✓	✓		✓	✓	✓		✓
St Edward's School				✓		✓	✓	✓	
The Railway	✓	✓		✓		✓	✓	✓	
Beckett's Fishing Lakes	✓			✓			✓	✓	✓
Mortesbury's		✓	✓			✓	✓	✓	✓

Every scenario is preceded by a 'knowledge check' of multiple choice questions. In the main these are self-check questions on legislation or procedure that relate to the scenario that follows. It is advisable to check your answers at the end of each chapter before attempting the questions within the scenario itself.

The scenarios usually finish at the point where the police officers are likely to complete their shifts. Of course, this is not normally also the end of the processes involved and each scenario has a short postscript that explains the likely long-term outcomes.

We also provide answers to the questions raised within each scenario. These answers are not intended to be prescriptive: in many cases there is no single right or wrong answer to a question, and if you are a student police officer you should always be guided by local force policy. However, the questions and answers are a good starting point to ensure that you are familiar with the issues involved and the skills required. In a number of answers reference is made to *Blackstone's Student Police Officer Handbook 2010*, also published by Oxford University Press. The Handbook provides further detail and explanation (but it remains entirely possible to complete the Workbook without reference to the Handbook). Each chapter concludes with a short puzzle related to the legislation and police procedures covered in the scenario.

We would be grateful for feedback on the contents of this Workbook, including any proposed corrections.

The authors of this Workbook have taken care to ensure the accuracy of the information contained within. However, neither the authors nor the publisher can accept any responsibility for any actions taken, or not taken, as a consequence of the information it contains. Any resemblance to people, locations, or events is entirely unintentional and coincidental.

References throughout the Workbook to IPLDP materials have not been reviewed or endorsed by the IPLDP Central Authority Executive Services.

List of Icons

Throughout the scenarios various icons are used to indicate to the reader where particular issues apply. The meaning of these symbols is as follows:

Forensic awareness is required, for instance to preserve delicate evidence or to prevent contamination from other sources.

The event portrayed in the scenario could provide an opportunity for the student officer to demonstrate competence, either directly to an accompanying officer or as stimulus material for the student officer to use in assessed written work.

Of course all officers need to have a constant regard for the wide diversity of people they encounter, but some situations require particular attention in terms of respect for diversity.

The health and safety of officers and the people they encounter is paramount. This symbol draws attention to particular aspects of health and safety.

In the heat of the moment an officer, despite his or her best intentions may be forgetful or be tempted to take procedural short cuts. The reader's attention is drawn to the very few instances where such event or considerations are portrayed in these scenarios.

And finally, just a reminder that a pen or pencil is required to jot down your responses to the knowledge check questions.

This shows that the words are spoken over a telecommunications system such as Airwaves, rather than face to face.

This indicates an officer's thoughts at the time.

1 | The Handy Store

�footprint forensic awareness required

✓ assessment opportunity

☺ diversity issues

▲ health and safety

▽? questionable practice

✎ a pen or pencil is required

Introduction

This scenario illustrates a very common crime, that of damage to property. Home Office research (Home Office, 2009a) using the British Crime Survey (BCS) and police recorded crime figures suggests that the majority of crimes are property-related. Vandalism accounts for 26 per cent of all BCS crime (two-thirds of which is vehicle vandalism) and criminal damage accounts for 20 per cent of the crimes recorded by the police. This equates to over 936,000 reports during the period 2008/09.

Here we describe and discuss the investigation into a spate of broken shop windows in a medium-sized town. Instead of simply reacting to calls by taking details for a crime report, the attending officers, colleagues, and supervisors in this scenario proactively investigate the latest incident of criminal damage, and successfully draw it to a conclusion using their available powers. A variety of policing skills, such as house-to-house enquiries and the use of targeted area searches to inform the investigation, are also portrayed. As with so many other incidents, the scenario reinforces the importance of the 'golden hour' after the offence has been committed. This is the most critical time in which to locate suspects, and to preserve and collect evidence.

Knowledge Check

✎ Before you look at this scenario, check your understanding of the underpinning legislation involved by attempting the following knowledge check. For the multiple choice questions K1 to K8 write down **one** of the letters a, b, c, or d as the answer to the question. Check your answers at the end of this chapter before beginning the scenario.

K 1 Which of the following **are not** prohibited articles for the purposes of making a search under s 1(1)(b) of the PACE Act 1984?

    a) Fireworks
    b) Offensive weapons
    c) Drugs
    d) Bladed or sharply pointed articles

K 2 Under what circumstances can you use s 1 of the PACE Act 1984 to search a person inside a dwelling or place of residence?

    a) When you have reasonable grounds to suspect the person is in possession of stolen or prohibited articles
    b) When the person is trespassing and does not have the consent of the resident to be there
    c) Under no circumstances at all
    d) Only if you have complied with GOWISELY

K 3 A person you are searching under s 1 of the PACE Act 1984 resists your attempts to search him/her after you have sought their cooperation to do so. What should you do?

    a) Give up and walk away
    b) Give them a receipt as it ended up being only a stop and account
    c) Use reasonable force to continue the search under s 117 of the PACE Act 1984
    d) None of the above

K 4 Which of the following offences can be racially aggravated under the Crime and Disorder Act 1998?

    a) Section 1 of the Criminal Damage Act 1971 (damage)
    b) Section 1(2) of the Criminal Damage Act 1971 (criminal damage, life endangered)
    c) Section 1(2) of the Criminal Damage Act 1971 (threats to damage)
    d) All of the above

K 5 In what ways can a suspect commit a s 3 Criminal Damage Act 1971 offence, that of possessing an article with intent to cause criminal damage?

    a) To have the article for use by her or himself
    b) To have the article to cause somebody else to use it
    c) To have the article to permit somebody else to use it
    d) All of the above

K 6 There is a list of offences under the Theft Act 1968 for which s 1 of the PACE Act 1984 can be used to search for prohibited articles used in the course of, or in connection with, committing those offences. Which one of the following offences is **not** included in that list?

    a) Burglary
    b) Taking a conveyance
    c) Robbery
    d) Theft

K 7 Which of the following factors **cannot** be used to form reasonable grounds for the application of s 1 of the PACE Act 1984?

    a) Previous convictions
    b) Age
    c) Appearance
    d) All of the above

K8 Which of the following 'excuses' would prevent a person from being found guilty of s 1 Criminal Damage Act 1971 (damage), s 1(2) Criminal Damage Act 1971 (criminal damage, life endangered), and s 1(2) Criminal Damage Act 1971 (threats to damage)?

  a) Lawful
  b) Legalized
  c) Legitimate
  d) Legal

The Handy Store Scenario

During the briefing at the start of an afternoon shift of patrol officers in Maidbury, the following information is given to the patrols via an electronic briefing. The information has been collated by the Research and Development Team at Maidbury Police Station using crime reports and intelligence.

Criminal Damage to Shop Fronts

- 4 Shop premises
- All front windows
- 17.00–22.00 each day for the past four days
- Location—Maidbury High Road area
- Current value in excess of £8,000

- Patrols requested to default to these hotspots between these times
- Local intelligence indicates the suspects are firing the ball bearings from a vehicle (details unknown) and live in the Stella housing estate

Q1 What offences under the Criminal Damage Act 1971 may have been committed in relation to these incidents and what powers under the PACE Act 1984 are available in relation to these offences?

At 21.00, officers Barden and Ferez (MA 10), are on mobile patrol in a marked police vehicle in Maidbury town centre when they receive the following message from Control over airwaves:

'Control calling MA 10, please attend the Handy Store, Maidbury High Road, Maidbury, see the owner Mr Patel reporting damage to his shop window by a thrown object. Suspects believed to be a driver and two passengers in a blue hatchback car, no descriptions, no index number. Direction of travel of the vehicle believed to be towards the Maidbury Industrial Estate.'

Two other patrols hear the deployment of MA 10 over Airwaves and volunteer to provide back-up if requested.

Q2   Where should the other patrols go?

The two officers attend the scene of the alleged crime and are met by Mr Patel at the front door of his corner shop. The shop window is badly damaged; there is a hole, with six large radiating cracks. They introduce themselves to Mr Patel. Pc Ferez takes a closer look at the window.

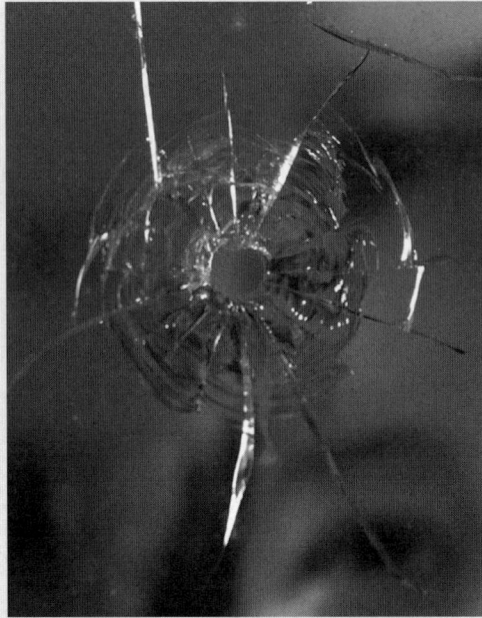

Depending on the type of glass, it will break in different ways when hit by a projectile. Here, the glass was 'float glass' so a neat hole has been made, but the radiating cracks mean there is a risk that large shards of glass may fall out, and these could cause serious injury or worse. Toughened glass would have shattered into thousands of tiny cubes and would be safer for a large area of glass.

. . . looks like float glass to me . . . shouldn't it be toughened glass for a shop window? . . . must check that later . . .

Q3   What is the responsibility of any police officer at the scene of such a crime?

Pc Ferez begins to draw a plan of the crime scene in his PNB and Pc Barden takes the lead in relation to the victim.

Q4   Consider Pc Ferez's sketches of the crime scene. What further details should he include on these diagrams?

21.02	Attended at Handy Store, Maidbury High Road,
	Maidbury. Saw Mr Patel. Complaint of criminal damage
	to shop window approx 5m x 2.5m. Hole in the middle approx
	2cm in diameter.—————————————————

till

window   *hole*   *shelves*

front door

Pc Barden	Can you tell me what happened please?
Mr Patel	I was inside the shop clearing up behind the till when I heard a loud bang. I thought I had been shot at it was so loud—I feel a bit shaken up really—it was so loud, but they've gone now . . .
Pc Barden	Do you feel well enough to give me some details for a crime report?
Mr Patel	Yes of course, go ahead.

As she questions Mr Edsen, Pc Barden imagines the first page of the typed up version of the crime report; this helps her to remember what to ask.

Maidbury Police ✦

Offence	CRIMINAL DAMAGE

Victim Details

Surname	PATEL		Forename(s)	SANJAY	
Gender	MALE	DoB	25/04/60		
Flat number	N/A	Building name	HANDY STORES	House number	N/A
Road name	MAIDBURY HIGH RD	District	N/A		
Town	MAIDBURY	County	MAIDSHIRE		
Post code	MD14 4LP	Telephone numbers: 0118118 743509			
Home: N/A		Business: N/A		Mobile: N/A	
Self defined ethnicity	ASIAN BRITISH				
Occupation	SHOP OWNER				
Injuries	N/A				
Previous victim	NO				
VSS accepted	Yes No	Victim Care leaflet given	Yes No		

Crime Details

Reporting officer	Pc BARDEN				
Station/department	Maidbury	Database ref. no.	1454/10		
Time crime reported	21.02	Date	10/05/09		
Crime committed on/between	Day	Mon	Date	10/05/09	Time	20.55

Venue Details

Flat number	N/A	Building name	HANDY STORES	House number	N/A
Road name	MAIDBURY HIGH RD	District	N/A		
Town	MAIDBURY	County	MAIDSHIRE		
Post code	MD14 4LP	Description	GROCERY STORE		

Modus Operandi Details

At the material time, unknown offender(s) drove past shop in town centre in unknown vehicle and fired a ball bearing from an unknown source at shop front window causing the window to be irreparably damaged.

Q5   What further details are likely to be required to complete the rest of the report?

While Pc Barden obtains the details for the crime report from Mr Patel she also confirms with him what he saw of the incident. He repeats what the officers know already from the call they received over Airwaves, and cannot provide many more details.

Q6   If Mr Patel was behind the window at the time the ball bearing was fired, could any other offence under the Criminal Damage Act 1971 be considered?

Mr Patel invites Pc Barden to perch on the stool behind the till so that she can fill in the rest of the crime report form. Mr Patel answers her questions quietly. He seems distracted and keeps glancing out of the window, sighing every so often. His wife comes downstairs with a dustpan and brush but he waves his hand at her impatiently to go away. Pc Barden writes as fast as she can while thinking ahead to the next question.

> *... is there a racist slant to this? ... well, he hasn't mentioned it ... I'll presume not ...*

Q7 What standards of professional behaviour has Pc Barden failed to reach here in relation to making this presumption?

Q8 Who decides if an incident is a racial one?

Q9 Can a s 1 Criminal Damage Act 1971 offence be racially aggravated?

Fortunately, Pc Barden's professionalism gets the better of her:

Pc Barden   Do you think your window was broken because of your ethnicity?

Mr Patel   Do you mean my race? No, no ... not at all. There's been a few other shops that had the same thing and they're owned by ... all sorts of people, no ... no way.

Pc Barden   Yes, there have been quite a few incidents of this sort reported recently ... Oh yes, as a victim of crime we have these two leaflets for you. This one, 'Victims of Crime', is produced by the Home Office and the other is from Victim Support. Have a read through them in your own time—they give some useful information and contact details of where to get further help if you need it.

Details about Victim Support

Your local Victim Support Scheme is:

You can also contact the Victim Supportline on:
0845 30 30 900

Or, if you prefer, you can write to the Victim Supportline at:
PO Box 11431, London SW9 6ZH

Further information about the help available to you as a victim of crime can also be found at **www.cjsonline.org**

Home Office
BUILDING A SAFE, JUST AND TOLERANT SOCIETY

Published by Home Office Communication Directorate.
May 2003. CC1.

Victims of Crime –
the help and advice that's available

CJS   The criminal justice system

The police will pass information about you to Victim Support so that they can offer you help and support, unless you ask the police not to.

Q10   Why might this leaflet be of limited use to the Patels?

Pc Barden	Anything else you want to say before we leave? Have you made arrangements to make the premises secure?
Mr Patel	No, I'll have to see to that—just a minute, while we were waiting for you I found this by the window—do you need it?

Mr Patel picks up a single ball bearing from a small dish on the back counter and shows it to Pc Barden.

Such large ball bearings are relatively unusual. The officers might consider investigating how and where the offenders obtained them to help to identify the suspects.

Q11   How will the ball bearing be referred to in any subsequent evidence?

Q12   How should the ball bearing be initially packaged at this stage, and then later in the investigation?

Meanwhile, MA 20 Pc Kilt and Pc Holma begin their house to house enquiries on Maidbury High Road, but on the opposite side of the road to the Handy Store—where they feel people would have had the best opportunity to witness the incident. They knock on the front door of each house. If there is a reply, they reassure the occupant that there is nothing to worry about before the officers explain that they are investigating an incident of criminal damage which occurred at the Handy Store a short while ago, and are trying to find out more about what happened.

Q13   In relation to the Criminal Procedure and Investigations Act 1996 Code of Practice and the Crown Prosecution Service (CPS) Disclosure Manual, what details, if any, must the officers record in relation to the enquiries?

> Having crossed to the same side of Maidbury High Road as the Handy Store, Pc Kilt and Pc Holma finally strike lucky with their house to house enquiries. In the terraced house next to Mr Patel's shop, a Mr Edsen was in his front room when the incident took place, and says he saw 'everything' and can remember all the details. The officers are invited into the house and led into the front room.

Officers should always be on the look out for any item or object that might be relevant to the case. Here, the attentive officers were able to spot the possible significance of these items amongst the clutter of the Edsens' living room.

Q14   Look at the above photograph. In relation to the Criminal Procedure and Investigations Act 1996, what 'material', ie objects in this photograph, can you see that may have some bearing on the evidence that Mr Edsen is able to supply, and what questions, if any, should the officers ask him in relation to the material/objects?

Pc Kilt draws a plan of the scene in his PNB while Pc Holma interviews Mr Edsen.

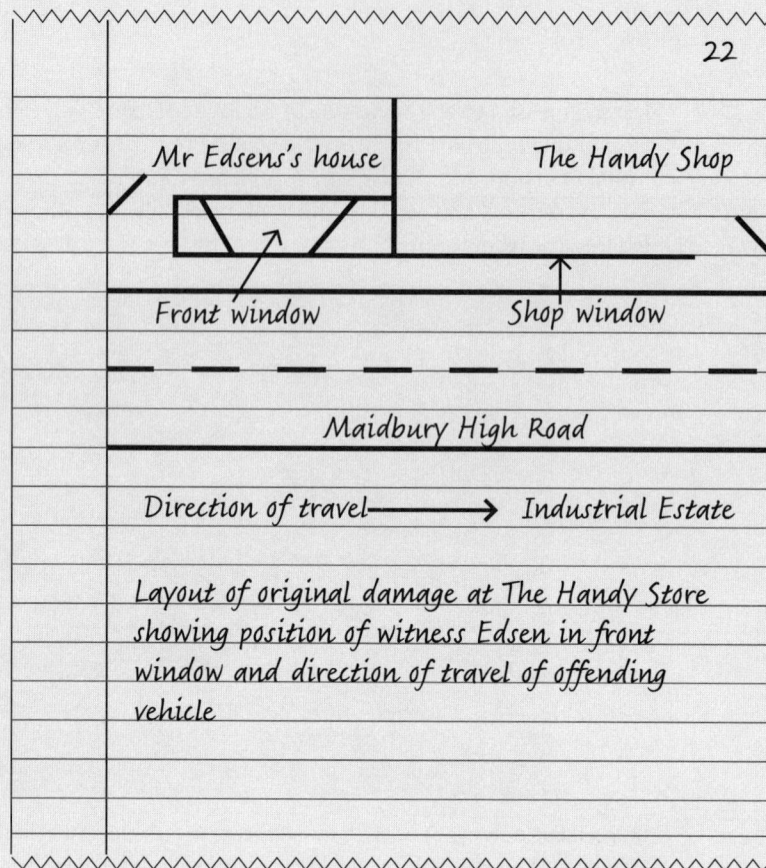

22

Mr Edsens's house   The Handy Shop

Front window   Shop window

Maidbury High Road

Direction of travel ——————→ Industrial Estate

Layout of original damage at The Handy Store showing position of witness Edsen in front window and direction of travel of offending vehicle

Mr Edsen explains to Pc Holma that, after he had finished some gardening, his wife had been helping him to get a splinter out of his finger using the magnifying glass by the window but had just put the hand lens down to go and turn the kettle off. (Pc Holma begins making notes in his PNB.) Mr Edsen said that he looked out of the window and saw a blue hatchback in the road outside, and it slowed down as it approached his house.

Pc Holma	Any particular reason for looking out of the window at that particular moment?
Mr Edsen	I heard the car coming. It's one of those cars with the loud music that you can't help but hear—before you can even see it . . .
Pc Holma	So you heard the car before you saw it?

Mr Edsen then went on to say that the rear nearside passenger window was open and that a 'young lad' was inside. The 'lad' then leaned out with a sling shot at arm's length, pulled back the pocket, and let it go. Mr Edsen said he ducked down immediately and also heard a very loud bang from the shop next door and the car sped off. When he looked out again he saw that the car had stopped further down the road and the youth who had fired the catapult got out and quickly ran into an alleyway across the other side of the road and disappeared from view.

Having heard Mr Edsen's account of the incident, Pc Holma realizes that recognition and/or identification of the suspect in the car may well be an issue in the investigation at some point in the future.

Q15 What checklist of information should Pc Holma obtain from Mr Edsen regarding the identification of the suspect? (Consider the case of *R v Turnbull*.)

Pc Holma knows that he needs to get more detail from Mr Edsen, particularly a description of the youth he saw firing the sling shot. Pc Holma gestures towards the glasses and asks Mr Edsen if they're his long distance glasses; Mr Edsen says not. They sit down on the edge of the sofa and Pc Holma suppresses a sneeze, and looks around for something to rest on while he writes. Mr Edsen pulls a small coffee table across, and moves the TV listing magazines onto a chair. Pc Holma gets ready to start writing.

. . . hope there's no cats here . . . my allergy's getting worse . . . don't want to be sneezing all over the place . . .

Q16 How should the description given by Mr Edsen be recorded (to ensure it complies with PACE Code of Practice D para 3.1 in relation to suspect identification by a witness)?

Pc Holma   I'm going to ask you to give me a description of the youth in the back of the car who later got out and ran down the alleyway. Can you clarify whether the person was a male or female, and tell me precisely what they were wearing on their head.

Pc Holma records Mr Edsen's replies in his PNB.

Q17 What type of questions and what style of questioning should be avoided? What questions and what style of questioning will illicit the most amount of information from Mr Edsen?

Q18 Suggest one technique that Pc Holma could use to ensure he gets as full a description of the suspect as possible.

Q19   Looking at Pc Holma's PNB entry, can you suggest one aspect of the suspect's physical features that Pc Holma has not covered?

hat	A male and no hat —————————————————
Hair	Fair, pulled back into a pony tail which was about six
	inches long and hanging down his neck at the back
Face	High forehead, bushy eyebrows, quite big ears,
	large nose, spotty face, large mouth, no facial hair,
	pointed chin, hollow cheeks, obvious cheek bones.————
clothing	Black t-shirt with some white design on the front ——
	(seen while suspect was seated in car) and dark
	trousers (seen only from a distance when suspect
	ran into alleyway)—————————————————
Hands/	Dirty hands, long thin fingers and dirty arms could
arms	be a mechanic or works on engines. No big rings on
	fingers—————————————————————
Sling	The 'Y' made of a silvery metal , red thick elastic and
shot	a black pocket —————————————————
Car	Blue hatchback, dirty, old, missing hub cap on the
	rear nearside, part index N363... make unknown———————

Pc Holma   How long ago did this all happen?

Mr Edsen   Well, you lot were here pretty quick, so it can only be about five or ten minutes ago.

Pc Holma requests Control give him the opportunity to make a broadcast to other patrols in the area and says:

> 'Broadcast, broadcast, your attention is drawn to the following vehicle, a hatchback colour blue, dirty, with a missing hub cap on the rear nearside, part index N363, made off from a criminal damage in Maidbury High Road towards the industrial estate between five and ten minutes ago. One white male in the rear decamped from the vehicle approximately 100 metres west of the Handy Store, Maidbury High Road into an alleyway on the north side. Male described as having fair hair in a pony tail, high forehead, bushy eyebrows, large nose, spotty face, no facial hair, pointed chin, pronounced cheek bones, stocky build, broad shoulders, dirty hands and arms wearing a black T-shirt and dark trousers. May be in possession of a silver metalled sling shot.'

Mr Edsen	Sorry officer, what was that?
Pc Holma	Nothing sir, just communicating . . . with my colleagues.

On hearing this, MA 10 Pc Barden requests permission to speak over Airwaves in order to add to the broadcast and says:

'Vehicle or suspect on foot may be in possession of one or more ball bearings approximately two centimetres in diameter.'

Two police officers, Pc Twain and Pc Lamst (MA 30) are deployed to conduct a search for the suspect who left the car.

Q20 Where would the logical start point be for Pc Twain and Pc Lamst to begin such a search?

As the two officers drive past the end of a cul-de-sac, they slow down and lean forward to get a good view past the trees. In the distance they spot a person who seems to fit the description broadcast by Pc Holma. He is walking away from the officers, at quite a brisk pace. Pc Twain asks his fellow officer to turn into the side street and stop the patrol vehicle about half way along. Pc Lamst is careful to drive slowly and quietly. As they approach on foot, they see that the person is a young male who matches the description perfectly. The suspect glances back and the officers know that he has noticed them. The suspect slows down, adopting a more leisurely pace. The officers call him over and introduce themselves.

Pc Twain	Hello there. Could you tell me please where you have just come from?
Young man	Nowhere . . . I've just left my friend Jason . . . we've been . . . swimming and I'm walking home. If it's the window you're asking about, I didn't see who broke it.

Q21 If this was the sum total of the encounter, does it need to be recorded to satisfy PACE Codes of Practice?

Q22 Was the response given to Pc Twain of any consequence?

Q23 Where should Pc Twain record what the young man said?

Pc Twain writes down what has been said.

		25
21.15		Millo Road Maidbury, stopped male and asked him to
		account for his presence in the area. Male, white,
		5'8" fair hair in a pony tail, high forehead, large nose,
		bushy eyebrows, spotty face, dirty hands and arms
		broad shoulders, pointed chin, pronounced cheek
		bones, stocky build, wearing a black t-shirt————————
21.16	Q	Could you tell me please where you have just come
		from? ————————————————————————————————————
	R	Nowhere like. I've just left my friend Jason ,we've
		been swimming and I'm walking home. I didn't see
		who broke the window honest. M Twain PC92643,
		S Lamst PC 87954— —————————————————————
	Q	Please read over the entry and check whether it is a
		true record of what we both said. If you agree that
		it is a true record, please write the words I agree
		that this is a correct record of what was said and
		sign your name here———————————————————————
	R	I agree that this is a correct record of what
		was said. Tom Mayler —————————————————

Meanwhile, Pc Lamst speaks to Pc Holma over Airwaves and informs him that they have stopped an individual fitting the description of the person who ran off from the car. Pc Twain then searches Mayler.

Q24 What could Pc Twain do apart from searching Mayler?

Q25 Under what legislation does Pc Twain conduct the search?

Q26 Give examples of the 'reasonable grounds' for the search in these circumstances.

Q27 In what way(s) must Pc Twain comply with the Codes of Practice and s 2 of the PACE Act 1984 for this search?

Pc Twain tries to comply with the Codes of Practice, but his concentration slips:

> *'My name is Pc 104553 Twain and I am from Maidbury Police Station. I am detaining you for the purpose of carrying out a search under s 1 of the Police and Criminal Evidence Act 1984. The grounds of my search are that your description is very similar to that of a young male provided by a witness to some damage caused to a window in Maidbury High Road a short while ago. Without prompting you have already mentioned in passing that you did not see who broke the window and although we are approximately half a mile away from the crime scene, it would be reasonable to believe that you have had sufficient time to walk to this location from the crime scene. The object of my search is to look for articles which could have been used to damage a window.'*

Q28   Pc Twain has not provided all the information required under the Codes of Practice. What has he left out?

Q29   What are the safety implications to be considered during such a search of persons?

Pc Lamst puts away his PNB and pen, ready to 'support' Pc Twain during the search, albeit not too obviously. He acts as 'cover' officer by constantly observing Mayler (trying to anticipate his movements—he may suddenly decide to resist) and to prevent injury to his colleague.

Pc Twain checks the ground around Mayler's feet before and during the search in case anything falls down during the process. Having systematically searched his top half, Pc Twain moves the back of his hand over Mayler's right jacket pocket and feels a small, hard, spherical object. Having explained what he is about to do, Pc Twain takes hold of Mayler's wrist and asks him to take the object out of his pocket. Mayler pulls out a metal ball bearing, two centimetres in diameter and places it in Pc Twain's free hand. The officer puts it in his own pocket.

Q30   Why does Pc Twain use the back of his hand over Mayler's pockets?

Q31   Is it acceptable for Pc Twain to put the ball bearing in his own pocket?

Q32   What should Pc Twain do with the ball bearing later?

Q33   For what reasons might it now be necessary to arrest Mayler?

Pc Twain says to Mayler, 'I am arresting you on suspicion of causing criminal damage to the Handy Store on Maidbury High Road approximately 20 minutes ago. The arrest is necessary because I wish to interview you at the police station to allow a prompt and effective investigation.'

Q34 What else should Pc Twain say to Mayler immediately after arrest?

Q35 What else should Pc Twain be considering in relation to Mayler immediately after arrest?

Apart from personal possessions, no other 'suspicious' articles have been found on Mayler so far. He is placed in a police vehicle and taken to Maidbury Police Station where he is introduced to the custody officer.

Meanwhile, the duty inspector has been listening to the developments surrounding the criminal damage incident over Airwaves. She knows from the electronic briefing that some of the other suspects are believed to be residents on the Stella housing estate, and she thinks it would make sense to check vehicles going in or out of the estate.

Q36 How should she arrange this?

MA 10 volunteers to service the road check; they have finished with Mr Patel.

Q37 What forensic investigative issues could be raised in relation to Pc Barden and Pc Ferez having attended the crime scene and the possibility of intercepting possible suspects at a road check?

Instead, Control deploys MA 40, Pc Chambers and Pc Alberg, to Moonstone Road which services the Stella housing estate. They decide that the most appropriate place to stop vehicles is a layby with clear views of oncoming traffic. They avoid the turning off the main road and the bend half way along Moonstone Road where the houses first start.

This road layout is ideal for a road check—lots of space, good visibility, and no nearby junctions.

They put up signs to reduce the speed of vehicles entering the checking area. Pc Alberg recalls his recent training on how to bring a vehicle to a halt safely and is pleased to have a chance to try it out—he gives clear indications to drivers of where to stop. Luckily the weather is not a problem so he doesn't need to make extra allowances for safe stopping distances.

After checking each vehicle, Pc Chambers indicates with a wave to each driver where to ease back out into the traffic flow safely.

Q38   What else do they need to check to make the road check as safe as possible?

They are aware that a blue hatchback had been associated with the incident at the Handy Store. It is not long before a blue hatchback with a missing rear hubcap comes into view.

Q39   What power, if any, have MA 40 in these circumstances to stop the vehicle?

The vehicle is successfully brought to a safe stop and Pc Chambers asks the driver to remove the ignition key and, along with the passenger, to step out of the car onto the pavement. He tells them that Pc Alberg is going to search them and their car.

Q40   Apart from searching the car and its occupants, what option(s) are available to the officers to prove or negate the driver's and passenger's involvement in the recent criminal damage?

Q41   What are the 'reasonable grounds' for the search?

Q42   What are the health and safety implications and considerations to be made regarding the search of such a vehicle?

As there is more than one suspect at the scene, Pc Chambers acts as cover officer for Pc Alberg while he carries out a s 1 PACE Act 1984 search of the driver and passenger, and inside the car.

In the rear nearside footwell Pc Alberg finds a plastic bag containing three large ball bearings, and located down the back of the seat, hidden to the eye of the cursory observer, he finds a sling shot. These items are all seized.

Pc Alberg decides to arrest the occupants of the car.

Q43   What considerations should be made in relation to seizing the ball bearings and the sling shot?

Q44   For what reasons might the arrest be necessary?

The two occupants of the vehicle are arrested and cautioned. The search is also completed (this time searching under s 32 of the PACE Act 1984 as the suspects have been arrested). The officers then take the suspects to Maidbury Police Station where they are introduced to the custody officer. The car is left locked and secure.

Outcome

The custody officer authorized the detention of all three suspects associated with the damage to the shop window at the Handy Store.

Seized items were placed into special property and as the officers were near the end of their shifts, a handover package was prepared so that interviewers would have information available to them at a later stage. Databases holding information on crime reports were interrogated to find similar crimes and in total ten shops and five local school buildings had been the target of similar attacks over the past week. Having sought legal representation, the three suspects were interviewed and admitted taking turns to drive the vehicle and shoot the ball bearings at the various locations.

The suspects were charged under s 1 of the Criminal Damage Act 1971. A decision was reached with the CPS that, due to the seriousness of the offence and the evidence available to the prosecution, each of the three suspects should be charged with criminal damage. The value of the property destroyed exceeded £5,000, and although this gave the defendants a right of trial on indictment at Crown Court, each of them pleaded guilty at magistrates' court. They were each given community service as part of a Community Order, fined, and ordered to pay compensation to the schools and shop owners.

The officers involved in the arrest of the suspects for the criminal damage at the Handy Store were highly commended by their BCU commander for their determination and professionalism.

Handy Store Answers

A1   The following offences could be considered:

- criminal damage under s 1(1) of the Criminal Damage Act 1971;

- possessing an article with intent to cause criminal damage under s 3 of the Criminal Damage Act 1971.

See Criminal Damage, *BSPOH 2010*, 10.21.1

There is a power to stop and search for prohibited articles used in the course of the destruction or damage of property. The power is available under s 1(2)(a) of the PACE Act 1984.

A2   If other patrols are available, either to be resourced by Control or on a voluntary basis, then one patrol could begin house to house enquiries in the immediate vicinity, while another patrol could begin an area search to try and locate the blue hatchback car.

A3   All of the following may need to be considered (not in any order of priority):

- welfare of the victim;

- preserve the scene;

- search for forensic evidence;

- seize forensic evidence;

- victim support;

- obtaining details for a crime report;

- health and safety of yourself and everybody around you;

- identification of suspects;

- asking Control to call out a boarding up company at the victim's request.

A4   He should also include the measurements of the position of the hole (eg how far is it from the ground or the edges of the window?).

A5   All of the following will be needed:

- property items: description and value;

- property items damaged: description and value;

- suspect/offenders: descriptions and names and addresses if known;

- crime log.

A6   The offence of 'criminal damage life endangered' under s 1(2) of the Criminal Damage Act 1971 if the person who destroys or damages the property is intending (or being reckless as) to endanger life. See *R v Steer* [1988] 2 All ER 833—the danger to life must come from the actual damage caused and not the act of causing the damage. In other words, in this situation the danger to Mr Patel's life would need to have come from the glass of the broken shop window and not from the ball bearing which broke the window in the first place.

See Criminal Damage, Life Endangered, *BSPOH 2010*, 10.21.2

A7   Any of the following might not have been met:

- honesty and integrity;

- equality and diversity;

- duties and responsibilities.

See Standards of Professional Behaviour, *BSPOH 2010*, 6.14.1

A8   ACPO's definition of a racial incident is 'Any incident in which it appears to the reporting or investigating officer that the complaint involves an element of racial motivation, or any incident which includes an allegation of racial motivation made by any person.'

A9   Yes, the offence is covered by s 30 of the Crime and Disorder Act 1998.

See Racially or Religiously Aggravated Criminal Damage, *BSPOH 2010*, 9.11.3

A10   Although their spoken English appears good, either one or both of the Patels might not be able to read English very well. The Victims of Crime leaflet is available in other languages, both paper-based and in electronic form.

A11   Mr Patel is the first person to have possession of the item after the suspect, therefore his initials will be used to exhibit the article, ie SP/1—his first name is Sanjay.

A12   The fact that Mr Patel has handled the ball bearing means it is unlikely that the suspect's DNA will be available on it. It is virtually impossible to take a fingerprint from the ball bearing. In plain terms, the ball bearing stands alone. Importantly, it may be possible to link it to other ball bearings in the possession of any suspects, so it should still be treated with care. At the scene,

Pc Barden would ideally place it in a rigid container and then into a Police Evidence bag. The rigid container may be a plastic pot or small cardboard box. Full details must be recorded on the bag's label, such as Mr Patel's exhibit identification number, the time and date of recovery, the address, and, crucially, the continuity part of the label should be completed to show Mr Patel gave custody of the exhibit to Pc Barden.

See Packaging Techniques, *BSPOH 2010*, 13.5.19

A13 All police officers have a responsibility to record and retain relevant material obtained or generated by them during the course of the investigation. Information gathered from house to house enquiries may be relevant to an investigation even though it does not contain any supporting evidence for the prosecution case against the suspect. When police officers carry out house to house enquiries, details of to whom they have spoken and what information, negative or otherwise, has been gained must be recorded in their pocket note book and retained to await a test for relevancy by an investigator, the officer in charge of an investigation, or the disclosure officer.

See Record, Retain, Reveal, and Disclose, *BSPOH 2010*, 12.6

A14 If Mr Edsen has corrected eyesight then this might be relevant to the investigation in regard to whether or not he was wearing his glasses at the time. Visibility and the strength of Mr Edsen's account of the incident may have some bearing on the offence under investigation (see Criminal Procedure and Investigations Act 1996 Code of Practice para 2.1). The officers should ask Mr Edsen if he has corrected eyesight. (And if he does, was he wearing glasses at the time?) A record should be made of his reply. In this case Mr Edsen informs the officers that his eyesight is good without the use of spectacles.

A15 The mnemonic ADVOKATE is a good way of ensuring the relevant information is recorded.

- Amount of time the suspect was under observation.

- Distance between the witness and the suspect.

- Visibility (eg, what was the lighting like, what were the weather conditions?).

- Obstructions to his/her view of the suspect.

- Known or seen before (does he/she know the suspect and, if so, how?).

- Any reason for remembering the suspect.

- Time lapse between the first and any subsequent identification to the police.

- Errors between the first recorded description of the suspect and his/her actual appearance.

See Evidence to be Gathered from a Witness, *BSPOH 2010*, 8.6.6

A16 Under the PACE Code of Practice D para 3.1(a) the description should be recorded in a visible and legible form before asking him/her to make any form of identification. It is known as a 'first description'.

A17 Closed and leading questions should be avoided. Open questions will elicit the most information and here are some examples:

- 'Describe to me exactly the features of his face.'

- 'Tell me in detail about the clothing he was wearing.'

A18 It's always a good idea to start at either the top of the body (or the feet) and work your way down (or up).

A19   He has not asked about his general build—for instance was he stocky, average, or skinny?

A20   The alleyway into which the suspect was seen to run is a very good starting point, and then for a distance along roads or paths equal to ten minutes of running or walking.

A21   Pc Twain is in a public place and asking the young male to account for his presence in an area, therefore a record of the person's self-defined ethnic background must be made and a receipt provided.

See Stop and Account, *BSPOH 2010*, 7.3.2

A22   Yes. On the face of it, if the young man becomes a suspect in the case, his comment appears to be capable of being used in evidence against him and is therefore a significant statement. This is because, firstly, his comment secures him to an alibi with his friend Jason. This may be a false name or false alibi, but either way the information may be relevant at an interview later. Secondly, the comment identifies him with probably being in the vicinity of the alleged damage which may be relevant to the offence. Consequently, a note should be made of the comment in a PNB, timed and signed by the maker. When practicable, the suspect should be asked to read the note and sign it along with anybody else who is present. At the beginning of any subsequent interview at the police station, the interviewer (after cautioning the suspect) must ask the suspect about any significant statement he/she made earlier.

See Significant Statements and Interviews, *BSPOH 2010*, 8.5 and 12.5.5.5

A23   He must record it in his PNB.

A24   There are probably sufficient reasonable grounds to suspect that Mayler has committed criminal damage because he fits the description given by the witness. His arrest might be necessary to prevent any prosecution for the offence from being hindered by his disappearance or to allow for a prompt and effective investigation through interview and search.

A25   He conducts the search under s 1 of the PACE Act 1984.

See Stop and Search, *BSPOH 2010*, 7.5

A26   The reasonable grounds to suspect that prohibited articles will be found in Mayler's possession include the following:

1. Mayler looks very similar to the description of the young male (given by Mr Edsen earlier) and having made an area search, nobody else appeared to fit the description so well.

2. Mayler has already mentioned a window being broken without any prompting by the officers.

3. Although half a mile away from the crime scene, it would be reasonable to believe that Mayler had had sufficient time to walk to his current location from the crime scene.

The prohibited articles would be those used in the course of, or in connection with, an offence of criminal damage.

A27   Under s 2 of the PACE Act 1984 and the Codes of Practice he must take reasonable steps to provide certain information to Mayler, represented by the mnemonic GOWISELY. A record of the search must also be made.

See Requirements Regarding the Search of Persons and Vehicles, *BSPOH 2010*, 7.5.5

A28   He has not told Mayler that he is entitled to a copy of the search record from Maidbury Police Station within the next 12 months.

A29   Mayler could cause Pc Twain injury as a result of using:

- physical force;

- a weapon he is carrying;

- a weapon he picks up;

- an object that he takes from Pc Twain, such as police personal safety equipment;

- transmitting an infection, such as hepatitis C, tuberculosis (TB), or influenza (flu);

- an infestation such as scabies;

- a needle injury.

        See Threat Levels and How they can be Reduced, *BSPOH 2010*, Chapter 6, Task 5

A30   If the pockets are close to the groin area (or in the case of females, the breast area), the use of the back of a hand will be less intrusive and possibly violating to the person being searched.

A31   On the face of it, there does not appear to be any problem with the ball bearing being left in Pc Twain's pocket. He is unlikely to be confused as to its source when he later removes it. As long as he does not lose it then this is acceptable—it is not practical to attempt to package it at the moment.

A32   Upon arrival at the police station it needs to be given an exhibit number and secured in a rigid container (if available) and then it must go into a Police Evidence bag. Obviously, Pc Twain needs to make a PNB entry regarding its seizure and the fact that he has searched Mayler—he will do this later—'as soon as reasonably practicable'.

A33   Mayler had possession of an article which may be linked to the damage of a window. There has been a series of other windows broken which may also have been damaged by the suspect. Evidence of his suspected involvement in that crime needs to be gathered through interview and search. His arrest is necessary to allow for a prompt and effective investigation through the use of questioning and search.

A34   He must caution Mayler.

        See When to Caution a Suspect, *BSPOH 2010*, 8.4.2

A35   He could complete the search of Mayler (this time under s 32 of the PACE Act 1984, as Mayler has now been arrested).

        See Searching a Suspect after Arrest, *BSPOH 2010*, 8.9.4

A36   A police officer of the rank of superintendent or above can authorize a s 4 PACE Act 1984 road check in writing. If such a police officer is not available, a road check may be authorized by an officer below the rank of superintendent (see s 4(5) of the PACE Act 1984). Any use of the power to impose a road check must be conducted in accordance with PACE Code of Practice A, which is concerned with stop and search.

        See Road Checks (s 4 of the PACE Act 1984), *BSPOH 2010*, 7.4

A37   Contamination from broken glass fragments around the vicinity of the shop adhering to the footwear and possibly to the officers' clothes. Whilst caution should always be exercised about transferring material from the crime scene onto suspects, in this case it is not an issue. The offenders in this particular incident, having fired a ball bearing from a sling shot from a car driving past the scene, will have no relevant trace evidence from the scene on their clothing or person. Therefore, if Pc Barden and Pc Ferez searched or arrested a suspect, they would technically contaminate the suspect with material relevant to the offence, but in reality it would have no defence 'mileage'. The CSI, when carrying out the forensic planning for a laboratory submission, would have no concerns over contamination. However, it must be noted that Pc Barden must rigorously ensure that the first exhibit is packaged and secured prior to seizing other (possibly identical) ball bearings from vehicles or suspects at the road check.

A38   The officers should:

- wear personal safety equipment including high visibility clothing;

- remain alert to the presence of vehicles at all times;

- reduce the risk to the general public by asking them to stay in or near their vehicles;

- considered the possibility that a vehicle may fail to stop at the road check;

- maintain communication with each other and be mindful not to become detached from the other officer(s) involved in the check;

- carry out the road check in an area which is well lit by street lamps if it is dark.

The road layout shown below would not be a good place for a road check.

There are no safe locations for a road check here as the road layout consists of several multiple junctions.

A39   To stop the vehicles they will use s 163 of the Road Traffic Act 1968.

See Powers to Stop a Vehicle, *BSPOH 2010*, 11.3

A40   The main alternative here is arrest. The officers' 'reasonable grounds to suspect' are that the vehicle fits the description of the blue hatchback involved in the recent criminal damage. Local intelligence was also available supporting the view that the suspects for the recent criminal damage of shop windows live on the Stella housing estate. The arrest would be necessary to allow the prompt and effective investigation of the offence or of the conduct of the people in question; the arrest would be for an indictable offence, and there is a need to enter and search any premises occupied or controlled by a person (the car) and/or search the person.

See Reasons that Make an Arrest Necessary, *BSPOH 2010*, 8.7.4

A41   The reasonable grounds to suspect that the officers will find prohibited articles in the car or on the persons have been discussed above; they will be very similar to the reasonable grounds to make an arrest. The prohibited articles would be those used in the course of, or in connection with, criminal damage.

A42   As Pc Alberg approaches the vehicle, he should think about:

- the driver attempting to move off in the vehicle;
- traffic passing by the location;
- if the engine is running;
- the driver making off;
- the location of the ignition key;
- the handbrake not being applied.

He could follow this sequence:

1. Speak to the driver and introduce himself.

2. Outline the reason for stopping the vehicle.

3. Ask the driver for his/her name and address and date of birth.

4. Ask the driver for his/her connection with the vehicle (is he/she the owner too?).

5. Ask the driver for details of his/her intended destination and the place where he/she began his or her journey.

6. Search the vehicle whilst considering the potential health and safety implications associated with:

   - moving parts inside the engine compartment such as thermostatically controlled cooling fans;
   - high temperatures associated with parts such as brakes, exhaust systems, radiators, and engines;
   - harmful liquids such as hydraulic fluids, battery acid, anti-freeze, and hot engine coolant;
   - sharp objects such as exposed tyre-cords, faulty bodywork, or drug paraphernalia, for example needles down the back of seats;
   - movement of the vehicle and anything in, on, or under the vehicle;
   - movement of other vehicles and persons nearby;
   - the surface on which the vehicle is positioned and the existence of harmful objects or substances.

A43   The ball bearings will preferably be packed out with polythene bags and placed into a rigid container and then sealed into a Police Evidence bag with full details of the seizure written on the label. Since it is unlikely that there are any tool marks or machine marks of relevance on the ball bearings it will not matter if they are packed together. There may be advantages in packaging one ball bearing loose within the Police Evidence bag, so that interviewer and suspect can see it during interview.

The sling shot will ideally be packaged in a large cardboard box with a plastic window on the lid. Special inserts are available to allow the weapon to be tied into the box securely. Once secured, the box is closed and paper signature seals are placed over the joint between lid and box body. The entire joint between lid and box must now be sealed with parcel tape, to prevent any material entering or leaving the box.

It is preferable that gloves and a mask are worn for this operation, since there is a possibility that a sample of ball bearings, and the sling shot, may be required for DNA analysis. Clearly, a number of patrol cars do not contain large amounts of packaging material, so this advice presumes a 'perfect world'.

Once packaged, the exhibits should be placed into a secure property store.

A44 The suspects have possession of articles which may be linked to the damage of a window. There has been a series of other windows broken which may have also been damaged by the suspects. Evidence of their suspected involvement in those crimes needs to be gathered through interview and search. Their arrest is necessary therefore to allow for a prompt and effective investigation through the use of questioning.

Test Yourself

And finally, solve these anagrams and fill the gaps to complete the s 1 Criminal Damage Act 1971 definition.

A person who without AWFUL CLUE SEX destroys or SAD GAME any property BOOTLEG GINN another TED GIN INN to destroy or damage any such PET OR PRY or being CRESS ELK as to whether any such PET OR PRY would be DEED STORY or damaged shall be guilty of an offence.

Answers to Knowledge Check Questions

K1 c   K2 c   K3 c   K4 a   K5 d   K6 c   K7 d   K8 a

Answers to Test Yourself

BOOTLEG GINN—Belonging to

PET OR PRY—Property

SAD GAME—Damages

AWFUL CLUE SEX—Lawful excuse

TED GIN INN—Intending

CRESS ELK—Reckless

THOU WIT—Without

DEED STORY—Destroyed

2 | The Burchers

👣 forensic awareness required

✓ assessment opportunity

☺ diversity issues

💧 health and safety

▽? questionable practice

✐ a pen or pencil is required

Introduction

This scenario involves a missing person enquiry and internet sexual grooming. The Child Exploitation and Online Protection Centre received over 5,000 reports relating to child protection issues during 2009 from members of the public (CEOP, 2009). Nearly 2,000 of these were from children, and the vast majority related to 'grooming'. Child sex offenders are reported to be using a combination of the internet and offline tactics to target and abduct young victims, and CEOP believes parents could and should do more to protect their children.

Knowledge Check

✐ Before you undertake this scenario, check your understanding of the underpinning legislation involved by attempting the following knowledge check.

In questions K1 to K8 inclusive write down one of the letters a, b, c, or d as the answer to the question. Then try the remaining questions. Check your answers at the end of the chapter before beginning the scenario.

K 1 Section 15(1) of the Sexual Offences Act 2003 (sexual grooming) only applies to children or young people of what age?

        a) Under 16
        b) Under 17
        c) Under 18
        d) Under 19

K 2 In relation to s 10(1) of the Sexual Offences Act 2003 (causing or inciting a child to engage in sexual activity), which of the following statements is true?

    a) The suspect must be aged 17 or over
    b) The sexual activity can include penetration and/or touching
    c) The offence is categorized as an indictable only offence
    d) The offence can only be committed by a male

K 3 In relation to s 15(1) of the Sexual Offences Act 2003 as amended (sexual grooming), which one of the following statements is true?

    a) The offence cannot be committed if the suspect travels with the intention of meeting the victim outside England, Wales, or Northern Ireland
    b) The offence can only be committed by a person aged 17 years or over
    c) The offence is committed if the suspect meets up with the victim on three occasions, twice planned and the third time by accident
    d) The offence is committed if the suspect has communicated with the victim on three occasions but they have never met

K 4 According to s 2(1) of the Child Abduction Act 1984, which of the following statements is false in relation to abduction of a child by another person?

    a) The abducted child must be under the age of 16
    b) The suspect does not commit an offence if he or she takes or detains a child with reasonable authority or excuse
    c) If the father or mother of the child were married to each other at the time of the child's birth either or both parents can commit the offence
    d) The suspect must detain the child for the purpose of keeping him or her from the lawful control of any person having lawful control of the child

K 5 In a missing person enquiry, which of the following may indicate the vulnerability of a person?

    a) Age
    b) Listed on the Child Protection Register
    c) Drugs or alcohol dependency
    d) Any of the above

K 6 When carrying out the unplanned seizure of a personal computer (PC) which of the following is an **incorrect** procedure?

    a) Do not take advice from the owner on how to turn the PC off
    b) Always turn the PC on or off to check that it is working
    c) Photograph the screen if it is displayed
    d) Allow a printer to complete its print run

K 7 What grading of risk does the ACPO *Guidance on the Management, Recording and Investigation of Missing Persons* (2005a, updated 2007) use to record missing persons?

    a) High, medium, or low
    b) Red, amber, or green
    c) Substantial, severe general, or severe specific
    d) Substantial, moderate, or low

K 8 Which one of the following is not a type of transaction according to Berne's theory of Transactional Analysis?

    a) Crossed
    b) Ulterior
    c) Simultaneous
    d) Complementary

The Burchers Scenario

Pc Biggs, MA 23, an experienced community police beat officer, is on late turn on Friday night and carrying out routine functions on his patch. It is 22.00 when he receives the following message from Control over Airwaves:

'Control calling—MA 23 please attend 11 Jonas Gardens where a minor, a 14-year-old girl Emma BURCHER (that's Bravo , Uniform, Romeo, Charlie, Hotel, Echo, Romeo) has been reported missing by her parents. She hasn't returned home from school—was expected back at 16.00.'

Pc Biggs is aware that the school is now probably closed for the weekend and so there would be little point in 'phoning the school receptionist'. Control also give Pc Biggs the Burchers' home telephone number—and he decides to ring ahead before visiting the family home.

Q1   Suggest why Pc Biggs thought it best to ring ahead.

His call is answered by Emma's mother, Mrs Burcher. Pc Biggs introduces himself courteously and gives his name, number, and station. He tells Mrs Burcher that he will visit them and take more details and try to help find their daughter. He tries to be reassuring.

Pc Biggs then goes to the Burchers' house. Mrs Burcher seems very worried and emotional, but Mr Burcher, Emma's stepfather, appears less concerned, and also seems reluctant to speak with Pc Biggs.

Pc Biggs	Mrs Burcher, you told me earlier on the phone that your daughter Emma has not returned home from school yet, is that right?
Mrs Burcher	Yes, it's not what she normally does, she's such a good girl she always comes straight home. Or phones me on her mobile . . .
Pc Biggs	Okay, I'm sure there is an explanation and I understand how concerned you might be, I'm a father myself and I know how worried I'd be. There are a few questions we need to go through—can we make ourselves comfortable somewhere—and could you turn the telly off for us please?
Mr Burcher	I suppose I'll have to watch the footy later then—I can't even record it—bloody satellite!

Pc Biggs then explains that he first needs to ask Mrs Burcher, and then Mr Burcher, some questions about Emma and the circumstances of her not returning home.

Q2   What information should he collect from Emma's mother at this stage?

	Mrs Burcher answers the questions fully before adding:
Mrs Burcher	She is such a quiet girl. I can't imagine where she would go after school, she normally comes straight home and goes to her room to go on the computer. It's not like her . . . and her mobile's turned off . . .
Mr Burcher	(interrupting) Of course it's like her, bloody selfish, spends more time on that computer than helping you, never cleans, cooks, or does nothing around the house. I've told her time and time again she is to help around the house—to help you—and not to sulk away in that bloody bedroom of hers.

Pc Biggs	Thanks Mr Burcher, if I can come to you in a minute, can we let Mrs Burcher answer for the moment and I will get to you shortly?
Mr Burcher	Well, make it quick then—I could still make the second half.
Pc Biggs	So, Mrs Burcher, did you see her go off to school this morning?
Mrs Burcher	Yes, with her bag, she was fine.
Pc Biggs	Was anything at all you can think of out of routine?
Mrs Burcher	No, it was our normal routine, she shouted 'Bye mum'—but then she did come back and give me a kiss and a hug that was a bit more, I don't know, longer, more with meaning now I think of it, normally it's just a rush out of the door.
Mr Burcher	More than I ever get, ungrateful she is for what we do for her, never a thank you . . .
Pc Biggs	Again, Mr Burcher, can we let your wife speak first?

(To Mrs Burcher) Would it help if we went somewhere else to chat about this?

Mrs Burcher	What do you think, Peter—should we go in the kitchen?
Mr Burcher	Suit yourself, I can put the telly on then, can't I . . . and, Sue, tell him about her sulking and scheming, little bitch always taking and no giving . . . make me a tea while you're out there. And tell him she won't call me dad— it's always 'him' or 'that bloke'. No discipline that girl, what she needs is a good . . .
Pc Biggs	(interrupting) I get the picture Mr Burcher, let's move to the kitchen.

Pc Biggs and Mrs Burcher settle themselves as best they can on the chrome stools at the breakfast bar in the kitchen.

Pc Biggs	Mrs Burcher—or can I call you Sue? Great, yes . . . I get the impression that Mr Burcher and Emma don't seem to get on very well—is there any truth in that d'you think? I know all families are different, but . . .
Mrs Burcher	Well, she never took to him after her father . . . she adored her father . . . he means well—he's been good to us—provides for us and well, perhaps he is a bit overbearing, but she ought to think of how much he does for us. Where is she . . . I can't stand the worry . . . where can we look . . . we must look for her . . .
Pc Biggs	I appreciate this is very difficult for you, and very upsetting, but we need to go through things carefully so we can find her as soon as possible. So, Emma should have got home from school at about what time?
Mrs Burcher	Between half past four and five o'clock.
Pc Biggs	Okay, and when she gets back she is normally at home with Peter—Mr Burcher—alone, until you get home at what time?
Mrs Burcher	It depends—not til after nine some nights because of my cleaning jobs.

Pc Biggs gradually gets a picture of the Burchers' family life. He is sympathetic to Mrs Burcher but avoids saying too much—letting her speak for herself. From his further questioning of Mrs Burcher this is what Pc Biggs discovers:

Emma is a 14-year-old girl, an only child living with her parents, both in their 50s. Susan (Sue) Burcher is Emma's biological mother and Peter Burcher is Emma's stepfather of some five years. Sue has not divorced or remarried, but she and her daughter Emma use the surname Burcher. Sue is almost embarrassed to say that Mr Burcher insists that Emma calls him 'Dad', and that Emma finds this troubling.

It emerges that, in her mother's view, Emma is a shy girl who has few friends and finds mixing with school friends difficult. Emma does not lead a very active social life—or at least she goes out 'hardly at all'. Emma's mother believes that a school friend of Emma's, a certain Kathy (could be Kathy Trimble) is the only friend that Emma appears to associate with (at school) and possibly confide in.

Pc Biggs need to decide how this all fits into the standard categories used by the police in missing persons cases.

. . . is anyone else involved . . . don't think so . . . lost? . . . medium risk?

Q3   At this stage, should Emma be categorized as a 'lost person', a 'missing person who has voluntarily gone missing', or as a 'missing person under the influence of a third party'?

Q4   What sort of questions could Pc Biggs ask Emma's mother to help determine the level of risk to Emma (high, medium, or low) as a consequence of Emma's disappearance?

Mrs Burcher then mentions that Emma has a computer in her bedroom and Emma had talked to her about how much fun it was using chat rooms and Facebook.

She goes on to explain that Emma keeps this part of her life much to herself and does not involve her parents in her computer 'world', spending 'hours' on the internet every evening. Mrs Burcher explains—almost laughing—that she and Mr Burcher 'haven't a clue' what she gets up to—but she suddenly looks worried and falls silent.

Pc Biggs suspects that Emma and her stepfather do not have a particularly easy relationship and might argue. Mrs Burcher confirms that Mr Burcher and Emma often argue—but 'Dad is never actually violent—he has never hit her—never—he wouldn't . . .'. But she says that Peter Burcher often berates Emma about her 'locking herself away' for hours and points out how she is 'not normal, doing normal things with her friends'.

Pc Biggs then decides it is time to ask Mr Burcher a few questions, despite Mr Burcher's apparent reluctance to become involved.

. . . easy does it with this one . . . coax it out of him . . . not the nicest man I've ever met . . . but still . . .

Q5   What theories of communication might Pc Biggs bear in mind when he questions Mr Burcher?

Pc Biggs returns to the living room, leaving Mrs Burcher in the kitchen.

Mr Burcher	There's no point in asking me any questions . . . I don't know anything and besides, shouldn't you be out looking for my stepdaughter instead of being in here harassing me?
Pc Biggs	Mr Burcher, I cannot begin to understand how you are feeling right now— this must be a really difficult time for you and your wife. She's very worried and upset, as I am sure you are. I want to provide the best opportunity for Emma to be found as quickly as possible and as such, you may well have

> information that your wife does not have access to. We need to work together to find Emma as soon as possible.
>
> **Mr Burcher**   Yeah, I see your point, let's get on with it. I don't think I can help you any more than my wife, but you never know . . . I'm sorry, but things can get a bit dodgy round here sometimes. Sorry. So what would I know that could help find her?

Pc Biggs now asks Mr Burcher the same set of questions he asked Mrs Burcher earlier, and his replies provide the same information as his wife gave earlier—with no real inconsistencies.

Mr Burcher delayed in reporting Emma as missing for a few hours as he thought she might have gone to a friend's house after school. He explained that Mrs Burcher had been out of the house earlier in the evening doing a cleaning job for an elderly lady and only returned at 8 pm, when she was told by Mr Burcher that Emma had not come home from school.

Pc Biggs nods and makes a note of the information Mr Burcher is providing. He now feels he has a more detailed picture of their family life and what is 'normal' for them.

Mrs Burcher returns to the lounge.

Q6   With the more detailed picture he now has, would it be reasonable to expect Pc Biggs to categorize Emma as a 'missing person, lost' or a 'missing person, voluntary' or an 'abductee' at this stage?

Pc Biggs steps outside for a moment and uses Airwaves to contact the police station in confidence—away from the parents. The Burchers also have a couple of moments of privacy to absorb the reality of the situation.

Q7   What information or intelligence might Pc Biggs be seeking from the databases held at the station?

It emerges that Mr and Mrs Burcher have a 'history' on the force databases. The police have been called to the house on one previous occasion some years ago to a 'domestic'; Mr Burcher had been drunk and had become particularly aggressive—more than Mrs Burcher could cope with on that occasion.

Pc Biggs reflects on this new slant to events:

> *. . . did something blow up between Emma and her stepfather when she got in from school . . . and mum wasn't there to calm it all?*

Q8   Given the circumstances described so far, should Pc Biggs class the risk to Emma as high, medium, or low?

Pc Biggs is also becoming increasingly concerned that Peter Burcher has a propensity to try and dominate other people, and is prepared to conflict openly with others. Pc Biggs remembers reading somewhere that domestic violence does not merely relate to physical acts of violence—assaults etc, and that there are other forms of abuse.

> *. . . has he done something to Emma? . . . is that why she's gone off . . . well, or maybe just part of it?*

Q9   Should Pc Biggs really be thinking in terms of domestic violence and abuse in relation to Emma; surely this applies only to partners and husbands and wives?

Q10   Is Pc Biggs right to consider a link between domestic violence and abuse and 'going missing'?

> Pc Biggs mentally puts to one side at this point the question of domestic violence and abuse, although he realizes this might feature at some stage in the future.
>
> *. . . must get back to the basic procedures . . . first things first . . .*
>
> Pc Biggs asks Mr and Mrs Burcher if he can have a quick look around the house. He looks in each room—thankfully there is not too much furniture and he can easily see that Emma is almost certainly not in the house.

Q11   Why is it important that Pc Biggs notes the extent and detail of his search?

> Out in the garden (a rather large garden), Pc Biggs notices a shed and a summer-house. He is beginning to wonder if something more serious might have taken place, and he suddenly finds himself thinking where a body could be concealed in the garden.

Q12   Should Pc Biggs search the garden area of the house for Emma (or her body)?

Q13   Should Pc Biggs even 'think murder' (the phrase used in the *Murder Investigation Manual,* ACPO, 2006) at this stage or would this be exaggerating the situation?

Q14   Suggest some fast-track actions that should be taken immediately.

> Pc Biggs now takes stock of the circumstances up to this point. Emma is a missing person but so far there are no obviously suspicious circumstances.
>
> *. . . don't even know if she was at school today—could we contact her friend, or the school somehow?*
>
> He decides to attempt to contact school staff to ask them about Emma (eg, did she attend school on Friday and did they have any useful suggestions that might help focus the investigation?) and also to try to contact Emma's school friend, Kathy Trimble.

Q15   Given that it is Friday night, how might Pc Biggs further these two lines of enquiry? Should he wait and see if Emma turns up, perhaps until early Saturday morning, before he begins to alert people?

> Through Airwaves communication with his local police station Pc Biggs requests contact be made with the relevant staff at the school and every effort be made to trace the whereabouts and address of Kathy Trimble.

. . . I hope this area's education office are more helpful than the last one . . . took ages to get anything useful out of them . . .

Q16 Are there any issues around the Data Protection Act 1998 that would prevent the school from accommodating Pc Biggs' request for school staff to release details of Kathy Trimble's home address or telephone number?

Q17 If the school staff do have issues over confidentiality or security of information, can you think of a practical remedy that would enable Kathy, once contacted, to talk freely with Pc Biggs without causing difficulties for the school?

Pc Biggs receives a message from his Control.

'School headteacher confirms that Kathy Trimble lives approximately two miles from your location, and is at home and is willing to speak to you about Emma.'

Pc Biggs makes a decision to interview Kathy himself and informs Control that he will visit the address given and interview her immediately. He notes the time in his pocket book and informs Mr and Mrs Burcher of his intentions and updates the 'activity log'.

Q18 Why is it important for him to update this 'activity log'?

On arrival at Kathy's house, Kathy is with her mother and they are both keen to assist Pc Biggs, even though it is late.

Pc Biggs	Kathy, Emma's mum and stepdad have told us that Emma is missing—they have not seen her since she left for school this morning—she was expected home at about 4 pm. Can you help us? Is there anything you know that might help put their minds at rest? I am sure you understand how they might feel.
Kathy	Her so-called dad won't care much, he never cares about Emma.
Pc Biggs	Why's that Kathy?
Kathy	He is a bully, he terrifies her and her mum, and she hates him.
Pc Biggs	I think I understand what you mean Kathy, but at the moment I need to speak to Emma myself as I may be able to help her and her mum if I can only speak to her. Can you help me with that?
Kathy	Not really—she left school at about quarter to four, the usual time—I don't know where she went after that.
Pc Biggs	Okay that's fine. How did she seem today?
Kathy	Well, I do think she was a bit excited today, she kept saying she couldn't wait for school to finish. I thought perhaps she was going out with her mum, but she didn't say.
Pc Biggs	Did you see her leave school yourself?
Kathy	Yes, she walked off towards her home as usual—except . . .
Pc Biggs	Go on.

Kathy	Well, I thought she was carrying a hold-all instead of her normal school bag—I thought maybe she had got a new one and I hadn't noticed before.
Pc Biggs	Can you describe it?
Kathy	Yes, you know, a blue hold-all with a shoulder strap about the size of a sports bag—one for carrying your kit in for sport.
Pc Biggs	Have you seen Emma with this bag before?
Kathy	No, she doesn't bring that one to school.
Pc Biggs	Okay, thanks Kathy, that really helps . . . but is there anything else that Emma has told you? Perhaps she speaks to you as a friend and tells you things she doesn't tell others? Is there anything like that?
Kathy	Well . . .
Pc Biggs	Kathy this could be really important and we really want to help Emma if we can . . . I know how you might have something that Emma does not want everybody to know—but it really is in her interests to share it with us—she might need our help.
Kathy	(Wringing her fingers and becoming a little distressed) I said I wouldn't tell anybody, she won't speak to me ever again.
Pc Biggs	Kathy, trust us with this, we will explain to Emma that we needed to know she was safe and you acted in her best interest, concerned for her safety.
Kathy	She is meeting a bloke for a modelling career and she does not want her mum and stepdad to know, they might stop her. Her dad would.
Pc Biggs	Okay, Kathy you are really helping us now, tell me in more detail about this man she is meeting, what exactly did Emma say?
Kathy	She just said she had been talking with him on the internet and he said he could introduce her to friends in the fashion business . . . and that she could have a great modelling career or something. She even sent him a photograph . . . I think. She never actually saw him though, it was all on the computer . . .

Pc Biggs spends some more time with Kathy and elicits all the information he can, reassuring her throughout that sharing this information is in Emma's best interest. Once Kathy has started explaining it all she seems almost relieved to be telling Pc Biggs. Her mum just stares at her and looks worried.

Pc Biggs leaves a contact number and asks Kathy and her mum to contact him if she thinks of any more details about what Emma might have said.

'I may need to speak with you again—is that okay—try and get some sleep now. Thanks for all your help, you've been very brave, well done. Mrs Trimble, thanks, very good, she's a great girl your daughter.'

Q19 The information put before him by Kathy has now raised other potential serious and sinister reasons for her disappearance: what might they be?

Q20   Does the information from Kathy change the perceived level of risk to Emma in the risk assessment process?

> Armed with this information and having informed his supervisor, who in turn has informed specialist child abuse officers, Pc Biggs is instructed to return to the parents' home and to secure Emma's computer—and to see if there is anything else of interest in her bedroom. Even though it is approaching midnight, he is not surprised to find that Peter and Sue Burcher are still up. They come to the door quickly, and let him in expectantly. Mrs Burcher looks drained and Mr Burcher seems to have less to say now.

Q21   What might Pc Biggs tell Mr and Mrs Burcher about the information from Kathy?

Q22   What sort of other items, other than the computer and associated equipment, might be of interest to Pc Biggs in Emma's bedroom?

> Pc Biggs decides to tell the parents about what Kathy has told him, about Emma's online 'friend' and her plans to meet him. He makes a note of the decision and his reasons in his PNB. Mr and Mrs Burcher receive the information quietly, and are clearly very concerned. Pc Biggs explains that he needs to take a look at Emma's room to help move the investigation on as fast as possible.
>
> Looking around in Emma's bedroom, it is clear that a bag and some clothes are missing. Pc Biggs also finds a building society passbook which shows that a withdrawal had been made the previous weekend and, in a drawer, a receipt for the recent purchase of some clothes. There is nothing else of much apparent immediate significance apart from the computer, a desktop PC which appears to be still on as it is showing a screensaver. Pc Biggs notices a hairbrush by the keyboard and makes a mental note of this.

Q23   What value might the hairbrush be of value to the investigation?

It might be tempting to try some obvious ones, such as 'Emma' but this should be left to the specialists.

> Pc Biggs moves the mouse of the computer and a password dialogue box appears on the screen. Stumped, Pc Biggs decides to contact his force Digital Forensic Unit for advice, but the office isn't open so he asks his supervisor what to do instead.

Q24   Why was it a good idea for Pc Biggs to seek advice after moving the mouse? What would the Digital Forensic Unit be likely to advise in these circumstances?

Pc Biggs takes the advice of his supervisor to leave the computer in situ overnight and to make sure that no one touches it.

> *. . . do I have to stand over it? . . . I've got other things to do . . . those specialists—why don't they work nights too? . . .*

Pc Biggs locks the door to Emma's room and then keeps the key 'for the specialist' and tactfully checks with the parents that there is no other key. Mrs Burcher looks very upset, and Pc Biggs tries to reassure her that it is all 'standard procedure'. Fortunately, she will have extra support soon; a Senior Investigating Officer (SIO), Detective Inspector Cullen, has been appointed to lead the investigation into Emma's disappearance and he has arranged for a family liaison officer, Jodie Franks, to attend in the morning.

DI Cullen also arranges for a computer forensic investigator to attend early the next day to recover Emma's computer and ancillary equipment such as USB memory sticks and CDs. Meanwhile Pc Biggs explains to Mr and Mrs Burcher that Jodie will come to the house first thing in the morning. The two officers then return to the station.

Q25   Why has the investigation been upgraded and a SIO become involved?

Q26   Why has a family liaison officer (FLO) been appointed at this point?

DI Cullen considers issuing a media release for the following morning, appealing for information about Emma's disappearance but decides that this is premature.

Q27   Suggest some reasons why DI Cullen delayed the media appeal.

It is now early Saturday morning but, before going off duty, Pc Biggs still needs to find the time to fully brief DI Cullen and to fully update his pocket book and live activity logs. Emma is now judged to be a high-risk missing person and the possibility of internet grooming for sexual exploitation remains a real possibility. But this is not Pc Biggs's and DI Cullen's only concern; they cannot dismiss the background information they have and the relationship between the stepfather and his partner, Emma's mum. DI Cullen knows there is a second hypothesis that needs to be thoroughly investigated and he will determine lines of enquiry that follow both possibilities, all being recorded in his policy file or decision log.

✓

> *. . . should be able to use some of this for my PIP Level 3 training . . . elements of that NOS Unit about managing major investigations . . . CI103*

Overnight, Emma's bedroom is a crime scene—a source of evidence, intelligence, or information that will throw further light on the sequence of events that led to her disappearance.

Q28   Why is the bedroom secured and cordoned?

By Saturday morning, Pc Biggs has handed over the ongoing investigation to specialist officers but stays in touch with the major enquiry team—he knows he will be tasked to assist them in any way he can. Specialist search teams are deployed and the house, sheds, and gardens are searched meticulously.

The officers searching her room recover a recent receipt for clothes in a drawer. Her computer is taken away by specialists and all the communications between her and a certain 'Richard' are soon discovered; they have arranged to meet in a hotel in London.

Later on the Saturday morning the officers find Emma alone in the room and take her into safe protection. 'Richard' returned to the room a little later in possession of an unopened packet of condoms. He was immediately arrested and taken into custody.

Outcome

The investigation (including interviews with Emma) reveals the following:

'Richard' is in fact a 42-year-old married man. Specialist digital forensic investigators find incriminating evidence on his home PC, evidence of paedophilia and downloading child pornography—some in the deleted files they manage to recover. He had been making online contacts with many young people, almost all girls aged 13–16 years; a long contact list of girls' addresses was found on his PC. Investigations in the vicinity of the hotel where Emma was found subsequently established that he had bought the condoms that Saturday morning.

Emma had met 'Richard' through an online social networking site. He befriended Emma online, and claimed to be 19 years old. Emma soon began to share more intimate information with him, including her feelings about her school and home life. The dialogue continued over several weeks. He suggested they should meet, and she agreed. Fortunately, the police officers found Emma in time; although clearly distressed, she had not been subjected to any sexual or physical assaults.

'Richard' was investigated for offences relating to downloading pornographic child images, 'sexual grooming', and abduction. He was subsequently charged under:

- section 1 of the Protection of Children Act 1978 (making and possession of indecent photographs of a person under 18 years). In the case *R v Bowden* [2000] 1 WLR 1427, 'making' was held to include downloading such images from the internet and storing them (either digitally or in a printed form);

- section 15 of the Sexual Offences Act 2003, for offences relating to grooming. He had communicated with her on more than one occasion, he knew she was under 16, he had arranged to meet her, he had met her, and he had the intent to commit a sexual offence. The fact that he had obtained the condoms while he had access to Emma demonstrated that he had a sexual motive (essential to proving the offence of grooming);

- section 2 of the Child Abduction Act 1984—she was under 16 and he caused her to go to the hotel, removing her from the lawful control of her parents.

He was found guilty on all three counts and was sentenced to three years in prison and placed on the sex offenders register for life. Emma is back at school. She and her friend Kathy are still very close, but Emma has also made a few new friends at school and spends less time alone.

The Burchers Answers

A1   Although most 'missing persons' such as Emma soon return home unharmed a small minority will have been abducted and/or been physically harmed (or even murdered). Hence, Pc Biggs' planned visit to the Burchers' home is possibly not simply a matter of taking an initial report but may also be the first (and possibly very important) stage in an ongoing serious investigation.

He has also made contact with Emma's parents to ensure that the parents know that their worries are taken seriously (as part of the Police Service's stated commitment to the community it serves). He certainly did not dismiss their concerns or imply that they are over-protective parents by using phrases such as 'she'll come home when she's hungry' or 'young people are like that these days, always staying over, she'll turn up when she is ready'. If, on the contrary, Pc Biggs had decided not to visit the home of Emma Burcher immediately he would also have informed the parents of the time (or date) that he or a colleague would be attending the Burchers' home.

A2   Pc Biggs should adhere to the advice given in the ACPO *Guidance on the Management, Recording and Investigation of Missing Persons* (ACPO, 2005a, updated 2007) and the minimum information he should gather in his initial report is Emma's full name, her age, her home address, her mobile number, her physical description, the location she is missing from, a description of the clothing Emma was last seen wearing, the circumstances of going missing, details of any vehicle or other transport used (eg, a bus from school), whether 'going missing' is out of character, and finally, the name, address, telephone numbers, and status of the person or persons reporting Emma missing (in this case, her mother).

See Missing Persons Enquiries, *BSPOH 2010*, 9.27.1

A3   It is too early for any kind of definitive categorization. However, the scenario so far suggests either a lost person or a missing person who has voluntarily gone missing. There is no information suggesting that a third party might be involved. The three categories Pc Biggs considers are those provided by ACPO for use in missing persons enquiries (see A2 above).

A4   His questions would be based on the ACPO guidelines and other documents. Hence Pc Biggs would ask Mrs Burcher whether Emma had shown any intent to harm herself, about Emma's general state of health, whether she had gone missing before (and if so, why?), etc.

So far, based on the information provided, he would probably have completed the following checklist:

Factor	Yes	No	Not known
Is the person likely to self-harm or attempt suicide?			✓
Is the person likely to be the subject of a crime in progress, eg abduction?		✓	
Is the person vulnerable due to age, infirmity, or any other factor?	✓		
Are the weather conditions inclement to the extent that this would seriously increase the risk to health, especially where the missing person is a child or an elderly person?		✓	
Does the missing person need essential medication or treatment not readily available to them?		✓	
Does the missing person have any physical illness, disability, or mental health problems?		✓	
Does the person have the ability to interact safely with others in an unknown environment?	✓		

Factor	Yes	No	Not known
Has the person been involved in a violent, homophobic, and/or racist incident or confrontation immediately prior to his/her disappearance?		✓	
Has the person been subjected to recent bullying?			✓
Has the person previously disappeared and suffered or been exposed to harm?		✓	

(Adapted from ACPO, 2005a, Appendix 3)

He might well conclude from this that he needs to ask further questions and make further enquiries to determine whether the risk is high, medium, or low.

A5   Although there are numerous theories relating to human communication, one that might be particularly useful in these circumstances is Transactional Analysis. According to this theory, people respond to each other depending on their 'ego' state and adopt characteristics of a parent (critical or nurturing), adult, or child (adapted or free). Here, Emma's stepfather may be scared, angry, frustrated, irritated, and upset. Consequently he might be feeling that Pc Biggs is like a 'critical parent' because, as a police officer, Pc Biggs represents authority and power. As for many people, this could reignite memories of previous bad experiences of feeling put down. If this applies to Mr Burcher, he may very well adopt the ego state of an 'adapted' child and become defensive and bad tempered. If Pc Biggs recognizes this in Mr Burcher, he might be in a position to manage the conversation and help Mr Burcher move on to a more adult frame of mind. In this case, Pc Biggs could make a real effort to avoid acting out the role of critical parent—he could adopt the ego state of an 'adult' and using a 'crossed' transaction would probably interrupt the flow and change the style of transaction.

See Effective Communication, *BSPOH 2010*, 6.18

A6   Emma is a definitely a 'missing person', according to ACPO definitions (that is, her whereabouts are unknown). But is Emma a 'lost' person? A lost person is somebody who is temporarily disorientated (due to age, as in young children, accident, injury, or illness) and would wish to be found. There seems no suggestion that Emma is likely to be in this type of confused state.

So, Emma is either a 'voluntary missing person' (who has control over their own actions but has decided to go missing, eg a person who wishes to leave home or run off) or an abductee, that is a missing person who has gone missing against their will, under the influence of a third party, eg abduction or murder. Either of these categories is possible on the available information so far; Emma may have left of her own accord or a third party—as yet unidentified—may be involved.

A7   Pc Biggs should initiate PNC checks on the family members, looking for any history that may give rise to concerns. Previous convictions and 'flags' of interest may be present on the PNC. (A 'flag' is a marker that further information is held securely on PNC or by other agencies, perhaps in confidence and not immediately available on PNC but through further enquiry). There may be 'warning' markers—an indication that an individual may be violent, a drugs abuser, a wanted person, or a warrant has been issued against a person—as well as other information.

A8   ACPO (2005a) recommend that the level of risk be categorized using the following criteria (as applied to Emma).

Level of risk	ACPO criteria applied to Emma	Comments
High	The risk posed to Emma is immediate and there are substantial grounds for believing that she is in danger through her vulnerability; or she may have been the victim of a serious crime; or the risk posed is immediate and there are substantial grounds for believing that the public is in danger.	It is possible that the risk to Emma is high but it is not likely. There is no history of significant vulnerability yet uncovered or any history of self-abuse, etc. In any event there would appear to be no grounds for fearing for the safety of the public.
Medium	The risk posed is likely to place Emma in danger or she is a threat to herself or others.	There are grounds for believing that there is a medium risk to Emma.
Low	There is no apparent threat of danger to either Emma or the public.	The risk to Emma cannot be classed as low given that 'going missing' is uncharacteristic of her and the concerns raised by her step-father's history and his relationship with Emma.

In the absence of determinable evidence, Pc Biggs decides that Emma is properly assessed as being a 'medium-risk' missing person and the response by the police should be measured and proportionate to this. However, this is a judgement call and may be assessed differently by others—unfortunately, sometimes influenced by anecdotes or individual experiences!

If in doubt Pc Biggs must share his concerns with his immediate supervisor and should never be afraid to declare that he 'does not know' what to do, what to say, or where to begin.

A9   Strictly speaking, the situation revealed so far does not seem to include domestic violence or abuse as far as Emma is concerned, because she is under 18 years. The shared ACPO, Crown Prosecution Service (CPS), and government definition of domestic violence is:

> any incident of threatening behaviour, violence or abuse (psychological, physical, sexual, financial or emotional) between adults, aged 18 and over, who are or have been intimate partners or family members, regardless of gender and sexuality.

(Home Office, 2009b)

Family members are defined as mother, father, son, daughter, brother, sister, and grandparents, whether directly related, in-laws, or step-family.

However, Susan Burcher may well be subject to domestic violence in terms of her psychological and emotional environment and may need ongoing support—in addition to any actions that may need to be taken as a consequence of Emma being missing.

A10   Yes, research has revealed a potential link between missing persons and domestic violence. The person reporting that an individual is missing may either not know that domestic violence may be an issue or may choose not to disclose the fact, at least initially.

Identifying that the missing person is a victim of domestic violence or child abuse, or is an offender, will determine the type and level of investigation to be undertaken. The missing person could be the victim of a domestic homicide. It is also possible that the person making the report could be attempting to locate the victim who has escaped from a violent situation or has killed the person and is trying to look innocent.

Police staff should, therefore, be alert to the possibility that the missing person is either a victim of domestic violence or an abuser. Specialist domestic violence officers (and child abuse specialists) should be informed when a domestic violence victim or suspect/offender is missing. Previous domestic violence records from police intelligence or from established links with other agencies (eg social services and education authorities) should be used to assist in the investigation. Such contact should respect the confidentiality process of the service provider and should not presume that information will be made available. See the ACPO guidance on investigating domestic abuse (ACPO, 2008) for further information.

A11 A note in the pocket book of the search areas and the extent of the search undertaken is recommended. If this is not done, it is more likely that certain places may be overlooked—each officer presuming that a potential hiding place had been checked by someone else.

A12 A cursory search is probably all that can be achieved at this stage in the incident but, again, looking to perhaps a long-term enquiry a 'full managed search' may be necessary (Cook and Tatersall, 2008, Appendix D) and the employment of specialist services required such as a police dog or POLSA search advisers.

A13 One of the fundamental facts to be determined in a missing person investigation is the reason why the subject has disappeared. ACPO guidance states that if the circumstances of a disappearance are found to be suspicious or unexplained then an officer must, if in doubt, 'think murder' (ACPO, 2005a, p 9).

Failure to apply such thinking in past cases has led to the loss of valuable investigative opportunities and could ultimately result in failure to trace the missing person or to establish sufficient evidence to convict a perpetrator.

The relationship between the missing person and the person making the initial report can also be important. Experience suggests that it would be wrong for investigators to always assume such relationships are as straightforward as they might initially appear; there have been numerous cases where the person reporting the crime and/or the missing person has been found to be the perpetrator of the crime.

See Missing Persons, *BSPOH 2010*, 9.27

A14 The immediate actions to be taken (based on ACPO, 2005b) include:

- trace and identify Kathy Trimble—Emma's last known sighting;

- trace and identify (from Kathy) any other school friends who spoke with Emma during the day;

- make a cursory search of bedroom—farewell notes (in case of suicide notes), clothing, suitcases, travel passes, passport, etc;

- make a cursory search of the house and garden (in case she has self-harmed);

- check with the hospital whether she is at A&E;

- profile family and identify relatives and extended family and contact as necessary.

Secondary actions for the next morning (involving other officers and depending on resources available) would include checking:

- CCTV at the school—identify and secure;

- H2H—neighbours at least.

Tertiary actions include checking:

- taxi offices/ranks (for travel from school or home address);

- CCTV in town centres, bus and railway stations, routes away from the school—begin to collate and identify for securing later;

- CCTV in the vicinity of the home address (community or local authority or private systems).

See Missing Persons Enquiries, *BSPOH 2010*, 9.27.1

A15 Pc Biggs should not wait until Saturday morning. Speedy lines of enquiry may quickly discover there is no alarm or cause for concern but delay can be serious or even tragic.

Pc Biggs should request a search of any databases available within the police station or held by the local education authorities to identify an initial contact for school-related emergencies. (However, local protocols and arrangements for emergency out-of-hours contact with educational establishments do vary from area to area.)

A16 It is perfectly legitimate for education authorities, headteachers, teachers, and caretakers to assist the police and provide personal details of pupils in cases that potentially involve a criminal investigation. Section 29 of the Data Protection Act 1998 allows organizations and individuals to give out personal information in order to trace a potential victim of crime or the perpetrator of a criminal offence (such as abduction).

A17 It is possible, of course, for a member of school staff to speak to Kathy Trimble direct and provide her with the information that alerts her to the ongoing situation and then invite Kathy to contact the police—providing a direct contact number to Pc Biggs. In this way the onus is on Kathy to make contact, but this approach often avoids difficulties in a situation where people working for an organization are concerned about sharing details they consider to be confidential to the employer.

A18 Depending on individual force systems, an incident or activity log (on an electronic database or in writing) records the incident and the police response to it. It is important that Pc Biggs records all the actions he has taken or intends to take as this informs his supervisors and specialist departments of the ongoing event. This system often allows 'flagging', that supervisors and specialists can be alerted of the need to monitor the officer's activities and in effect to supervise him from a distance. In other words, the incident is automatically drawn to the attention of others.

Furthermore, an activity log provides a comprehensive audit of police response enabling a retrospective review of any actions taken to date. This might avoid duplication of effort, identify new lines of enquiry, or require a higher level of response and logistical support. Finally, such systems enable 'trigger plans', that is, if certain factors or criteria apply then subsequent action should follow automatically. For example, if a missing person cannot be accounted for after, say, 24 hours, then this would automatically call for (or trigger) the investigation being upgraded, informing the NPIA Missing Persons Bureau, and bringing in an investigating officer (IO) or a senior investigating officer (SIO).

A19 There is the possibility that Emma is the victim of abduction, possibly for the purposes of sexual exploitation. If this is suspected to be the case then consideration will be given to implementing Child Rescue Alert and involving the NPIA Missing Persons Bureau.

A20 Yes, it would be appropriate to reassess the risk as 'high'.

A21 Sharing the information gained from Kathy is going to be difficult. It will alarm Mrs Burcher and quite possibly Mr Burcher and there is also the issue of confidentiality towards Kathy. The balance is one to be carefully thought out and if necessary any doubts shared with supervisors. It might be an issue that should be passed to other specialist officers or the Family Liaison Officer (FLO) who should be skilled in dealing with emotive issues and responding to parental concerns and upset. But Pc Biggs is an experienced officer and he seems to have made progress in his relationship with Mr and Mrs Burcher. He knows that the sooner he can acquaint them with the facts, the sooner they may divulge information to him that is essential to the progress of the investigation. The parents might not appreciate the relevance of some of the information they have, as they do not know all the facts of the investigation.

Such decisions (on how much to tell the parents) and the reasons for them are often called 'policy' decisions. They should be recorded so that any enquiry at a later stage about 'what happened and why' can examine the decisions objectively. This type of decision should be recorded in writing as it facilitates accurate recall of thought processes, priorities, and concerns and helps with good decision-making. Leaving the recording to a later time and date often results in the reasoning being less clear.

The disciplined process of recording actions and decisions encourages careful thought processes. A suitable strategy and approach is more likely to be composed in this way. In this case Pc Biggs decides he will share his information with Mr and Mrs Burcher and emphasize to them that Kathy was extremely helpful.

A22   A diary perhaps—had she written about what she was planning?—her personal items, eg her mobile—a bag, make-up—are they missing? He could also assess the amount of clothing in drawers and on hangers—is any clothing missing? He will need to know if a bag similar to the one described by Kathy is missing. Mrs Burcher could help him with all this, under the direction of Pc Biggs. He will need to look for any indication that Emma was planning to spend some time away.

A23   The hair in the hairbrush (and residue on any toothbrush) may be valuable sources of DNA if the incident becomes one of a sinister nature or a serious crime enquiry. Thought should be given to the recovery of these items, however, as being insensitive in the manner this is achieved may cause unnecessary distress and alienate the stepfather still further.

A24   It was wise to take advice as the forensic recovery and examination of digital equipment, such as computers, is a specialist area of forensic investigation. Inappropriate techniques used to collect computer-based evidence may lead to evidence being irretrievably lost or later being ruled inadmissible in the case of any criminal prosecution.

In this case the Digital Forensics Unit are likely to advise Pc Biggs to:

- photograph the screen showing the password protected screensaver;

- photograph any other components associated with the computer, eg printers, iPods connected to a USB port, etc (if Pc Biggs has no camera available then he will be advised to make a note of any messages on the screen and make a sketch plan of the computer set up—base unit, monitor, modems, etc);

- disconnect the power to the computer base unit by pulling out the power lead from the back of the base unit (not from the socket in the wall);

- look for any written notes in Emma's bedroom (eg a 'post it' note under the keyboard) which might give information about the passwords that she used;

- make notes in his PNB concerning the actions he has taken (eg moving the mouse) and the times at which these occurred.

A25   The case has become more serious because of the mention of modelling and meeting a man over the internet (a classic form of grooming and abduction).

A26   Jodie Franks will be of great assistance to Pc Biggs as an ongoing relationship needs to be established between the police investigators and the family. As soon as possible, whilst Pc Biggs' focus is on completing immediate enquires, she will be able to keep the family aware of ongoing enquiries and provide support to both sides of the incident. The FLO will initiate an SIO request for Mr and Mrs Burcher to move out of the house to a relative nearby while the search of the property takes place and the bedroom is secured. The family will understand the need for a photograph of Emma, if this is carefully explained, and Jodie Franks will be able to help here.

A27   He decides that this is premature as this may also alert the suspect and events would be out of his control. It could put Emma at risk. He chooses to accelerate enquiries on the computer to trace 'the man' and intercept him as soon as possible.

Generally, the timing of any publicity broadcasts is critical, for example the next local news event may be the most advantageous in jogging people's memories. Delay is likely to disadvantage the enquiry and willing members of the public may forget what they saw or heard over time. However, it is still perhaps too early to excite the press and radio but the media strategy will form part of the forward planning.

A28 This restricts movement in and out of the scene until the specialist CSI and computer forensic teams have completed the task of searching for forensic evidence. Pc Biggs had locked the room, presuming the parents had told the truth and that neither of the parents would go into Emma's room over night.

Test Yourself

Across

2 The offence of rape includes penetration of the . . .
4 An informal term for a sexual assault.
6 One category of presumptions about consent.
9 Child victims may find it hard to accuse this relative.
10 Scientific term for an opening in the body.
12 May constitute a sexual assault.
15 No defence for a sexual assault.
17 Under the Sexual Offences Act 2003, using the lavatory is a . . . act.
18 Essential part of rape.
19 Used for penetration but not rape.

Down

1 Several photographs can be combined to produce a new image known as a . . . photograph.
3 Minimum age for offender under s 7 of the Sexual Offences Act 2003.
5 Under s 63 of the Criminal Justice and Immigration Act 2008, a pornographic photograph of bestiality is known as an . . . pornographic image.
7 Photographs covered under s 1 of the Protection of Children Act 1978.
8 The symptomatic stage of HIV infection.
11 A . . . of a reward may be offered to a prostitute.
13 Informal term for a person who controls prostitutes.
14 Professional, touches intimate parts but not sexually.
16 Can only be committed by a man.

Answers to Knowledge Check Questions

K1 a   K2 b   K3 d   K4 c   K5 d   K6 b   K7 a   K8 c

Answers to Test Yourself

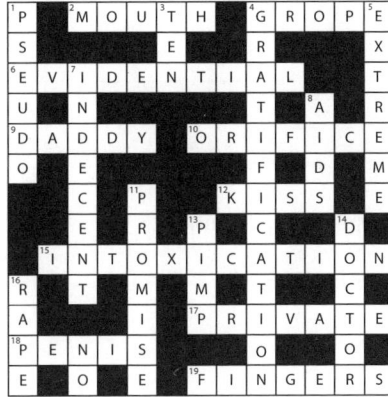

Dovestone Road

🦶   forensic awareness required

✓   assessment opportunity

☺   diversity issues

⬤   health and safety

▽?▽   questionable practice

✏   a pen or pencil is required

Introduction

In this scenario, two experienced police officers, Pc Jones and Pc Nabil, attend a drink and drive related road policing incident in Sholsbury, an average-sized town in northern England. Research carried out by the Institute of Alcohol Studies (2009b) indicates that approximately 50 per cent of convicted drink drivers have blood alcohol levels in excess of 150 milligrammes per 100 millilitres of blood, and about 12 per cent of these drivers are convicted of a second offence within ten years. Drivers of all ages cause accidents associated with drink driving, but the highest rates per 100,000 licence holders occur in young men aged up to 34, particularly between the ages of 20 and 24. Just over half of the convictions for drink driving are for people under 33, but the average age of drink drive offenders is higher than that of other serious traffic offenders. Within the category of convicted drink drivers, 40 per cent have previous convictions for other types of offences, and drink drivers are twice as likely (as a member of the general public of the same age and gender) to have a criminal record.

This scenario portrays a number of investigative procedures relating to being unfit through drugs and the detection of driving above the prescribed limit of alcohol including the preliminary testing, evidence gathering for post-incident drinking (hip-flask defence), and hospital procedure.

Knowledge Check

✏ Before you undertake this scenario, assess your understanding of the underpinning legislation involved by attempting the following knowledge check.

Questions K1 to K7 inclusive are multiple choice so you should select **one** of the letters a, b, c, or d as the answer—and write it down. Check your answers at the end of this chapter before beginning the scenario.

K1 An intoxicated woman is asleep in the driver's seat of a car, with the engine not running and the car keys in her lap. In relation to ss 4 and 6 of the Road Traffic Act 1988, she is:

    a) In charge of a vehicle
    b) Attempting to drive
    c) Driving
    d) Using a vehicle

K2 Which one of the following is a motor vehicle for the purposes of the Road Traffic Act 1988?

    a) Pedal cycle
    b) School bus
    c) Electric wheelchair
    d) Go-ped

K3 Which vehicle would be regarded as mechanically propelled but would not be classed as a motor vehicle?

    a) Forklift truck
    b) Family car
    c) Milk float
    d) London taxi cab

K4 Which legislation provides the power of arrest for being unfit to drive under s 4 of the Road Traffic Act 1988?

    a) Section 24 of the PACE Act 1984
    b) Section 4 of the Road Traffic Act 1988
    c) Section 5 of the Road Traffic Act 1988
    d) Section 17(1) of the PACE Act 1984

K5 What is the most appropriate course of action of a police officer towards a person who fails to provide a specimen of breath for a preliminary breath test under s 6A(1) of the Road Traffic Act 1988 when they are **not** suspected of having alcohol in their body, for example after an accident?

    a) Arrest the person for failing to cooperate with a preliminary breath test under s 6D(1) of the Road Traffic Act 1988
    b) Arrest the person for failing to cooperate with a preliminary breath test under s 24 of the PACE Act 1984
    c) Report the person for failing to cooperate with a preliminary breath test under s 6(6) of the Road Traffic Act 1988
    d) There is nothing that should be done

K6 When requiring a person to provide a specimen of breath for a preliminary breath test under s 6A(1) of the Road Traffic Act 1988, which of the following statements is **false**?

    a) A constable does not need to be in uniform to administer a preliminary breath test after an accident has occurred
    b) A constable must be in uniform to administer a preliminary breath test unless an accident has occurred
    c) A constable does not need to be in uniform to require a person to cooperate with a preliminary breath test
    d) A constable must be in uniform on all occasions to administer a preliminary breath test

K7 Under s 5 of the Road Traffic Act 1988, what is the prescribed limit of alcohol per 100 millilitres of blood?

    a) 35 milligrammes
    b) 35 microgrammes
    c) 80 milligrammes
    d) 107 microgrammes

Dovestone Road Scenario

It's 22.00 and Pc Jones and Pc Nabil are on mobile patrol in the town centre when they hear the following broadcast from Control over Airwaves:

'Your attention is drawn to a black Ford saloon with a partial index number of QQ51 seen in Ashbury Road in the last five minutes. The driver, male, age about 40 years, is believed to be driving with excess alcohol having just left the Dog and Duck public house in Ashbury Road, direction of travel unknown.'

Q1   Where should they begin their area search in order to locate this vehicle?

But a couple of minutes later, the two officers are requested by Control to attend the scene of a three-vehicle injury road traffic collision in Dovestone Road, Sholsbury near the junction with Cherry Street. Dovestone Road is a main road with a mix of shops, takeaways, and terraced houses, approximately three miles from Sholsbury town centre. On arrival there is considerable traffic congestion, and fire and rescue services are already at the scene.

Three vehicles are involved: a black Ford (index number QQ51 KUL) seems to have run into the back of a pale-coloured van, causing considerable damage to the rear of the van; the van has collided with the rear of a green hatchback causing frontal damage to the van and damage to the rear of the hatchback.

In line with ACPO policy, driver training is required before police officers are permitted to drive marked police vehicles at high speed using this warning equipment.

As the officers prepare to get out of the car, they hear loud music with a heavy bass beat from the direction of the vehicles. Pc Jones shakes her head and glances at Pc Nabil—who deliberately does not respond. He already knows what she feels about loud music.

The paramedics are busy looking after a casualty inside the ambulance.

Q2   What should be the first considerations at any incident?

The person sitting in the driver's seat of the van appears to be calm and unhurt. As he is looking over in their direction, Pc Nabil seizes the opportunity to gesture to him to turn off the music, and directs Pc Jones to find out about the casualty from the ambulance crew.

One of the ambulance crew tells her that the casualty is the driver from the hatchback, and that she is unconscious but breathing on her own. They also tell Pc Jones that the casualty smells of intoxicating liquor.

... have to speak with her later ... I wonder which hospital she's going to? ...

As Pc Jones turns back towards the van two young men from the group of onlookers call out that a man from the Ford ran off, and they keep pointing at one particular house. Pc Jones goes over to speak with them.

Q3 What information, if any, should Pc Jones record, and where?

Then another witness comes forward and speaks to Pc Jones, and says that she saw the driver from the van throw something into the gutter by a drain and then get out and kick it down between the bars of the drain cover. Pc Jones records the witness's details in her pocket note book and takes a quick look down between the bars of the drain—the light from her torch glints back from a long way down. She concludes there is nothing she can easily retrieve for the moment.

Q4 What other sources of evidence may be available to the officers?

Other officers now arrive at the scene and begin to direct the traffic around the vehicles involved in the incident. Pc Jones quickly tells Pc Nabil about what the witness said about the van driver and the small package, and then they go over to the van to speak with the driver.

Q5 What should the officers ask the driver first, before asking any further questions?

One of the newly arrived officers comes over to Pc Jones and asks about the width of the pinch points down one of the side streets where they are directing the traffic. Pc Jones goes over to explain the road layout—she knows these side streets well.

Pc Nabil begins questioning the driver from the van.

Pc Nabil	Good evening, my name is Pc Nabil. Thanks for turning off your music. Are you ok? Were you driving this car when it was involved in this collision?
Driver	Yeah ... just my luck, it running into me like that ... huh ...
Pc Nabil	What's your name? ... and I need to see your driving licence please.
Driver	Right—why? ... I dunno ... I'm not so sure I've got it on me today ...
Pc Nabil	Because you have been involved in an accident, I require you to produce your licence now, and failing to do so may make you liable to prosecution.
Driver	Oh right ... maybe it's in here ... here it is ... officer.

Q6 What power, if any under these circumstances, has Pc Nabil to require the driver to produce his driving licence?

Pc Nabil observes the driver to be generally unsteady, with slurred speech and glazed eyes. He notes down the details of the driving licence. The driver number is **CHAPM 506208C63LY**.

Q7   Using the driver number, what is his date of birth, and does the licence confirm that the van driver is male?

Pc Jones comes back over and at Pc Nabil's request carries out a PNC check—a nominal search for the driver's details using his name and then a vehicle search using the van's index number. The nominal check shows a Stuart Chapman, born 20 June 1958, as known, not currently wanted, with a warning sign of drugs, two records of convictions for unlawful possession of drugs, and a record of a street warning for unlawful possession during the last two years. The vehicle search shows the registered owner as a Stuart Chapman, residing at the address shown on the driving licence. The local police intelligence database has a record of a Stuart Chapman recently involved in a domestic incident with his wife, Vicki Scott.

Q8   Has Pc Nabil the power to require Chapman to provide a specimen of breath for a preliminary breath test?

Q9   In order to require a breath test, does Pc Nabil have to suspect that Chapman has consumed alcohol?

Q10   Does Pc Nabil need to be in uniform to request and administer the preliminary breath test?

Q11   Does Pc Nabil need to wait before carrying out the test?

Pc Nabil assembles the test kit. It's a new one he has only used a couple of times before.

. . . I can do this from memory now . . . no need for those instructions any more!

He says to Chapman:

'Now you need to take a deep breath and blow into this bit—just one long breath—don't stop until I say so.'

The test is negative, but Pc Nabil reflects on Chapman's general behaviour and condition, his previous convictions for unlawful possession of drugs, and the witness's assertion that he had deliberately disposed of a small package after the collision.

. . . drugs . . . unfit to drive?

Q12   What section of the Road Traffic Act 1988 covers driving while unfit to drive, and what types of vehicle does it cover?

Q13   What power of arrest would be used, and for what reason is the arrest necessary?

> Pc Nabil arrests Chapman and cautions him on suspicion of the offence. One of the other officers takes him to the police station in a patrol car.
>
> The two officers now turn their attention to the driver of the Ford. Pc Jones contacts Control and requests a PNC check on the Ford. The registered keeper is shown as Daniel Wood of 161 Dovestone Road, Sholsbury—the house which the witnesses pointed out earlier. A check of the local intelligence database confirms Wood as the occupant at the address and that he regularly uses the vehicle.
>
> Pc Nabil leads the way over to the house. The front door is ajar so they knock, but there is no reply. They wait and then knock louder and call out.

Q14   What power of entry, if any, do the officers have?

> Pc Nabil steps inside and sees a man standing in the dark facing the wall, swigging from a glass bottle. From the back he fits the description provided by the witness earlier. Pc Nabil indicates to Pc Jones to wait by the door—he wants to keep it low key—but is also aware of his own safety.
>
> | | |
> |---|---|
> | **Pc Nabil** | Good evening. We are investigating a road traffic collision that has recently occurred just outside here. What's your name please? Are you ok? |
> | **Wood** | Get out of my house. |
> | **Pc Nabil** | I have reason to believe that you were driving a black Ford saloon, index number QQ51 KUL when it was involved in a collision a few minutes ago just outside. I am requiring you to provide a specimen of breath for a breath test ... (pauses) ... and failure to do so may make you liable to arrest and prosecution. |
> | **Wood** | Look, I've just had a few snifters ... to calm my nerves ... |
>
> Wood half turns to face Pc Nabil, rolls his eyes and sighs heavily. Pc Nabil asks him to put the bottle on the table. He complies and sits down with his eyes closed and looking very tense. Pc Nabil reaches out quietly and moves the bottle away, noting a strong smell of intoxicating liquor.
>
> *... have to wait a while for this one ... hope he doesn't kick off ...*
>
> Although Pc Nabil cannot be sure if the liquid in the bottle contains alcohol, it is reasonable for him to assume it does, and since he has seen Wood drinking from the bottle in the last few minutes, Pc Nabil must wait before administering the breath test. He glances at his watch and notes the time. This delay could be awkward; Wood might become impatient and aggressive, but Pc Nabil decides to use this time to record some of what Wood has already said, and to caution him.
>
> *... checking he gets the caution might take a while ... just what we need! ...*

Q15   Has Wood made a significant statement?

Q16   Why is it particularly important for Pc Nabil to wait before administering the test?

Q17   How could Pc Nabil use ideas from transactional analysis to influence the tone of the exchanges between himself and Wood?

> Pc Nabil explains the caution, but it doesn't go that well.
>
> **Pc Nabil**   Do you understand that anything you say now could be referred to in court and used as evidence against you?
>
> **Wood**   What are you going on about now? I … I … I'm not going to any court!

Q18   What should Pc Nabil do if Wood appears not to understand the significance of the caution? How might this influence the case if it subsequently goes to court?

> Pc Nabil then asks Wood about the type and quantity of alcohol he has recently consumed. Wood's replies are brief, bad tempered, and (despite Pc Nabil's attempts to clarify) contradictory. Pc Nabil notes them down word for word in his pocket note book.

Q19   What further information will Pc Nabil require in order to calculate the likely alcohol level in Wood's blood at the time of the collision, and what form will he use back at the station?

> Pc Nabil checks that 20 minutes have elapsed and then assembles the breath test kit again. He guides Wood through what to do, and the result of the test is positive.

Q20   What piece of legislation provides the power of arrest under these circumstances?

> Pc Nabil arrests Wood on suspicion that the proportion of alcohol in his breath or blood exceeded the prescribed limit at the time of the accident. Pc Nabil indicates to Pc Jones to seize the bottle. He marks the level of liquid in the bottle with a sticky label. The screw-top is missing so Pc Jones sticks a label over the top of the bottle and holds it upright in a Police Evidence bag to try and avoid spillage.

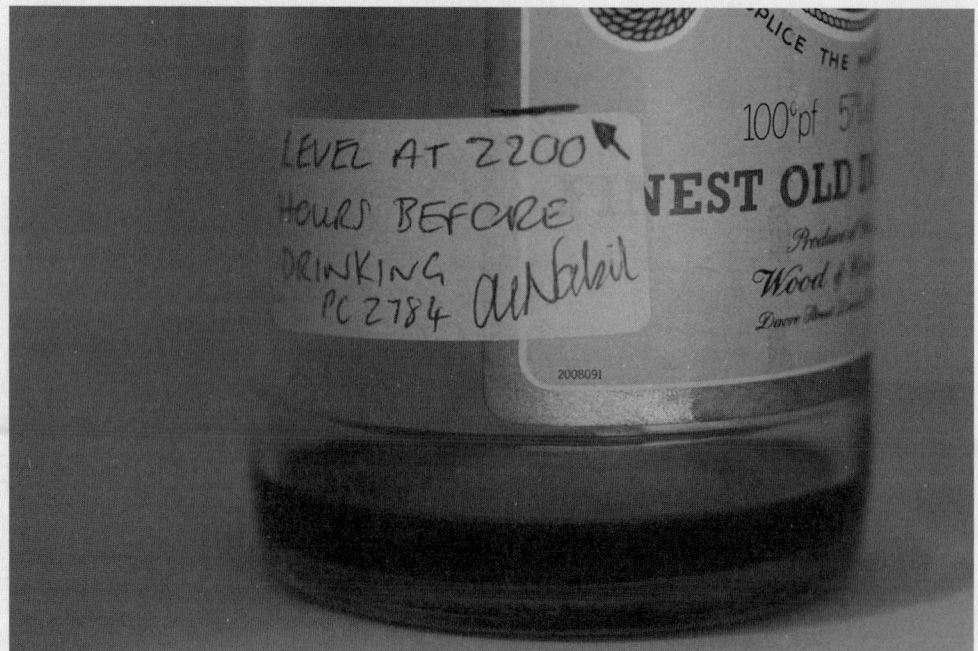

It is important to mark the bottle clearly for the purposes of laboratory analysis.

Q21   What details should Pc Jones note before leaving the house?

Q22   What will they do with the seized items?

> Before going back to the station with Wood, Pc Jones carries out a PNC check on the green hatchback. The registered keeper is Vicki Scott. Pc Jones requests that Control arranges for an officer to go to the hospital to carry out a hospital breath test procedure on the driver.

Q23   Which legislation provides police officers with the power to investigate drink or drugs related driving offences at a hospital?

Q24   What is the definition of a 'hospital' and of a 'patient'?

Q25   Before a preliminary test can be required from a hospital patient, does the officer need to notify anybody?

Q26   What type(s) of preliminary tests can be carried out on hospital patients?

> The breath test is positive so the officer arranges for a blood sample to be taken.

Q27   Who will take the blood sample?

Q28   Does anybody need to be notified of the proposal to make the requirement for the blood sample to be taken?

Q29   What happens to the blood sample?

> The officer returns to the station and tells Pc Jones that Scott fainted while the blood sample was being taken and that he had not obtained her permission to have it tested—he was going to do that after the sample had been taken. He had waited a while but she had not regained consciousness when he left the hospital. He also reported that the doctor in charge of the case seemed rather tetchy with him.
>
> Later that day Pc Jones receives a call from the hospital that Scott has regained consciousness. Before she goes to the hospital she checks with the force medical examiner that he had indeed taken the blood sample, and had arranged for the crime scene investigator to store the blood.
>
> Pc Jones finds the ward and sees Scott in the bed in the corner. She is awake. Pc Jones steps back before Scott spots her.

Q30   What should Pc Jones do before speaking with Scott?

> Scott is awake but still a bit drowsy. She is able to confirm her name and invites Pc Jones to look at her driving licence—fortunately the ambulance crew had brought her bag in the ambulance. Scott seems to have forgotten that she participated in a breath test earlier, and that she had already shown her licence to the other officer.

Q31   Why does Pc Jones check with Scott that the address on the licence is correct?

> Pc Jones then mentions the blood sample taken earlier, and explains that it needs to be tested. Scott seems upset but agrees to cooperate and gives permission for the sample to be tested. Pc Jones then explains that she needs to ask her about the accident, and interviews her under caution. She also explains that the test results will take a couple of weeks to come back, and depending on the test result, she may be prosecuted for the offence of driving after consuming so much alcohol that the proportion of it in her blood exceeded the prescribed limit, and if so will receive a letter in the post at her home address.
>
> Once the results of the evidential tests are known, a decision can be made as to what offences will be considered for prosecuting one or more of the drivers. Already it is clear that Wood could be prosecuted for failing to stop after an accident because he left the scene of the collision without furnishing details to the other drivers.

Q32   Under what legislation is it an offence to fail to stop after an accident?

> Back at the police station, Chapman's detention is authorized and the investigation into his suspected driving under the influence of drugs begins.

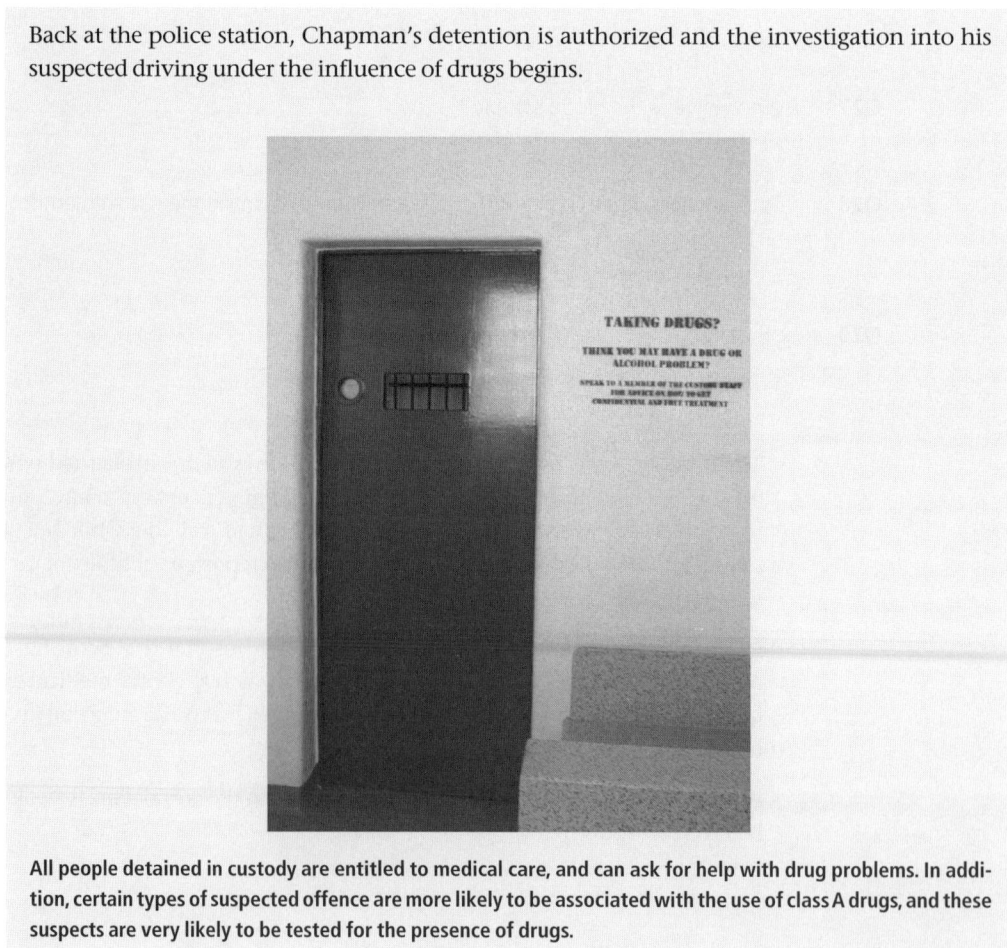

All people detained in custody are entitled to medical care, and can ask for help with drug problems. In addition, certain types of suspected offence are more likely to be associated with the use of class A drugs, and these suspects are very likely to be tested for the presence of drugs.

Chapman agrees to have evidential blood samples taken and is subsequently bailed to return to the police station pending analysis.

The detention of Wood is also authorized and the station breath test procedure is carried out, although he still maintains he had only drunk alcohol after the incident.

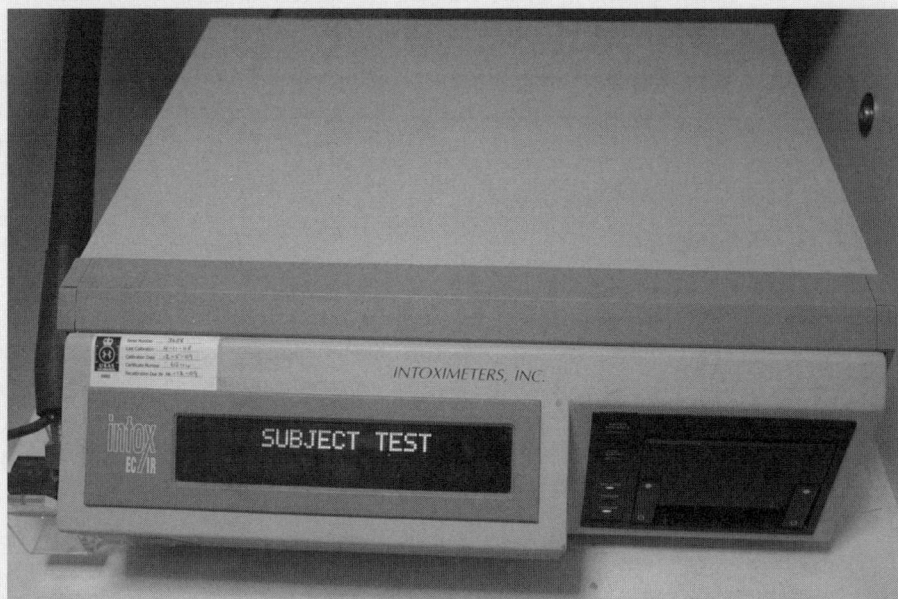

This equipment is used for evidential breath tests for alcohol—clearly not one of the portable devices now increasingly used by some police organizations.

The lower of the two readings indicates that he had 121 microgrammes of alcohol per 100 millilitres of breath, above the prescribed limit. MG DD forms are completed with information required for the laboratory to make a back-calculation. He is bailed pending the results from the laboratory.

Outcome

The results of the lab tests and the back-calculations showed that at the time he drove into the back of Chapman's van, Wood had 152 milligrammes of alcohol per 100 millilitres of blood, above the prescribed limit. Witnesses from the Dog and Duck described Wood and how much he had drunk prior to leaving in his black Ford saloon—he had indeed been the subject of the police broadcast just prior to the collision. On his return to the police station he was charged under s 5 Road Traffic Act 1988 (driving above the prescribed limit) and s 170 RTA 1988 (failing to stop). He pleaded guilty in court and was fined and disqualified from driving for one year. As for Scott, the result of the analysis of the evidential blood samples taken from her in the hospital indicated that she had 102 milligrammes of alcohol per 100 millilitres of blood. She too appeared in court, pleaded guilty to s 5 RTA 1988, driving above the prescribed limit and was fined and disqualified from driving for one year.

Chapman was charged under s 4 RTA 1988, being unfit to drive through drugs. Laboratory results indicated that he had significant traces of amphetamine sulphate in his blood. At court he pleaded guilty and was fined and disqualified from driving for one year.

After interviewing all the drivers it emerges that the most likely sequence of events was that Chapman came to an abrupt halt colliding with the rear of Scott's car, having been driving far too closely behind his estranged wife's vehicle for some distance. Wood was unable to stop in time and ran into the back of Chapman's van. Other witnesses came forward to confirm that they had seen what they had believed to be a road rage incident in the surrounding area involving Chapman's van and his estranged wife's hatchback.

Dovestone Road Answers

A1 According to research from Scotland, 88 per cent of people who drove after consuming alcohol said they were driving home. 51 per cent stated they were on a journey that was between one and five miles in length that was 40 per cent of the time on roads that were mainly quiet and lit in rural towns or villages (Scottish Government, 2007).

Based in part on this information, but also using their local knowledge, the officers' area search should focus on an area in a five-mile radius of Ashbury Road, on quiet, lit roads. As patrolling officers they will probably be familiar with routes around town that are often used to avoid city centres, colloquially known as 'rat runs'. Some drivers may believe that away from city centres, the police presence is likely to be less and that the chance of 'random' stops might be lower than on main roads.

A2 The preservation of life is a priority. The officers should wear high visibility clothing at all times and protect the scene from further danger by placing warning signs to slow the traffic nearby.

A3 The identity of the driver of the Ford is unknown and therefore according to PACE Code of Practice D, a record should be made of any witness's first description of a potential suspect, preferably in one of the officers' pocket note books.

As this information may be relevant evidence of a crime, the details of the two men and any other witnesses (such as other bystanders) should also be recorded to comply with the Criminal Procedure and Investigations Act 1996 (CPIA) and the associated Codes of Practice.

This incident may result in a criminal investigation and the police officers involved here are therefore investigators, and hence they must follow the CPIA Codes, such as recording information and retaining records of information and other material. Pc Nabil and Pc Jones do not know for certain whether an offence has been committed or if the case will go to court or what evidence might be needed. Early on in an incident, deciding how to proceed with the enquiry and what evidence to collect is not easy; these skills will be developed over time.

A4 CCTV footage of the scene may be available, and might provide important evidence. The officers must make every effort to retrieve the recording as soon as possible; it may be automatically deleted by the recording authority after a certain period of time, depending on their operating procedures.

A5 The officer asks the driver to get out of the car partly to ensure that the driver cannot drive off. One alternative would be to ask for the keys to be handed to one of the officers. The officer is also provided with the opportunity to observe the driver, to see if he or she is unsteady or drunk.

See Unfit to Drive through Drink or Drugs, *BSPOH 2010*, 11.16.2

It is safer for all persons concerned to stand on the pavement away from vehicles, particularly as the vehicles may be dangerous due to damage sustained in the recent collisions.

A6 Section 164(1) of the Road Traffic Act 1988 provides the power to request to see a driver's licence and it applies when a person is reasonably believed to be the driver of a motor vehicle at the time of an accident.

See Requesting to See a Driver's Licence, *BSPOH 2010*, 11.4.2

A7   The number shows that the person is a male born on 20 June 1958:

- **5**06208 shows the year of birth as 1958;

- 5**06**208 shows that the person was born in June and is male; five has not been added to the second digit;

- 506**20**8 shows that the date of birth was the 20th of the month.

See Information Shown on Driving Licences, BSPOH 2010, 11.4.1

A8   Yes, s 6A of the Road Traffic Act 1988 provides Pc Nabil with the power to require a person who he reasonably suspects of driving a motor vehicle at the time of an accident to cooperate with a preliminary breath test.

See Preliminary Tests, BSPOH 2010, 11.16.4

A9   In this case, it is not necessary to suspect the influence of alcohol as it is sufficient that this person is suspected of driving a motor vehicle when it was involved in an accident.

A10   As the person to be tested is suspected of driving a motor vehicle when it was involved in an accident, the officer does not need to be in uniform to either request or administer the preliminary breath test.

See Preliminary Tests, BSPOH 2010, 11.16.4

A11   Pc Jones should ask the suspect if he has smoked or drunk alcohol in the last 20 minutes. If not, there is no need to wait. Failing to ask these questions will not invalidate the test or the result, but the results may be considered as less reliable and this could influence the outcome of a subsequent court case.

See Preliminary Breath Tests, BSPOH 2010, 11.16.4.1

A12   This offence is covered in s 4 of the Road Traffic Act 1988, and can involve any mechanically propelled vehicle.

See Unfit to Drive through Drink or Drugs, BSPOH 2010, 11.16.2

A13   The power of arrest in these circumstances is given under s 24 of the PACE Act 1984 and the necessity for the arrest would include the prompt and effective investigation of the offence such as gathering further evidence from the suspect, eg blood or urine samples and/or evidence from a medical practitioner regarding whether the suspect is fit or unfit to drive.

See What to do after a Preliminary Test, BSPOH 2010, 11.16.4.2

A14   The officers have powers of entry in this situation, for two separate reasons:

- first, there has been an accident in which they reasonably suspect a person has been injured (the driver of the hatchback has been taken to hospital so is likely to be injured);

- alternatively, the officers have information that Wood has been drinking alcohol so it is reasonable for them to suspect that he has committed a drink driving offence.

This power of entry in order to administer preliminary tests is given in s 6E of the Road Traffic Act 1988. A power of entry will be required to enter any premises, unless consent has been obtained from a person who has authority to give it. Consequently, it makes no difference whether a door is open or closed.

The table below shows the powers of entry and arrest that apply in suspected incidents of drink driving.

Offence	Power of entry	Power of arrest
Unfit to drive	section 24 of the PACE Act 1984	section 17(1)(c)(iiia) of the PACE Act 1984
Over the prescribed limit	section 6D(1) of the Road Traffic Act 1988	section 6E of the Road Traffic Act 1988 provides the power of entry (only after an injury accident) to: • require a preliminary breath test; • arrest for failing to provide a preliminary breath test; • arrest on suspicion of driving with excess blood alcohol.

See Preliminary Tests, *BSPOH 2010*, 11.16.4.2

A15   No. Although Wood has stated that he has consumed some alcohol recently, he has not said where or when. On the face of it these comments do not appear to amount to admission of guilt or to be evidence that could be used against the suspect. Further questioning will be required at interview to clarify whether he was involved in the collision and whether he was referring to drinking before or after the collision.

See Unsolicited Comments by Suspects, *BSPOH 2010*, 8.5

A16   Pc Nabil has seen Wood drinking a liquid that he suspects may contain alcohol. The manufacturer's instructions are to wait a period of 20 minutes before administering a test, because residual alcohol in the mouth from drinking intoxicating liquor and recent smoking of a cigarette or cigar can distort the accurate measurement of breath alcohol levels.

See Preliminary Breath Tests, *BSPOH 2010*, 11.16.4.1

A17   It could be that Wood is transacting in the child ego. Pc Nabil should certainly not use terse language or sarcasm (parent ego state) because this will increase the risk of this exchange developing into a full-blown child–parent–child transaction, complete with anger, defensiveness, and aggression. However, if Pc Nabil instead adopts the adult ego state (and speaks in terms that contain reasoning, logic, and common sense), then a crossed transaction will take place and this might bring Wood into a more adult frame of mind, avoiding a parent–child–parent transaction. Outlining the seriousness of the situation and the injury to the driver of the hatchback may help.

See Transactional Analysis, *BSPOH 2010*, 6.18.1

A18   Pc Nabil must ensure he has explained the caution in terms that Wood is most likely to understand, but if Wood still does not seem to understand, the investigation should nonetheless be continued. Pc Nabil must record in his pocket note book what was said by both himself and Wood in relation to the caution. As long as a court is convinced that Pc Nabil did his best to help Wood to understand the caution this will not affect the case.

The caution will be explained in full again when Wood is interviewed at the police station.

See Cautions, *BSPOH 2010*, 8.4

A19   In order that a back-calculation can be made by laboratory analysts, it is vital that evidence of all the alcohol consumed post-incident is seized. There will be little opportunity to return to the house at a later stage to retrieve further evidence. Later, back at the police station, Pc Nabil will need to find out the suspect's weight, height, and age (this can be calculated from his date of birth, but he should also ask, just in case there is any discrepancy) and information relating to any medical conditions, food consumption in the preceding six hours, and any medication taken regularly or taken in the preceding four hours. Pc Nabil should also note the suspect's general 'build'. All this information will be recorded on form MGDD/D.

See Allowing for the Delay between the Offence and Taking Samples, *BSPOH 2010*, 11.16.5.3

A20   Section 6D(1) of the Road Traffic Act 1988 provides the power of arrest. A positive result from a preliminary breath test directly justifies arrest; Pc Nabil should tell the suspect the result of the test and that he is under arrest on suspicion that the proportion of alcohol in his breath or blood exceeds the prescribed limit. The reason for the arrest is not the result of the breath test.

See What to do after a Preliminary Test, *BSPOH 2010*, 11.16.4.2

A21   She should note descriptions of the intoxicating liquor that has been consumed, such as the alcohol percentage proof and the volume of liquid left in the bottle and an estimation of the volume consumed.

It is important that the bottle and any drinking glasses are appropriately marked by the officer in such cases so that the laboratory is fully aware of what was drunk, in what quantities, and at what time. It is not sufficient to say that the suspect had 'two shots' or a 'swig' from a bottle. If the bottle cannot be identified then the officer needs to identify the brand of alcohol which has been drunk.

A22   They will contact the CSI or Scientific Support Unit representative who will ensure the paperwork and exhibits are in order before forwarding everything to the laboratory.

A23   Section 9 of the Road Traffic Act 1988, which relates specifically to patients in hospitals.

A24   The Road Traffic Act 1988 defines a hospital as an institution which provides treatment to patients. Generally, a patient is a person who is on hospital grounds either waiting to receive treatment or actually receiving treatment, however, a person whose treatment is complete is not considered to still be a patient. Whether a particular person is a patient is a question of fact for a court to decide.

See Drink-driving, Drugs, and Admission to Hospital, *BSPOH 2010*, 11.17

A25   Yes. The medical practitioner in immediate charge of Scott's case must be notified of the proposal to make the requirement and given the opportunity to object. Scott will also be asked to cooperate with the test and warned that if she fails to do so, she will be reported for an offence under s 6(6) of the Road Traffic Act 1988.

See Obtaining Samples from a Hospital Patient, *BSPOH 2010*, 11.17.1

A26   Preliminary tests that can be carried out on hospital patients include breath tests for alcohol, impairment for drink or drugs, and for the presence of drugs under ss 6A(1), 6B(1), and 6C(1) of the Road Traffic Act 1988, respectively.

A27   The force medical examiner should be called to take the sample. Under no circumstances must the doctor in charge of Scott's case take the sample.

A28   Yes. The medical practitioner in immediate charge of Scott's case must be notified of the proposal to make the requirement for the blood test and given the opportunity to object (even though he has been previously notified of the proposal to make a requirement for a preliminary breath test and was given the opportunity to object to that). Scott should also be asked to cooperate with the test and warned that if she fails to provide a specimen, she will be reported for an offence under s 7(6) of the Road Traffic Act 1988.

A29   The blood sample will be sent to the forensic laboratory. The officer should contact the CSI to make the arrangements, or alternatively it could be sent via registered post. Policy varies between forces.

A30   Pc Jones needs to ask the medical practitioner in immediate charge of the case if he objects to Scott being asked for permission to analyse the blood sample taken earlier; Scott might not even know that the sample had been taken.

See Unconscious Patients and Tests for Drugs or Alcohol, *BSPOH 2010*, 11.17.2

A31   Pc Jones knows that the case will involve sending documents to Scott by post.

A32   Section 170 of the Road Traffic Act 1988.

See Providing Information after a Reportable Accident, *BSPOH 2010*, 11.12.2

Test Yourself

And finally, complete the following crossword about driving under the influence of drugs or alcohol.

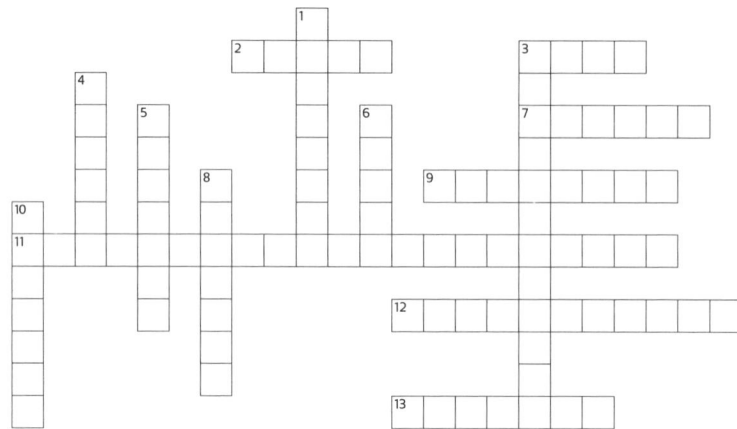

Across

2 Body sample for which the legal limit is 80 mpg alcohol per 100ml sample.

3 the case-file form for drink driving cases.

7 Minutes to wait after drinking before a preliminary breath test.

9 Month of birth for driving license 452171.

11 Type of vehicle referred to in s 4 of the RTA 1988.

12 This breath test cannot be used as evidence in court.

13 Must be given by a hospital doctor before the drunk patient fives a blood sample.

Down

1 Patient drink drivers can never be arrested here.

3 Type of vehicle referred to in ss 5 and 6 of the RTA 1988.

4 Place for a s 4 RTA 1988 offence.

5 Mode of trial for driving while unfit through drink or drugs.

6 Power provided by as 17(1)(c)(iiia) of PACE 1984 provides this power for s 4 of the RTA 1988.

8 A police officer must be in this to administer a preliminary breath test.

10 Must be avoided before taking a breath test for alcohol.

Answers to Knowledge Check Questions

K1 a   K2 b   K3 a   K4 a   K5 c   K6 d   K7 a

Answers to Test Yourself

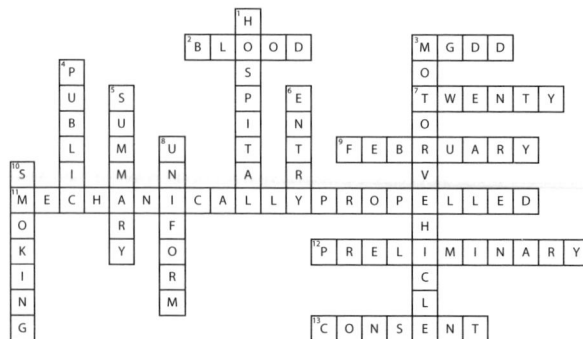

4 | The Stella Estate

👣   forensic awareness required

✓   assessment opportunity

☺   diversity issues

🌢   health and safety

▽?   questionable practice

✎   a pen or pencil is required

Introduction

This scenario features the problem of anti-social behaviour in residential areas and under-age drinking in places to which the public have access. According to the IAS (Institute of Alcohol Studies) 84 per cent of 12–17 year olds have drunk alcohol at some point. For the majority of those aged 12–15, drinking is occasional, however, about one in ten reported drinking at least once a week on average. As might be expected, drinking increases with age; over half of those aged 16–17 drank alcohol at least once a week.

The latest survey data suggests that in relation to so-called 'binge drinking', girls have caught up with and, in some cases, overtaken boys. Beer and lager are the most popular drinks among under 18s and to a lesser extent spirits, wine, and 'alcopops'. Approximately one in six of all 12–17 year olds have been involved in some form of anti-social behaviour during or after drinking, with the majority getting into a heated argument and frequent drinkers more likely to have been involved in anti-social behaviour. Finally, 20 per cent of young people who drink alcohol said they had asked someone else to buy alcohol for them.

This scenario aims to explore police powers both to deal with anti-social behaviour and to confiscate alcohol from young people. It also provides an insight into investigating offences of public disorder.

Knowledge Check

✎ Before you undertake this scenario, assess your understanding of the underpinning legislation involved by attempting the following knowledge check.

Questions K1 to K8 inclusive are multiple choice so you should select **one** of the letters a, b, c, or d as the answer—and write it down. Check your answers at the end of this chapter before beginning the scenario.

K1 Section 50 of the Police Reform Act 2002 gives a constable the power to request the name and address of a person acting in an anti-social manner. Section 1 of the same Act defines 'anti-social manner' as behaviour which causes or is likely to cause:

    a) Harassment
    b) Alarm
    c) Distress
    d) All three of the above

K2 Under s 5 of the Public Order Act 1986 a person is guilty of an offence if he/she uses disorderly conduct within the hearing or sight of a person:

    a) Who might be caused harassment, alarm, or distress
    b) Who is likely to be caused harassment, alarm, or distress
    c) With intent to cause harassment, alarm, or distress
    d) Who is caused harassment, alarm, or distress

K3 Under s 28(1) of the Crime and Disorder Act 1998 a basic offence becomes racially or religiously aggravated if the offender demonstrates hostility towards the victim of the offence based on the victim's membership or presumed membership of a racial or religious group. At which point must the suspect demonstrate the hostility?

    a) Before, at the time, or after committing the basic offence
    b) At the time of committing the basic offence only
    c) After committing the basic offence only
    d) Before committing the basic offence only

K4 Under s 1 of the Confiscation of Alcohol (Young Persons) Act 1997 a constable may require a person to surrender anything in his/her possession which he or she reasonably believes to be alcohol (or a container for alcohol) if the person is in a relevant place. Which of the following is **not** a relevant place?

    a) A seating area in a fast food establishment
    b) Licensed premises
    c) A private dwelling to which the person has unlawfully gained access
    d) A bus

K5 Under s 12 of the Licensing Act 1872, a person commits an offence if he or she is found drunk, but in which location?

    a) On the pavement adjacent to any road
    b) In a pedestrian precinct
    c) In licensed premises
    d) All of the above

K6 For a person to commit the offence of 'being drunk and disorderly' under s 91(1) of the Criminal Justice Act 1967, where must the person be at the time?

    a) In any licensed premises
    b) In any private place
    c) In any public place
    d) In any highway

K7 Under s 7(3) of the Children and Young Persons Act 1933 it is a constable's duty to seize any tobacco or cigarette papers in the possession of a person apparently under the age of:

    a) 18
    b) 17
    c) 16
    d) 15

K8 Under s 146(1) of the Licensing Act 2003 (selling alcohol to children) which of the following statements is true?

    a) The offence is committed only if the alcohol is sold in licensed premises and to a child

    b) The offence is committed if the alcohol is sold to a child who is under 17 years, in any place

    c) The offence is committed only when the alcohol is sold and never when it is supplied

    d) The offence can be committed anywhere

The Stella Estate Scenario

RESTRICTED

Maidbury Police

Operation Alcopop
Operational Order

1. Information:

1.1 The Stella Housing Estate recreation ground has been targeted by groups of under-age drinkers in the last three weeks.

1.2 Local residents have been making several complaints of rowdiness, anti-social behaviour, noise and litter.

1.3 The source(s) of the alcohol is not known.

1.4 Previous attendance by police and the local authority at the ground has made no contact with the youths.

1.5 The group appear to be highly organised with children of even younger years being used as spotters for police and local authority interventions.

1.6 Rubbish discarded by the group includes soft drink bottles thereby indicating that these receptacles are being used to hold alcohol covertly.

1.7 Local residents have counted between 10 and 20 members of the group at any one time.

1.8 There are several exit and entry points to the recreation ground.

1.9 Occurrences have been observed between the hours of 20.00 and 22.00 hours daily.

2. Intention:

2.1 The intention of Operation Alcopop is to confiscate the alcohol in possession of the young people and to identify the source(s) of the alcohol whenever possible.

2.2 Offences disclosed will be dealt with at the discretion of the officers attending.

3. Method:

3.1 Each patrol supervisor will designate a uniform mobile patrol containing two officers from core section to be in the area of the Stella Housing Estate recreation ground between 20.00 and 22.00 hours.

3.2 The call sign of the designated patrol will be MA 11.

3.3 A marked police vehicle will be made available for Op Alcopop by the patrol supervisor.

3.4 There are no extra resources available for this operation.

3.5 Force control room will deploy MA 11 to any call in the immediate area relating to youths and anti-social behaviour.

3.6 Once deployed, MA 11 will ascertain if other patrols are available to provide further assistance if required.

3.7 MA 11 will submit any intelligence gained regarding this group and their activities via a 5x5x5 report.

3.8 Consideration will be given to citizen focus and public reassurance through the use of foot patrol whenever possible.

4. Administration:

4.1 Deployments, including refreshment times, will be at the discretion of the patrol supervisor.

4.2 The Control Room Supervisor in consultation with the Patrol Sergeant will undertake co-ordination of MA 11.

4.3 All 5x5x5 intelligence reports will be submitted through line supervisors.

4.4 Any person arrested as a result of this operation will be taken to the custody area at Maidbury Police station.

4.5 Alcohol testing strips will be issued to officers deployed on Op Alcopop.

4.6 No overtime is available for this operation.

5. Risk Assessment:

5.1 The Stella Housing Estate recreation ground is poorly lit apart from the main footpaths.

5.2 The group appear to congregate on hard-standing areas within the grounds.

5.3 The ages of the group appear to be 14–16 years.

5.4 No intelligence has been received to indicate that weapons are carried by members of the group.

6. Communications:

6.1 MA 11 will use the Maidbury BCU Airwaves channel and not the operational channel.

7. Health and Safety:

7.1 All officers engaged on Op Alcopop will be given a copy of this operational order.

7.2 All officers engaged on Op Alcopop will be briefed by the patrol supervisor and have the opportunity to ask questions about the operation.

7.3 Officers will wear high visibility clothing at all times when away from the patrol vehicle.

7.4 Consideration will be given to the safe handling of liquids and containers at all times.

7.5 The safety of the general public will be considered at all times throughout this operation.

7.6 Consideration will be given to the welfare of young individuals who appear to be heavily intoxicated.

Q1 What offences and powers are available to deal with the problem described in the Operational Order reproduced above?

At 21.00 MA 11 Pc Kaleen and Pc Smithson are on patrol in Bronswell. It is the first time that Pc Smithson has been on mobile patrol in the evening—he is only eight months into his training. He looks about, glancing out of the windows and in the rear view mirrors. Pc Kaleen notes his eager attentiveness and reflects that this is all new for him. But for Pc Kaleen it is just another Friday night—his mind wanders back to his recent application for promotion to sergeant, after his successful OSPRE result.

It is a warm dusk, and street lights have just begun to flicker into action.

They receive the following message from Control over Airwaves:

'Control calling MA 11. Please attend Bronswell Square. Report from a Mr Langford, local neighbourhood watch coordinator, of some anti-social behaviour reported to him by some local residents there. Believe you are part of "Operation Alcopop" to deal with such incidents this evening?'

Bronswell Square is at the centre of a small 1970s housing estate of low-rise blocks of flats and semi-detached and terraced houses with on-street parking—the area has something of a bad reputation. Pc Kaleen recently attended an alleged shoplifting incident at the licensed convenience store. He recalled the run-down feeling of the area; a scruffy grassed area with a climbing frame and a couple of broken swings at one end, and a few concrete block bench seats.

Q2 Should the officers go to see Mr Langford before going to Bronswell Square? What are some possible advantages and disadvantages of calling at his home? What alternatives are there?

It is not the first time Pc Kaleen has attended anti-social behaviour incidents on this housing estate. Using his local knowledge, Pc Kaleen recognizes that Mr Langford's address is some distance away from Bronswell Square so he decides to call in on him on the way to the incident.

Mr Langford explains that this summer, possibly because the convenience store has stayed open later, young people (mainly males) have taken to meeting up in the square in the evenings talking, laughing, and sitting around, but that later on they play ball games, sometimes extending into the front gardens of the neighbouring houses. The noise levels rise as the young people call to each other across the square, and they also play 'tag' using the front gardens of the houses and flats as a 'circuit'. They drum out a rhythm on the metal frames of the climbing frame and swings and later, as night falls, local residents suffer anonymous door-bell ringing, upturned refuse and waste containers, graffiti on walls, and minor damage to property.

The more elderly residents suffer the most, particularly in the ground-floor flats. Windows are banged or tapped, and some young people put their heads through open windows making noises at the people inside. Such is the attraction of the activities in Bronswell Square that the local youths are joined each evening by 15 to 20 other young people aged between 14 and 16, presumably from neighbouring estates; their hooded garments effectively hide their faces from casual onlookers.

The residents have only just begun to address the problem, having suffered a great deal so far. They had been reluctant to contact the police and until now only vented their anger and frustration on the local neighbourhood watch coordinator.

Pc Kaleen confirms with the coordinator that there have been a number of calls from local residents reporting this incident and that they will attend the area and deal with whatever situation confronts them. However, this is the first occasion that Pc Kaleen has been made aware of incidents of anti-social behaviour in Bronswell Square.

Using his local knowledge, Pc Kaleen directs Pc Smithson to one of four entry points to Bronswell Square and, from a footpath from an adjoining garage block, they gain a vantage point from which they can observe the situation.

It is just as Mr Langford had described; young people running around and shouting, and banging on the climbing frames in the abandoned playground area. Pc Smithson finds the metallic drumming noise has a particularly threatening feel to it, and wonders how the local residents cope. After a moment or two, the two officers walk to the centre of the square, where three young people are emerging from a scuffle. Their eyes meet and the noise level drops around the square.

The two officers shine their torches on their cap badges and uniform to help them to be identified. Many of the youths who had been running around the square, now find exit points and disperse away from the area. Pc Kaleen introduces himself and his colleague to the three remaining young people. He asks them for their names.

Q3   What legislation is available to the officers to identify the young people involved should they be reluctant to answer questions?

The officers have reason to believe as a result of their own observations that these youths are acting in an anti-social manner.

Q4   What is the legal definition of an 'anti-social manner'?

They also conclude (from the earlier account of telephone messages from the local residents to the neighbourhood watch coordinator) that the behaviour has been going on for some time. They decide, for the purposes of intelligence and to try to prevent future occurrences of the behaviour, to establish the names and addresses of the youths remaining in the vicinity.

'We're here because of complaints from local residents who are feeling distressed, alarmed, and harassed by your behaviour this evening, and they have also told us about similar problems with young people on other occasions—but we are not saying that must have been you. But this evening we've been standing here watching and it's obvious that the noise coming from these climbing frames and from people running around the area and shouting and calling out is anti-social. Please can you each give me your name and address. These will be recorded permanently in my pocket note book and also entered onto a database in case anything like this happens again.'

The three young males stand quietly and two give names and addresses. Pc Smithson notes down their responses. The third one refuses to give his name and address, claiming he has a right to respect for his private life under 'Human Rights'.

Q5   In respect of the Human Rights Act 1998, does the youth have a legitimate claim? How could the officers deal with this situation and what offences might the youth be committing?

> Pc Kaleen asks him to step to one side and leaves Pc Smithson with the other two who have started protesting that they weren't causing much of a disturbance and that the main protagonists have gone. Pc Smithson hopes to build a rapport with the two youths, and asks them where else they could meet up to play football without disturbing other people.
>
> Pc Kaleen knows that to avoid escalating the situation he will have to proceed carefully with the youth who is refusing to give his name and address.

Q6   What forms of authority might Pc Kaleen use to solve this problem?

Q7   How will the officers' attitude and behaviour influence the outcome of this situation?

> The officers having used their knowledge of the law, and their authority, the youth provides his name and address. There is no evidence of alcohol therefore the youths are asked to leave the area.

Q8   How could the officers have dealt with the situation differently if an authorization under s 30 of the Anti-social Behaviour Act 2003 had been in place in the area?

> The two officers resume their patrol in the local area on foot to provide some public reassurance. A number of local residents make conversation with the two officers and thank them for the work they have done so far. Pc Kaleen takes the opportunity to test Pc Smithson's knowledge of how partner agencies could deal with the problems in Bronswell Square.

Q9   How could inter-agency and partnership initiatives be employed to relieve this situation and help the local residents?

> Pc Smithson has lots of ideas, and excitedly moves from one to the other—youth clubs, refurbishing the playground, community support groups . . . Pc Kaleen listens and wonders at his optimism. They move away from the square and take a route that follows the grassy area bordering on the local school playground. Pc Smithson is soon explaining how communities can be brought together through school sports clubs, and Pc Kaleen is about to interrupt and ask him which approach is most likely to be employed for the Stella estate when he receives another call from Control over Airwaves:
>
> *'Control calling MA 11, please attend the St Luke's recreation ground. Report of 15 to 20 youths being anti-social, consuming alcohol.'*
>
> Pc Kaleen calculates that the recreation ground is a couple of minutes' drive away and so they return to Bronswell Square to collect their patrol car.
>
> On arrival at the recreation ground the officers identify a group of about 20 young people, including some from the group they dispersed half an hour earlier. They all appear to be under 18 years of age and two youths are drinking from plastic bottles and seem unsteady on their feet.

Male or female and is it just cola?

Q10   What legislation is available to the officers to deal with the activities of these young people?

Although the two apparently drunk young males are holding soft drinks bottles, the officers reasonably suspect those bottles to contain alcohol. The suspicion is based on their observations that the youths are unsteady and that their speech is slurred. The youths keep chanting and whooping as Pc Kaleen questions them, and he begins to get impatient. There is also a strong smell of intoxicating liquor in the air; he feels confident of his suspicions and wants to get on and calm things down.

Q11   If Pc Kaleen had felt less than confident about his suspicions, what other methods are available to test that the soft drinks containers did in fact contain alcohol?

Q12   What legislation is available to the officers to deal with young people with alcohol in their possession?

Pc Kaleen draws the two young males aside to speak to them:

'I suspect you are under 18 years of age and in possession of alcohol. This is because there is a strong smell of intoxicating liquor in the air and you are unsteady on your feet, your eyes are glazed, and your speech is slurred. Please give me those soft drinks bottles as I suspect they contain alcohol. I also need your names and addresses. I must warn you that failure to comply with either of these requests without a reasonable excuse is an offence for which you may be arrested.'

Q13 Why has Pc Kaleen phrased it in this rather formal way?

The two young people seem less confident now, and they hand over the bottles to Pc Kaleen for disposal. Pc Kaleen asks them where they obtained the alcohol, but they refuse to say.

Q14 How should Pc Kaleen dispose of the alcohol, and what record does he need to make of his actions?

Pc Kaleen also completes a search form as this is policy in his area (although he has not technically conducted a search). The form records details such as the details recorded in the PNB, where the alcohol was obtained, and details of the parent/guardian.

Q15 In relation to the Confiscation of Alcohol (Young Persons) Act 1997, does MA 11 have any other options regarding the two youths?

Q16 Under what circumstances would the officers need to keep the bottles?

Pc Kaleen tells the youths he is going to keep the bottles to show their parents.

Some of the rest of the group have wandered off, but glancing up from the search form, Pc Kaleen can't help but notice two younger youths who are kicking something against a wall some distance away over by a garage block. He indicates to Pc Smithson that he should go over and have a word with them. As Pc Smithson approaches he hears them giggling and notices that they are smoking what appear to be hand-rolled cigarettes. He can't detect the characteristic smell of cannabis but judges that the two boys are no more than 14 years old.

Q17 What legislation if any is available to support Pc Smithson in relation to young people and cigarettes?

Having been initially rebuffed by one of the young people earlier on in the evening when he requested a name and address, Pc Smithson is hesitant to ask them to hand over the tobacco or cigarettes, in case they refuse. He does not want to appear as if he is unable to be professional, and wonders if Pc Kaleen has seen that they are smoking.

. . . if he hasn't noticed . . . I'll just leave it . . . maybe this is discretion . . .

Q18 Can police discretion be used in this way in these circumstances?

Pc Smithson's professionalism gets the better of him and with a logical, clear, and assertive tone to his voice, he requests that they hand over their tobacco or cigarettes. Still smirking, they hand over a crumpled packet of rolling tobacco and offer their two half-smoked cigarettes.

Pc Smithson declines the two lit cigarettes and tells them to stub them out and put them in the nearby bin.

Q19 How should Pc Smithson dispose of the packet of rolling tobacco and record his actions?

> He asks the boys to sign the record, although this is not a legal requirement. He then conducts a brief search of the boys as this is policy in the area, and tells them he is going to inform their parents about the incident. They don't look particularly concerned about this, but Pc Smithson is relieved that they have complied with his requests.
>
> Pc Kaleen now asks the rest of the group to leave the area, but keeps back the two youths who had the alcohol. As the group disperse he says quietly to the remaining two:
>
> *'Right you two, as you have been found with alcohol and you are under 18, then under s 1AB of the Confiscation of Alcohol (Young Persons) Act 1997 we can legally remove you back to your home. Let's be off—and start to make our way back now please.'*

Q20 Should the two young people decide not to comply, can they be removed by reasonable force if necessary?

> Pc Kaleen knows how to get to the street where they live but to give them a chance to be compliant he allows the two young people to lead the way out of the recreation ground. As they approach a bend in a small alleyway, a voice calls out:
>
> *'I've got you your bottles you wanted—call it a tenner—and the receipt.'*
>
> A young man appears in front of them in the alleyway. He starts at the sight of the two police officers, and the two young people suddenly look away and try to pull back. The man rapidly regains his composure. One of the young lads hangs his head and seems close to tears.

Q21 What offence, if any, do you suspect the man may have committed if he has bought alcohol for the two young people? Are there any powers available to require him to surrender it?

> Pc Smithson feels more confident now and remembers that s 1(1) of the Confiscation of Alcohol (Young Persons) Act 1997 also applies to persons over 18 years of age. He decides to seize the bottle from the young man.

Q22 What could Pc Smithson say to the young man in order to seize the alcohol under s 1(1) of the Confiscation of Alcohol (Young Persons) Act 1997?

Q23 What offence might Pc Smithson suspect the man to have committed?

The young man gives his name and address, but appears unwilling to hand over the vodka to the officers, claiming it is his to take home and that he didn't call out about anyone paying for it. Pc Smithson explains the offences that he suspects the young man to have committed and again outlines the consequences of failing to give up the bottle of alcohol. The man reluctantly hands over an unopened half bottle of cheap vodka, 37.5 per cent ABV, muttering under his breath.

Pc Kaleen interrupts the stream of obscenities, making a logical, calm, and assertive request for the man to calm down and keep quiet, and reminds him that he is in a serious situation and should avoid making it any worse.

Q24   In relation to the two young people, can they be allowed to go home alone as the officers now have to deal with the man with the vodka?

Q25   How should the officers respond to the obvious distress of one of the young people?

Pc Kaleen asks the man and the two young people to walk to the entrance of the alleyway. Pc Kaleen then carries out computer checks to verify the man's identity and makes contact with the parents of the young people. Pc Smithson begins a pocket note book entry noting down what has been said so far, what has happened, the suspect's name and address, and that the bottle of vodka has been seized for evidential purposes.

The man gives a bona fide address which is verified on the voters' register. He has a photo driving licence in his possession, and the officers also call the telephone number he supplied for his home address on Airwaves and speak to a relative. This all confirms his identity. He has no previous convictions on the police national computer or any record on the local intelligence databases. Pc Kaleen judges that it is not necessary to arrest him.

Q26   Under what circumstances could Pc Kaleen have chosen to arrest the man? Explain why it might have been necessary to make an arrest.

Q27   Pc Kaleen chooses to ask the suspect questions in relation to an offence, so what must he first of all say to him?

Q28   What question(s) about the offence of buying or attempting to buy alcohol for a young person (aged under 18 years) might Pc Kaleen want to put to the suspect?

Q29   What should Pc Smithson do with the bottle that has been seized?

Q30   What other evidence might Pc Smithson ask for from the suspect?

Pc Smithson interviews the man and notes down his responses in his pocket note book. He takes care with the seized items and secures them about his person in the best way possible.

. . . more for the special property store . . . now for a PND . . .

Q31   What other methods of disposal could the officers consider apart from arrest or a PND (penalty notice for disorder)?

Q32   What are the circumstances in which penalty notices for disorder can be issued?

> Pc Smithson points out the offence of buying or attempting to buy alcohol for a young person (aged under 18 years) to the suspect. He then offers the suspect the opportunity of dealing with the matter by way of a penalty notice for disorder.

Q33   Why must he ensure he has a full PNB entry on this matter?

> Pc Kaleen waits with the two young people and asks them where they go to school and how they get there to put them at ease while they await the arrival of their parents. He speaks with them so that he is close enough to Pc Smithson to hear what he is saying as he issues the PND.
>
> A small crowd of people have gathered nearby to see what is happening; some were passing by and others have come out of the local houses and flats. The parents of the two young people appear on the scene and Pc Kaleen informs them of the recent events while Pc Smithson completes the PND. The parents thank the officers for their help and take their children home. At the end of the process Pc Smithson reports the suspect for the offence of buying or attempting to buy alcohol for a young person (aged under 18 years) and cautions him once more using the 'now' caution. He then gives the young man the opportunity to read the interview record and to sign it in order to comply with PACE Code of Practice C para 11.11. He reads through it and signs it as correct.
>
> Suddenly an adult male lurches forward from the group, laughing and saying:

'What we got here then, a meeting of the Klu Klux fucking Klan . . . yeah . . . an' got ourselves a black plod to hang—huh.'

> Pc Smithson looks up from the PND form and steps a little closer to Pc Kaleen. Someone jeers from the crowd, which then falls silent. Pc Smithson looks the man in the eye and says:

'That is offensive and racist, and I suspect you of committing an offence.'

> The man looks round at the crowd and rolls his eyes but says nothing. Pc Kaleen then cautions him. Someone coughs and laughs, and people begin to chat quietly again.

Q34   What offence(s) could the officers be considering, in relation to the man causing harassment, alarm, or distress?

Q35 Were the man's words sufficient for Pc Smithson to be harassed, alarmed, or distressed?

Q36 Consider the words used by the man. Do they demonstrate hostility based on the victim's membership (or presumed membership) of a racial or religious group?

Q37 Can a successful prosecution be brought for racially abusing a police officer?

✓   Pc Kaleen steps back so that Pc Smithson can arrest the man.

> *. . . ideal opportunity for him really . . . he can use this in his SOLAP . . . and I'll sign off some of those arrest criteria for him soon . . .*

Pc Smithson arrests the man on suspicion of using racially aggravated words which were alarming, harassing, and distressing. He also cautions the man again, and then searches him carefully.

Q38 Which part of the PACE Codes of Practice lists the reasons that could make an arrest necessary?

Q39 What grounds might he have for believing the arrest to be necessary?

Q40 Why does he search the suspect?

Outcome

The male suspected of racially aggravated harassment, alarm, or distress was later interviewed but chose to make no comment in the presence of a legal representative. Statements were obtained from members of the public who witnessed the incident and a decision was made to charge the suspect with offences under s 31(c) of the Crime and Disorder Act 1998 (racially aggravated harassment, alarm, and distress) as well as s 5 of the Public Order Act 1986 (non intentional harassment, alarm, and distress). He was charged with this second offence to cover the eventuality that the racially aggravated aspect of the s 31 offence could not be proved—there is no opportunity to return an alternative verdict of guilty of the basic public order offence in a magistrates' court. The defendant pleaded not guilty at the hearing but the prosecution case was eventually proved after the evidence available from witnesses had been heard. The defendant was found guilty of the racially aggravated offence. He was fined £500 and ordered to pay costs.

The PND issued for s 149(1) of the Licensing Act 2003, buying or attempting to buy alcohol for a young person (aged under 18 years), was duly paid by the suspect thereby negating the necessity for the case to be heard at court.

Thanks to Pc Kaleen and Pc Smithson, the young people who had alcohol confiscated from them were given closer supervision by their parents and the smokers decided to wait until they were older before trying cigarettes again.

The Stella Estate Answers

A1 The following offences could all be used:

- section 5 of the Public Order Act 1986;
- section 12 of the Licensing Act 1872 (drunkenness);
- section 91(1) of the Criminal Justice Act 1967 (drunk and disorderly);
- section 146(1) of the Licensing Act 2003 (selling alcohol to under 18s);
- section 149(3) of the Licensing Act 2003 (buying or attempting to buy alcohol on behalf of under 18s).

The following powers could all be used:

- section 50(1) of the Police Reform Act 2002 (obtaining name and address);
- section 7(3) of the Children and Young Persons Act 1933 (seizure of tobacco);
- section 1 of the Confiscation of Alcohol (Young Persons) Act 1997.

A2 The officers could go straight to the caller as a matter of courtesy, citizen focus, and professional policing, but it is not always achievable operationally, due to other priorities such as attending the scene.

In terms of the possible advantages and disadvantages of calling in on him, if the suspects saw the officers visiting Mr Langford (and they are in uniform so are very likely to be noticed), the suspects will be highly suspicious of his involvement and he might face intimidation or retribution. On the other hand, he might welcome the reassurance and support.

Alternatively, the officers could:

- contact Control to establish Mr Langford's opinion on whether they should call;
- contact Mr Langford directly via Airwaves;
- ask Control to contact Mr Langford;
- visit him later, possibly as part of a series of door to door interviews to avoid him being singled out or, where possible, in plain clothes to help protect his anonymity;
- arrange to meet him in a neutral location.

See Working with Intimidated Witnesses (CJS, 2006)

A3 Section 50(1) of the Police Reform Act 2002 (obtaining name and address).

See Power to Require Name and Address of a Person Acting in an Anti-social Manner,
BSPOH 2010, 9.12.1

A4 Section 1 of the Crime and Disorder Act 1998 states that an anti-social manner is that which 'caused or was likely to cause harassment, alarm or distress to one or more persons not of the same household as [him/herself]'.

A5 The right to respect for private and family life is a qualified right within the Human Rights Act 1998 and so before interfering with such a right the officers need to ask themselves if their actions are lawful, permissible, necessary, and proportionate. The power to require the name and address of the individual is lawful, and in this situation it is in the interest of the public and also proportionate against the rights of the individual, and therefore the officers' interference appears to be permissible. The officers could inform the individual of these conclusions and point out to him that failure to give his name and address when required to do so is an offence under s 50(2) of the Police Reform Act 2002.

See Human Rights, *BSPOH 2010*, 5.12

A6 The main forms of personal authority open to Pc Kaleen are:

Form of authority	Explanation	Pc Kaleen's possible actions
Epistemic	Authority from knowledge (knowing more than the next person).	Pc Kaleen could reiterate why he thinks it is necessary to ask for these details and to what use the details will be put.
Natural	(Sometimes called 'charismatic authority'.) Derived from personality, demeanour (non-verbal communication).	Pc Kaleen could stand in a confident way, making eye contact with the youth, but physically non-threatening. He could speak slowly and deliberately to the youth.
De facto	(From fact.) Authority that exists through convention rather than as a matter of right.	Pc Kaleen might diplomatically remind the youth that the police 'have a job to do' just like most people.
De jure	(From right.) Authority as a matter of right.	He might remind the youth of the legislation and Codes of Practice that are being employed in these circumstances.
Moral	Authority that arises from a moral high ground.	Pc Kaleen might take care not to use patronizing or dismissive language or to swear back, eg address the youth in a polite fashion even though this might not be reciprocated.

See The Main Forms of Authority, *BSPOH 2010*, 5.5.2

A7 A person's attitude will often influence the way that person behaves, and the behaviour will often affect the attitude and ultimately the behaviour of a second person. This can be a never-ending circle; the behaviour of the second person will once again ultimately influence the attitude of the first, and so on. If either person is unable to control a negative attitude the exchange may escalate to outright conflict.

Using the theory of transactional analysis, you might be unwittingly acting in the style of a critical parent, or the youth might automatically see any police officer as a critical parent. If the youth then responds in a free child ego state you might be provoked to 'come down hard' and behave in an over-domineering manner (ie critical parent). Potentially, this situation could be the beginning of conflict between you and the young person. It is vitally important therefore that you recognize the significance of your attitude and behaviour at the earliest opportunity and as a professional police officer take the responsibility of breaking the chain of events. You could use a 'crossed transaction' to change the style of the transaction and to treat the youth as a responsible adult, which may trigger him into a more adult frame of mind, and bring about a satisfactory conclusion.

The exchange of attitude and behaviour between people is often represented by a model called Betari's Box (source unknown) whereby one person's attitude affects their own behaviour, which in turn affects a second person's attitude, and eventually affects their behaviour also.

See Transactional Analysis, *BSPOH 2010, 6.18.1*

Police officers are likely to deal with people in conflict situations, and should seek to minimize conflict. It is vital, therefore, to adopt a professional attitude always and apply standards of professional behaviour at all times.

A8   Any person under 16 and unsupervised by an adult could have been removed to his/her place of residence. Older members of the group could have been directed to disperse and those not living in the locality to leave the area and not return for up to 24 hours.

See Dispersal and Removal Powers for Antisocial Behaviour, *BSPOH 2010, 9.12.4*

A9   The local council might have a key role to play.

- Are they responsible for the play area? Can it be refurbished to attract back the residents who no longer use it? The Architectural Liaison Officer can redesign some of the problems associated with play areas.

- Could they ensure prompt collection of litter so that it cannot be thrown around?

- Could they look at the lighting and ascertain if the area is well lit at night and therefore acting as a magnet for people to hang around?

- Could they ensure that graffiti is cleaned up regularly before it has been up too long?

Any of all of the following could also be considered.

- Find out who is responsible for the housing estate. If the people committing the anti-social behaviour (ASB) are tenants then there may be a clause in their parents' tenancy agreements that ASB can affect their tenancy. The local neighbourhood officer/PCSO could liaise with them.

- Hold a PACT (Partners and Community Together) meeting—at a time when the young people are not in attendance so that the community priorities are clearly identified.

- Inform section teams and the force control room that the calls to this area are a priority so that intelligence reports can be submitted to ascertain the identities of all the young people involved. This would confirm if there is a real problem or only a perceived problem. It is important to remember that the young people may be being blamed for merely being young.

- Residents—provide reassurance patrols at the times when problems have been identified. Engage with residents and offer diaries so that they can log the problems. Ensure they have contact details of local officers/PCSO/community warden.

- Community—hold a litter clear up to get the play area re-established as a community space. Hold an open day at the play area incorporating a mobile police station, partnership representation to allow the community to reclaim the space.

- Youth workers—find out why the young people are congregating there. Are there any facilities nearby that they could use for sports, is there a cost implication to the young people? What would they like to see built—youth shelter or youth club? Co-opt them onto any plans for such development—get them involved.

- Environmental Health—deal with the nuisance noise issues.

- Local shop—has intelligence identified alcohol as an issue? If yes, then work with the owners to eradicate this problem. Involve them in the development processes—could they sponsor the litter clear up?

- Licensing/trading standards—if underage alcohol sales are a problem.

- Support groups—is there a residents' group that the local team can work with?

- Neighbourhood Watch—consider starting a more localized scheme and supporting its development.

- Help the Aged (or similar)—is there a local community group for the elderly? Link in with them to provide reassurance, engagement, and crime-reduction advice.

- Schools—do the young people all go to one school? Work with the school on a citizenship programme designed to show why this behaviour is anti-social. Perhaps involve the elderly people in some form of inter-generational programme designed to improve understanding on both sides.

- Primary schools—provide some educational classes/assemblies on ASB/litter, etc in a positive manner so as to try to get them thinking about these problems at an early stage.

- Media—ensure positive enforcement is publicized to this community and to the wider public—tackle the fear of crime. Also publicize community projects.

- Probation—use a community payback scheme to get offenders clearing up this mess.

- Restorative Justice—low-level interventions at an early stage so that the offenders can see the impact of their ASB.

- CCTV—is there one on the square? Is one needed?

A10 The following could all be considered:

- Confiscation of Alcohol (Young Persons) Act 1997;

- section 12 of the Licensing Act 1872 (drunkenness);

- section 1 of the Criminal Justice Act 1967 (drunk and disorderly).

See Alcohol and Young People, *BSPOH 2010,* 9.4
See Drunkenness as an Offence, *BSPOH 2010,* 9.3.2
See Drunk and Disorderly Behaviour, *BSPOH 2010,* 9.3.3

A11 In some police organizations alcohol test strips are available. These are a highly sensitive method of detecting the presence of alcohol in drinks.

Permission for use of the image kindly granted by Tests4health
(<http://www.tests4health.co.uk/index.php?productID=167>)

Test strips are convenient, accurate, and easy to use—and yet another item for the police officer to carry whilst on patrol.

A12 Section 1 of the Confiscation of Alcohol (Young Persons) Act 1997 provides an opportunity for alcohol to be confiscated from young people.

See Legislation Relating to Alcohol and Young People, *BSPOH 2010,* 9.4

A13   Section 1 of the Confiscation of Alcohol (Young Persons) Act 1997 outlines the process and the offences connected with the confiscation of alcohol from individuals under the age of 18. When an officer requires a person to surrender anything in his/her possession which is, or which the officer reasonably believes to be, alcohol or a container for alcohol, and to state his/her name and address, a number of criteria must first of all be satisfied. These are outlined within the phrasing that Pc Kaleen has used, and having to include all these requirements has made his words sound quite formal.

See Legislation Relating to Alcohol and Young People, *BSPOH 2010*, 9.4.1

A14   Each force policy may be different, but the following is a guide:

- Pc Kaleen needs to safely discard the alcohol in the presence of the persons from whom it was seized. He empties the bottles into the gutter.

- He makes a pocket note book entry recording the quantities and type of alcohol from each person. Although there is no legal requirement, he asks each person handing over a bottle to sign, acknowledging the disposal of the alcohol. One person refuses to sign so he makes a note of this against his record of the person's name and address.

A15   As the officers have made a requirement to the young people to surrender anything in their possession that they reasonably believe to be alcohol, they may remove the person to his/her place of residence or a place of safety (under s 1AB of the Confiscation of Alcohol (Young Persons) Act 1997).

See Alcohol and Young People, *BSPOH 2010*, 9.4

A16   If the person is arrested, the containers of alcohol would need to be retained as evidence and then disposed of following the result of the case. It is unlikely that the alcohol would be returned to the suspect/parent or guardian following release from custody, and so it could be disposed of in a similar way to having been confiscated on the street, ie tipped down a drain.

A17   Section 7(3) of the Children and Young Persons Act 1933 states that it is the duty of a constable in uniform to seize any tobacco or cigarette papers in the possession of a person apparently under the age of 16 years found smoking in any street or public place.

See Cigarettes and Young People, *BSPOH 2010*, 10.17.1

A18   In his 'Report into the Brixton Disorders', Lord Scarman refers to discretion as 'the art of suiting action to particular circumstances' (Scarman, 1981, para 4.58). In this situation Pc Smithson has so far decided not to take the cigarettes from the two teenagers, and based that decision on the earlier unrelated incident which has made him feel less confident. However, in these circumstances it would be very difficult for Pc Smithson to justify the use of discretion. This is because according to Action on Smoking and Health, two-thirds of smokers start before the age of 18 and in England one in seven 15-year-olds are regular smokers: 12 per cent of boys and 19 per cent of girls (ASH, 2009). The police have a moral obligation not to encourage smoking among young people. In addition, the Children and Young Persons Act 1933 clearly states that it is the **duty** of 'a constable in uniform to seize any tobacco or cigarette papers'. As such, Pc Smithson is not carrying out his duty if he decides not to seize the tobacco or cigarettes because he is not confident to do so, and is therefore failing to maintain one or more of the Standards of Professional Behaviour. These could include:

- honesty and integrity;

- orders and instructions;

- duties and responsibilities;

- discreditable conduct.

See Discretion, *BSPOH 2010*, 5.4.8 and 5.7
See Standards of Professional Behaviour, *BSPOH 2010*, 6.14

A19   Each force policy may be different, but the following is a guide:

- He should destroy and safely discard the tobacco or cigarettes in the presence of the persons from whom it was seized. Pc Smithson tips the tobacco into a bin, shaking the packet to make sure it separates into fragments.

- He should record the quantities and types of tobacco or cigarettes seized in his pocket note book.

One way of disposing of the tobacco.

A20   Yes. In case law regarding s 30 of the Anti-social Behaviour Act 2003, if the young person is unwilling to go voluntarily, the word 'remove' has been held to mean 'take away using reasonable force if necessary' *(R (W) v Commissioner of Police for the Metropolis and another, Secretary of State for the Home Department, interested party* [2004] EWCA Civ 458).

See Dispersal and Removal Powers for Antisocial Behaviour, *BSPOH 2010,* 9.12.4

A21   He may be suspected of committing the offence of buying alcohol on behalf of an individual under 18; an offence contained in s 149 (3) of the Licensing Act 2003. He can be required to surrender the alcohol as a result of a requirement made under the Confiscation of Alcohol (Young Persons) Act 1997.

See Alcohol and Young People, *BSPOH 2010,* 9.4

A22   He could say:

> I suspect you are in possession of alcohol because of what you are carrying and because of what you have just said to these two young people. I also suspect that you intend the alcohol should be consumed here in the recreation ground by these young people who are under the age of 18. Please give me the bottle as I suspect it contains alcohol. I also need your name and address. I must warn you that failure to comply with either of these requests without a reasonable excuse is an offence for which you may be arrested.

A23   Buying or attempting to buy alcohol for a young person (aged under 18 years) under s 149(1) of the Licensing Act 2003. This is an offence for which a penalty notice for disorder can be issued.

A24   Once the decision has been made to remove the young people to their place of residence it may be argued that the officers have a duty of care towards them. (This is especially so if they were intoxicated through alcohol and as such they could be considered as vulnerable. If a young person appears so drunk that they are incapable of carrying out normal bodily functions they may be at risk of significant harm and steps must be taken to protect their welfare. Under these circumstances it might be necessary to take that young person into police protection using s 46 of the Children Act 1989.)

Even though these young people are not highly intoxicated, the officers do not simply leave them to make their own way home.

See Police Protection, BSPOH 2010, 10.17.3

A25   The situation has escalated for the young people. Not only have they had alcohol confiscated but they have obviously been asking an adult to purchase it for them. Due to the duty of care the officers must show towards them, but mindful of having to deal with another suspect and the process which must be undertaken with him, the officers could ask Control to contact their parents and request them to attend, or the officers may be able to contact the parents themselves using Airwaves.

A26   Two elements must exist to make an arrest lawful, and these are given in PACE Code of Practice G para 2.1. The first element to satisfy is that the man is suspected of having committed a criminal offence. The second element concerns whether Pc Kaleen has reasonable grounds for believing that the arrest is necessary, such as:

- to prevent the man causing physical injury to the young people through the purchase of alcohol on their behalf; and/or

- to allow the prompt and effective investigation of the offence; it is necessary to obtain evidence by questioning him in relation to his purchase of alcohol on behalf of the two young people (eg to negate his defence of not knowing they were under 18).

See Arrest Without Warrant, BSPOH 2010, 8.7

However, PACE Code of Practice G para 1.2 points out that arrest represents an obvious and significant interference with the right to liberty under the Human Rights Act 1998. PACE Code of Practice G para 1.3 emphasizes that any arrest must be justified and consideration given to whether the objectives can be met by other less invasive means. In other words, just because an arrest can be made should never be a reason for making one.

See Human Rights, BSPOH 2010, 5.12

If an arrest had been necessary then an option to give street bail may also have been considered under the provisions of s 30A(1) of the PACE Act 1984. There are four considerations to be made:

- the **nature** of the offence;

- the **ability** to progress the investigation at the station;

- your **confidence** in the suspect to answer bail;

- the **level** of awareness and understanding of the procedure by the suspect.

The following questions should also be considered when deciding whether to grant street bail:

1. What type of offence has been committed and how serious is the offence?

2. What has been the impact of the offence?

3. Would a delay in dealing with the offender result in loss of vital evidence?

4. Is the arrested person fit to be released back onto the streets?

5. Does the arrested person understand what is happening?

6. If released on bail, is the arrested person likely to commit a further offence?

7. Am I satisfied that the arrested person has provided a correct name and address?

See Bail Elsewhere than at a Police Station—'Street Bail', BSPOH 2010, 8.15.5

A27   PACE Code of Practice C para 10.1 states 'a person whom there are grounds to suspect of an offence [. . .] must be cautioned before any questions about an offence, or further questions if the answers provide the grounds for suspicion, are put to them if either the suspect's answers or silence, [. . .] may be given in evidence to a court in a prosecution'. PACE Code of Practice C para 10.2 goes onto say 'whenever a person not under arrest is initially cautioned, or reminded they are under caution, that person must at the same time be told that they are not under arrest and are free to leave if they want to'.

See Police Cautions, *BSPOH 2010,* 8.4

A28   Questions might include:

1. The name/brand and percentage proof of the alcohol.

2. How much it cost.

3. Where it was bought from.

4. Whose money it was bought with.

5. What was the reason it was purchased.

6. Who it was bought on behalf of.

Section 149(6) of the Licensing Act 2003 offers a defence to a person charged with an offence of buying or attempting to buy alcohol for a young person (aged under 18 years). The defence is that he/she had no reason to suspect that the individual was aged under 18. To negate that defence, the following questions might be considered:

- How old are the people for whom the alcohol was bought?

- How did the suspect ascertain or estimate their age?

A29   He should take it to the police station where it will be bagged, labelled, and put in a special property store.

See Seizing Exhibits, *BSPOH 2010,* 13.5.8

A30   He asks the young man for the till receipt, which shows that the purchase had taken place.

Cooper Wine
and Beer
Supplies

21 Bronswell Street
Stella Estate
CV45 6YH

Date 15 December 2009 Time 21:10
124/854/247
VAT No 5678644789

Receipt No 648496

Vodka Shooter   50cl   1.99
Vodka Shooter   50cl   1.99
Vodka Shooter   50cl   1.99
Vodka Shooter   50cl   1.99
West Co cider   50cl   0.99

Cash sale   8.95
Tendered   10.00
Change   1.05

Paid in full

You must be over 18 to buy alcoholic drinks
and cigarettes. ID may be required if you
appear to be under 25.
Thank you for calling! Your manager today
is Derek Underhill

A31   Pc Smithson could report the suspect for the offence. This is one of the less intrusive means which PACE Code of Practice G para 1.3 describes, and as his identity and address have been verified, this is an option if the objective is to provide the opportunity for him to be considered for prosecution. It will also provide the opportunity for other evidence to be collected, such as statements from the two young people.

See Methods of Disposal of Arrested Suspects, *BSPOH 2010*, 8.15.1

A32   To be in a position to issue a notice, the officer must have reason to believe the person has committed an offence for which a PND can be issued and must have gathered enough evidence to prove the offence. In this case there would be a necessity to negate the defence available to the suspect.

The suspect must be able to comprehend what is happening. Factors to consider could include the suspect having a reasonable understanding of English, or not being too drunk and incapable. The suspect must also be amenable and cooperating fully. If the person is suspected of having committed two or more related offences at the same time, then a PND cannot be issued.

See Penalty Notices for Disorder, *BSPOH 2010*, 8.15.2

Here the suspect is 19 and Pc Smithson is satisfied with the validity of the suspect's given age, identity, and address. The suspect in this scenario meets the criteria for issuing a PND.

A33   If the suspect does not pay the fine or elects to have the case heard in court, evidence would then be required that the man has committed the offence, and to negate any defence.

> Guidance on how to complete PND forms is available at <http://police.homeoffice.gov.uk/ publications/operational-policing/PenaltyNotices_March105.pdf>

A34   They could use s 5 of the Public Order Act 1986 and s 31(1)(c) of the Crime and Disorder Act 1998 (racially aggravated non-intentional harassment, alarm, or distress). They could also consider s 4A of the Public Order Act 1986 and s 31(1)(b) of the Crime and Disorder Act 1998 (racially aggravated intentional harassment, alarm, or distress). Final consideration of which offence the suspect would be prosecuted under would very much depend upon his intentions and prosecution guidelines. It is unlikely that s 4 of the Public Order Act 1986 and s 31(1)(a) of the Crime and Disorder Act 1998 (racially aggravated fear or provocation of violence) would apply as the suspect does not appear to have intended to cause fear or provocation of immediate unlawful violence.

> See Public Order Offences, *BSPOH 2010*, 9.7

A35   In this instance the language used would support the view that the suspect intended his conduct to be threatening, abusive, or insulting and was used in the hearing or sight of several people who are likely to be caused harassment, alarm, or distress, including two police officers. Considering the case of *DPP v Orum* [1989] 1 WLR 88, a police officer can be harassed, alarmed, or distressed; however, it is a question of fact to be decided in each case by the magistrates, taking into account the familiarity which police officers have with incidents of disorderly conduct.

Here the words used include references to an American militant organization that has used violence and intimidation throughout its history, and to hanging. These words would be untypical for police officers to witness in incidents of disorderly conduct and therefore would be alarming or distressing to them.

A36   Yes. The language and the meaning of the words appear to support the view that the suspect was voicing his opinion in racial terms by referring to the colour of Pc Smithson's skin. These words appear to be capable of demonstrating racial hostility but it would still be a question of fact for the court to decide.

> See Racially or Religiously Aggravated Offences, *BSPOH 2010*, 9.11

A37   Yes. For example, in *R v Jacobs* [2000] 28 Dec CACD, a suspect made racist remarks against a police officer and was successfully convicted of an offence under s 31(1)(c) and (5) of the Crime and Disorder Act 1998 (racially aggravated non-intentional harassment, alarm, or distress).

A38   The reasons that could make an arrest necessary are given in PACE Code of Practice G para 2.4.

A39   Here, he might consider the arrest is necessary in order to:

- prevent him from suffering physical injury due to his intoxication;
- allow the prompt and effective investigation of the offence; it is necessary to obtain evidence by questioning him in relation to his intentions.

> See Reasons that Make an Arrest Necessary, *BSPOH 2010*, 8.7.4

A40   He should search him for any items that he might use to cause physical harm to himself or any other person, such as a police officer involved in his arrest or transport to the station.

> See Searching a Suspect after Arrest, *BSPOH 2010*, 8.9.4

Test Yourself

And finally, solve these anagrams to fill the gaps to create the definition of s 5 of the Public Order Act 1986.

A person is guilty of an offence if s/he:

(a) uses RANGE TEN HIT abusive or GUN LIST IN words or A HUB OVER I, or disorderly A HUB OVER I, or (b) LAD IS SPY any writing sign or other visible NEAREST ONE TRIP which is threatening, A BUS VIE or insulting within the hearing or sight of a person likely to be caused NASH ARM SET, LAMAR or distress thereby.

Answers to Knowledge Check Questions

K1 d   K2 b   K3 a   K4 b   K5 d   K6 c   K7 c   K8 d

Answers to Test Yourself

RANGE TEN HIT—Threatening

A BUS VIE—Abusive

GUN LIST IN—Insulting

A HUB OVER I—Behaviour

LAD IS SPY—Displays

NEAREST ONE TRIP—Representation

NASH ARM SET—Harassment

LAMAR—Alarm

5 | St Edward's School

---

forensic awareness required

assessment opportunity

diversity issues

health and safety

questionable practice

a pen or pencil is required

Introduction

If you are a student police officer, your area is likely to contain a number of schools and colleges and your local authority or county council may have agreements or 'Memos of Understanding' relating to incidents on their school premises, such as fights, robberies, and drug abuse. Typically, your area will also have a number of schools which have a poor reputation or are 'on the wrong side of the tracks', and knife carrying (whether for status, to facilitate crime, or for self-defence) is likely to feature. A 2005 survey (conducted by MORI for the Youth Justice Board with a sample size of 5,463 pupils) revealed that a frightening 32 per cent of pupils aged between 11 and 16 admitted to having carried a knife in the preceding 12 months (YJB, 2005).

Knowledge Check

Before you undertake this scenario, assess your understanding of the underpinning legislation involved by attempting the following knowledge check.

Questions K1 to K9 inclusive are multiple choice so you should select **one** of the letters a, b, c, or d as the answer—and write it down. Check your answers at the end of this chapter before beginning the scenario.

K 1 Which of the following would not constitute an offence of robbery under s 8(1) of the Theft Act 1968?

      a) Immediately before stealing, the thief uses force on a person
      b) At the time of stealing, the thief uses force on a person
      c) Immediately after stealing, the thief uses force on a person
      D) In order to steal, the thief uses force on a person

K2 Which of the following is a true statement in relation to the offence of carrying an offensive weapon under s 1 of the Prevention of Crimes Act 1953?

    a) The offence can be committed in private and public places

    b) The offence cannot be committed by a person under 17 years of age

    c) The offence cannot be committed by a person carrying the weapon who has lawful excuse or reasonable authority

    d) An offensive weapon is any article intended, adapted, or made for causing injury

K3 Which of the following cutting-blade lengths of a folding knife would not constitute an offence under s 1(1) of the Criminal Justice Act 1988?

    a) Less than 7.62 centimetres

    b) Less than 8.62 centimetres

    c) Less than 6.72 centimetres

    d) Less than 10.0 centimetres

K4 Besides good reason and lawful authority, s 139A(4) of the Criminal Justice Act 1988 provides four specific defences to carrying an offensive weapon on school premises. Which of the following is not one of those defences?

    a) Use at work

    b) Recreational purposes

    c) Religious reason

    d) Educational purposes

K5 Which of the following incidents would not constitute an offence of robbery under s 8(1) of the Theft Act 1968?

    a) Immediately before stealing a purse, the suspect used force on the owner of the purse

    b) Used force on a person at the time of committing the offence of taking a vehicle without the owner's consent (under s 12 of the Theft Act 1968)

    c) Used force on a person at the time of stealing a vehicle which was later dismantled and the parts sold separately

    d) In order to steal an iPod, used force on the owner

K6 Which of the following statutory provisions provides a power of search in relation to the offence of carrying an offensive weapon?

    a) Section 1 of the Criminal Justice Act 1988

    b) Section 1 of the Prevention of Crimes Act 1953

    c) Section 1 of the Police and Criminal Evidence Act 1984

    d) Section 1 of the Violent Crime Reduction Act 2006

K7 Which of the following articles would fit the definition of a bladed article under s 1(1) of the Criminal Justice Act 1988?

    a) A locking pocket knife with a 5 centimetre blade

    b) A kitchen knife

    c) A craft knife with a retractable blade

    d) All of the above

K8 A teacher has an offensive weapon in his possession on school premises. Within the meaning of s 1 of the Prevention of Crime Act 1953, at what times would this constitute an offence under s 139A(2) of the Criminal Justice Act 1988?

    a) Only during school hours for pupils

    b) At all times

    c) Only during school terms

    d) At all times during term time apart from when the teacher is on the premises between the hours of 9 pm and 6 am

K 9 Can police enter a school to search for knives?

    a) Yes, but only if the headteacher believes that there are knives on the premises

    b) No, it is the headteacher's responsibility to arrange for school staff to conduct such a search

    c) Yes, under the Violent Crime Reduction Act 2006, if a police officer suspects that weapons are held on school premises

    d) Yes, but only if a police officer has good reason to believe that bladed weapons are in the possession of certain named pupils

St Edward's School Scenario

Pc Almeda and her tutor, Pc Bentley, are called to St Edward's School on Friday afternoon at 2 pm. As they enter the gate, Mr Hanley, the headteacher, comes striding across the playground and immediately informs them that one of the pupils has been robbed at knifepoint after a fight in the playground.

They make their way through a maze of corridors, double doors, and covered walkways. Mr Hanley gestures expansively—new science block, sports hall—his office is in one of the new blocks past the dining hall. As he rushes along he glances back over his shoulder every now and then, telling the two officers that the boys had been brought to him by Mr Klein, a geography teacher, who had 'witnessed the whole incident' in the playground. Mr Hanley suddenly stops and turns to the officers to emphasize that he had interviewed the two boys himself, following school procedures, to find out what had happened and that, in his opinion, a robbery had definitely occurred, and that's why he knew that the police should be called.

Pc Almeda is already feeling a bit confused about who said what, to whom, and when.

> . . . *can't really ask now . . . we need to sit down and get this all clear . . . Hmmm, bit niffy, those toilets . . .*

Mr Hanley invites the two officers into his office and leans over to shut the door, hurriedly drawing forward two armchairs. Pc Almeda spots a knife on Mr Hanley's desk.

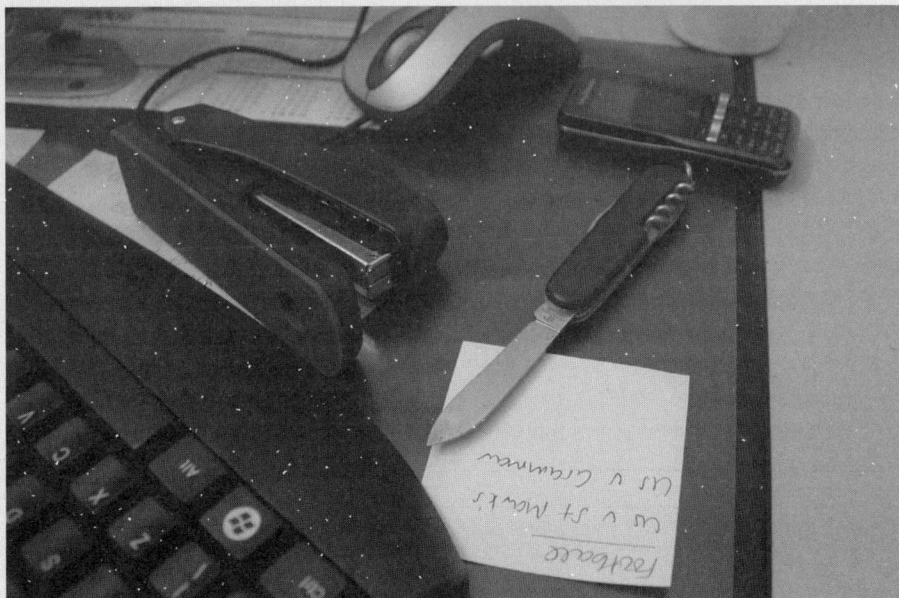

Kilbey's knife—allegedly. The officers will want to establish the length of the blade.

☺ Mr Hanley then excitedly provides three 'potted versions' of the events, one from each of the boys and the other from Mr Klein. The knife is from one of the boys. Pc Almeda is still not quite sure what happened and who saw what—or whether Mr Hanley seems to be the right kind of person to be a headteacher.

. . . this doesn't quite make sense . . . here we go . . .

Pc Almeda makes a full pocket note book entry of the first account of the incident provided by Mr Hanley as she understands it, including direct quotes he attributes to either of the two pupils, and gets Pc Bentley to cast his more expert eye over it.

Q1 What type of evidence are these quotes, and how can such evidence be used?

Mr Hanley says that James Kilbey, in year 9, told him that when he was on his way home the previous day, his iPod was taken by Mark Sangster from year 12.

'Sorry to interrupt you Mr Hanley, but how old are each of these boys?'

Mr Hanley looked momentarily confused but after glancing at his papers, stated that Kilbey was 14 and Sangster was 16. He then resumed his retelling of Kilbey's account.

Kilbey had said he had been walking past some shops when Sangster and four other boys came out of a shop a little further on and looked back at him, and then stopped (he could see them laughing) and waited for him to walk past. As he got close, the five boys spread out across the pavement to block his way and one of them asked him if he had an iPod or money. There was a short conversation when he was asked the same question again by two of the others, and then a further five or six other boys ran across the road from the bus stop opposite to join the group. The 11 to 12-strong group then surrounded him, 'jostling me' and when he did not produce his iPod they took his drink (from his blazer pocket) and snatched a packet of crisps out of his hand. Several members of the group went into his other pockets and Sangster removed 'his' (Kilbey's) iPod and walked off, and the others followed. Kilbey claimed he was not particularly scared or threatened but was definitely annoyed and that, of course, it was 'out of order' but that there were too many of them to deal with there and then. So, today in the playground, Kilbey 'sorted it out' and claimed that he merely took his own property back by force, which of course 'is only right'. When asked if he had a knife at school, Kilbey confirmed that he owned a folding pen-knife with a two-inch blade and said that he uses the knife in his art class for moulding clay.

Q2 The previous day, was the offence of robbery committed against Kilbey? (Assume he told the truth about what happened on his way home after school.)

Q3 List all the points that would be required to conclude that a robbery had occurred.

Q4 Which Act and section of the Act covers the offence of robbery?

Q5 Provide the legal definition of robbery as stated in the relevant legislation.

According to Mr Hanley, Mark Sangster said that 'nothing' had happened the previous day. Mr Hanley said he could not get Sangster to say any more about it but he was keen to talk about his version of what had happened today in the playground. Sangster had claimed that Kilbey had approached him and threatened him with a knife to make him hand over the iPod. Mark Sangster told Mr Hanley that the iPod was his own, and that Kilbey 'must be crazy' for thinking it was his. Sangster said that Kilbey had said, while pointing a knife at him:

> 'Give me that iPod or I'll stick you with this.'

Mr Hanley also said that Sangster had said the following words:

> 'I wouldn't have said anything, because I'm not a grass, but Mr Klein saw it happen so he dragged us both into the office.'

According to the headteacher, Mr Klein was unequivocal: he said Kilbey was threatening Sangster with a knife. Pc Almeda is keen to speak with Mr Klein but Mr Hanley says he is not available until later.

Q6 Assuming Sangster is telling the truth about the events in the playground, what offence has been committed against him? Consider s 5 of the Theft Act 1968 before you decide!

Q7 Putting aside possible robbery, has Kilbey committed any other offences in relation to carrying the knife at school?

Q8 Who decides if a defence offered by a suspect is to be accepted and that an offence has not in fact been committed?

Mr Hanley suddenly looks worried and asks the officers if all knives are illegal in schools—the builders are using craft knives to repair the roofing felt on the caretaker's shed—and he is certain that the caretaker has some knives locked away—and what about the knives in the kitchens—and the police officer who brought a 'dagger' into school during last year's anti-knife campaign . . .?

Q9 What do the officers say to Mr Hanley in order to allay his fears?

Mr Hanley looks relieved and smiles, opening the door of his office and gesturing the officers out into the corridor. They glimpse Kilbey through the open door of the medical room being tended by an anxious-looking school nurse. Kilbey's hand is bleeding profusely and she keeps pressing a large wad of gauze against it and then removing it to have a look. As the officers approach they see he has a deep clean cut on his palm. Pc Almeda notices drops of blood on the floor and wonders why the boy is not lying down.

> . . . he must have lost a fair amount of blood . . . the other boy's clothes may be stained . . . evidence . . . but where is he?

Q10 Given the circumstances, would it be reasonable for the officers to presume the cut was made during the incident in the playground?

Q11   What can the forensic laboratory do with the knife to establish its involvement in the offence?

Q12   How might the presence of blood on Sangster's clothing help with the investigation?

> Pc Bentley believes, based solely on what Mr Hanley has said, that Kilbey should be arrested. Neither of the officers have spoken to the two boys.

Q13   On the information provided here, should Kilbey be arrested?

Q14   If Pc Bentley believes it is necessary and justifiable to arrest Kilbey, must the arrest be carried out immediately?

Q15   If Kilbey is taken into custody, his age will mean that he needs an appropriate adult present. Who could be an appropriate adult for him?

Q16   Being 14 years of age, what additional rights does Kilbey have whilst in custody?

> The school nurse examines the cut on Kilbey' hand. She says he needs to go to hospital because the injury is deep and requires stitches.

Q17   Should one of the officers take him in a patrol car?

Q18   If Mark Sangster needs to go to the police station to be interviewed (as a suspect or a witness), can he go in the same patrol car later?

Q19   Why might fibre evidence not be very useful in any investigation of these incidents?

Q20   Is it appropriate to arrest Sangster? For what?

> Pc Bentley arrests Kilbey on suspicion of robbery. After medical treatment (monitored by Pc Bentley as Kilbey is in custody) he is taken to the police station where he is met by the custody officer and Mrs Kilbey.
>
> Pc Bentley hands over all the paperwork and copies of their PNB entries and briefs the DC responsible for the case. She agrees that the ownership of the iPod is a pivotal point of the investigation into the alleged robberies or assaults. Pc Bentley suggests that establishing who owns the iPod would be a 'nice little project' for Pc Almeda, and the DC nods enthusiastically.

Q21   How could Pc Almeda prove who owns the iPod, assuming it was bought through a legitimate retailer?

> The officers also brief the late turn CSI, who has been tasked to deal with the physical evidence. As they go off duty, the custody officer informs them that Kilbey is about to be interviewed.

Q22   What must be done if Mr Klein is interviewed as a witness and he provides an account but not a witness statement?

Q23   Sangster is a victim aged under 17, so how will he be interviewed and statemented?

Q24   Sangster is under 17 so an MG 2 form may be required. What is an MG 2 form?

Outcome

> As a result of the incidents at St Edward's, Mr Hanley held a week-long series of events in the school (which included hard-hitting workshops) that focused on the sometimes tragic consequences of carrying knives. Parents and guardians of students at the school were also invited to become involved, and there were contributions from the local police and national organizations and charities.
>
> Following the interview with Sangster, the other boys involved in the initial incident in the street (during which Kilbey's iPod was taken) were arrested and interviewed. They each admitted their involvement in the incident. Together with Sangster and Kilbey, all the youths under investigation were referred to the local Youth Offending Team (YOT). The YOT assessed the boys in terms of any previous involvement in crime (they had none), their health (one of the boys was identified as having undiagnosed ADHD), their educational level (generally average for their age), and their family circumstances (one boy was living apart from his parents). The boys were also encouraged to consider their attitudes towards their own behaviour and towards other people; they claimed they did not realize their behaviour had much effect on other people. The YOT made a number of recommendations to the court and the boys were each made a subject of a one-year Supervision Order, with specified activities set by the YOT including six months' compulsory participation in an Intensive Supervision and Surveillance Programme. The YOT also worked with the parents of the boys in an attempt to reduce the likelihood of any subsequent offending.

St Edward's School Answers

A1   This is, of course, 'hearsay' evidence which may not be admissible in court. The value of the information is as intelligence—eg did anybody mention where the knife could be found or the presence of other witnesses?

A2   If Kilbey is telling the truth then a theft has certainly occurred, but only if 'jostling' is considered to be use of force. In the case of *R v DPP, B v DPP* (2007) EWHC 739 (Admin) the defendants, R and B, appealed against a robbery conviction where a group surrounded a boy and stole from him. Whilst the boy was not injured or threatened, the trial judge was clear that a group in these circumstances implied a threat of force and that the pushing and pulling amounted to force. In applying this case to Kilbey, the resilience he displayed is irrelevant: it is the intention of the suspect that matters.

See Robbery, *BSPOH 2010*, 10.4

A3　To prove that a robbery had occurred, all the following would be required:

- theft;

- dishonesty;

- appropriation;

- property;

- belonging to another;

- intention to permanently deprive;

- force (at the time of the theft).

See Robbery, *BSPOH 2010,* 10.4

A4　Section 8(1) of the Theft Act 1968.

See Robbery, *BSPOH 2010,* 10.4

A5　'A person is guilty of robbery if he steals, and immediately before or at the time of doing so, he uses force on any person or puts or seeks to put any person in fear of being then and there subjected to force.'

A6　This could be considered as a robbery but Kilbey may offer a defence because he believes there was no theft as he is making a 'claim of right'. This means he may claim the property is his and that therefore he was lawfully retrieving it. Case law provides some guidance here in *R v Skivington* [1967] 1 All ER 483. Skivington went to his wife's employer's offices and demanded her wages whilst threatening a staff member with a knife. He was given two wage packets. He was subsequently charged under s 23(1) of the Larceny Act 1916. At trial he stated he had an honest belief that he had a right to the money and the judge instructed the jury that they should be satisfied with the 'honest belief'. This meant there was no dishonesty, and therefore no theft, and consequently no robbery.

Remember, it is the role of the court (rather than the police) to consider any defence. However, as part of an investigation a police officer may wish to proactively negate any defence that seems likely to be proffered at trial, perhaps by interview or the use of other forms of evidence.

A7　He has offered a reason for possession of the knife (the art class) and the burden of proof falls upon him: he would need to offer this 'fact' in his defence and provide evidence to support it, probably from the art teacher in question.

See Bladed Weapons in Schools, *BSPOH 2010,* 9.19.3

A8　The CPS will consider whether a defence should be considered and whether the defendant should be charged (applying the full code test), but ultimately the court decides. Despite the fact that there appears to be a prima facie case for the legitimate carrying of the knife it is the role of the defence to establish that Kilbey had a good reason for doing so.

A9　The officers explain in general terms that knives are allowed if they are to be used by a person in order to carry out his/her work or for another lawful purpose.

A10　Yes. You have heard three accounts that all state that Kilbey had been involved in an incident where a knife had been used and the cut is straight edged—it looks like a knife wound.

A11　The main thing to do would be to test the blade and hinge mechanism for the presence of human DNA. Any recovered DNA could then be compared to Kilbey's DNA (although this would not **prove** he was cut by his own knife today). A comparison to Sangster's DNA, if favourable, may suggest he was cut today (but, of course, he would need to be injured—not mentioned in any of the accounts).

A12 If Kilbey's blood is found on the clothing it will certainly be of assistance in the investigation, but it would not prove that Kilbey was cut in the incident in the playground; there may be a separate explanation for the presence of Kilbey's blood on Sangster's clothing.

A13 Any arrest must be necessary and justified. Here, the necessity could be to protect a child or vulnerable person from the suspect or to allow the prompt and effective investigation of the offence, or of the conduct of the person in question. It is justifiable to arrest Kilbey because there seems to be a reasonable suspicion that he has committed a crime.

A14 No. The officer can decide when and if to arrest the suspect; there is no obligation to arrest him immediately, or at all.

A15 In the case of a juvenile an 'appropriate adult' means:

- the parent, guardian, or, if the juvenile is in local authority or voluntary organization care, or is otherwise being looked after under the Children Act 1989, a person representing that authority or organization;

- a social worker of a local authority.

Failing these, an appropriate adult could be some other responsible adult aged 18 or over who is not a police officer or employed by the police. It may be that a teacher can fulfil this role, but common sense dictates that it should not be the headteacher (who has already 'interviewed' the boys).

A16 In addition to the rights of any adult held in custody, Kilbey will require an appropriate adult and to be kept apart from adult prisoners (eg in a detention cell).

A17 For medical reasons, the fastest option is best. The officers have been advised that he needs treatment and to ignore this would be reckless, but Kilbey's injury is not life-threatening, so he does not need an ambulance. He can go in a patrol car.

A18 Mark Sangster should not travel in the same car afterwards (even if it has been valeted) in case Kilbey has left wet blood in the car, which could later contaminate Sangster's clothing.

A19 In an enclosed population such as a school where nearly everyone wears the same uniform, fibre evidence is not normally considered to be very useful as there will be lots of identical fibres on many people and objects.

A20 It may be appropriate to arrest Mark Sangster for robbing Kilbey who allegedly had his iPod stolen and was jostled by a number of youths. Sangster was allegedly chief amongst them. We need to consider necessity again and perhaps apply discretion and employ alternative methods: he could be invited to the police station or a summons could be issued.

A21 If one of the boys has the receipt, then this may assist, but receipts typically do not bear the serial number of the article to which they apply. The receipt may also have been discarded. Friends and relatives may be able to support any claim to ownership, especially if the iPod is scratched or otherwise demonstrably unique. The content of the iPod's files may assist if the 'owner' can provide a list and the owner's home PC may bear digital evidence relating to the specific iPod, such as play lists.

A22 The conversation with Mr Klein must be recorded in full, and the written notes must be retained. Later, the content of the notes must be revealed to the Crown Prosecutor.

See Retain, Record, Reveal, and Disclosure, *BSPOH 2010*, 12.6

A23 Achieving Best Evidence (ABE) needs to be considered because there is a presumption that it will be carried out. The First Officer at the Scene (FOAS) must be aware of this and must know how to deal with the witnesses surrounding the offence.

A24 It is the Initial Witness Assessment form and it flags up the potential for the use of special measures for cases involving vulnerable or intimidated witnesses such as those with a mental disorder, impairment of intelligence, or a physical disability. (An intimidated witness is one who is in fear or is the complainant in a sexual offence case.)

Test Yourself

And finally, a chance to review your knowledge relating to offensive weapons.

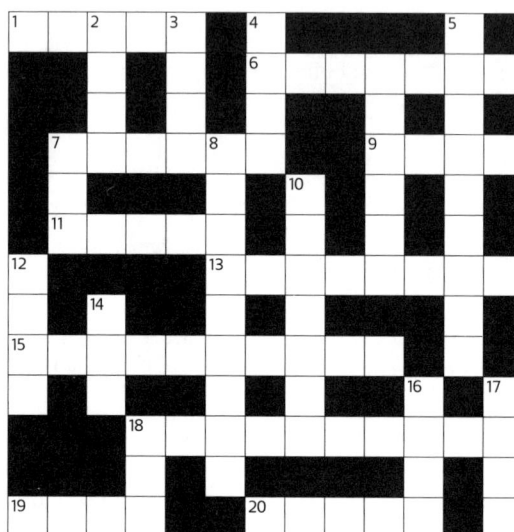

Across

1 Defensive weapon used by the police.
6 Converted from an innocent item into a weapon.
7 A joiner could use this to repair a window in a street and not commit an offence.
9 A lot of this is no excuse.
11 If so, it isn't covered by s 139.
13 Weapon, hand held with protruding spikes between fingers.
15 Place of learning not covered under s 139A(6) of the Criminal Justice Act 1988.
18 Part of a school according to s 139A(6) of the Criminal Justice Act 1988.
18 Essential part of rape.
19 Long story, spun out.
20 Scots knife is tucked in here.

Down

2 Members of this religion sometimes carry a small rigid knife.
3 Form a protective cage around the lungs and heart.
4 A mellowed suspect may get out on this.
5 The accused in court.
7,14 Places to leave an offensive weapon.
8 Mode of trial for carrying a knife on a train.
10 Better to do this for your business than for others' weapons.
12 Maximum years in prison for an offence under s 1 of the Criminal Justice Act 1988.
16 Lethal weapons.
17 Tool for smoothing rough-cut wood.
18 A very small pointed article.

Answers to Knowledge Check Questions

K1 c   K2 d   K3 a   K4 b   K5 b   K6 c   K7 d   K8 b   K9 c

Answers to Test Yourself

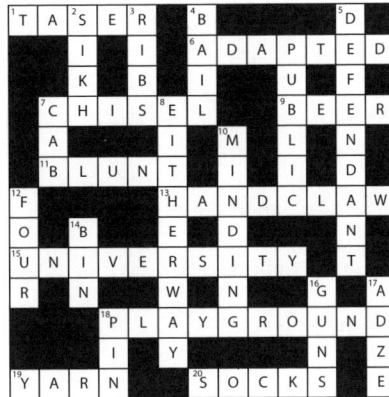

Crossword solution:

Across: 1 TASER, 6 ADAPTED, 7 CHISEL, 9 BEER, 11 BLUNT, 13 HANDCLAW, 15 UNIVERSITY, 18 PLAYGROUND, 19 YARN, 20 SOCKS

Down: 1 TAKA, 2 SIB, 3 RI, 4 BAILIFF, 5 DEFENDED, 8 ELI, 10 MILID, 12 FOUR, 13 HEDN, 14 BENWNY, 16 GUN, 17 ADZE

The Railway

👣 forensic awareness required

✓ assessment opportunity

☺ diversity issues

💧 health and safety

▽? questionable practice

✎ a pen or pencil is required

Introduction

This scenario illustrates the police response to a relatively common crime in England and Wales, that of violence against the person. According to the Home Office (2009a), figures from the British Crime Survey (BCS) and police-recorded crime statistics both estimate that violent crime represents around one-fifth of all crime. The Home Office report suggests that weapons were used in 21 per cent of violent crimes; knives were used in 7 per cent of violent incidents, and glasses or bottles in 5 per cent. Firearms were used in only 1 per cent of incidents. Between the 2007/08 and the 2008/09 BCS interviews, the use of knives and glasses or bottles remained constant while the use of 'hitting implements' decreased.

Increased concern about groups of young people and their relationship to violent crime in the UK has been widely reported in the media and also reflected in research evidence (Bullock and Tilley, 2002; Bennett and Holloway, 2004 cited in Hodgkinson, 2009). The Youth Justice Board observed that the use of the term 'gang' risked glamorizing violent group behaviour (2003) therefore we will use other terms here. According to the Joseph Rowntree Foundation (2008), territoriality among young people has been identified as one of the foundations of violent behaviour in groups of young people. It defines territoriality as 'a social system through which control is claimed by one group over a defined geographical area and defended against others' (Joseph Rowntree Foundation, 2008, p 2).

The scenario portrayed below involves a possible act of revenge conducted by one group of young people against another, partly in response to perceived territorial infractions. It illustrates a number of offences against the person and public order offences. It also demonstrates the use of intelligence, arrest and search powers, scene preservation, and gathering forensic evidence.

Knowledge Check

Before you undertake this scenario, check your understanding of the relevant legislation by attempting the knowledge check questions. Write down either a, b, c, or d as your answer to each of the multiple choice questions K1 to K8. Check your answers at the end of this chapter before beginning the scenario.

K1 For the offence of violent disorder under s 2(1) of the Public Order Act 1986 to be proved, how many people need to be present together and use or threaten unlawful violence?

a) One or more
b) Three or more
c) Four or more
d) Twelve or more

K2 Which of the following statements is not true in relation to the *mens rea* required to commit s 3(1) (affray) or s 2(1) of the Public Order Act 1986 (violent disorder)? A person is guilty of either offence only if he/she:

a) Uses towards another person threatening, abusive, or insulting words or behaviour
b) Intends to use violence
c) Threatens to use violence
d) Is aware that his/her conduct may be violent or threaten violence

K3 Which of the following 'harms' are sufficient to prove an offence of actual bodily harm under s 47 of the Offences Against the Person Act 1861?

a) Psychiatric injury/illness or psychological damage
b) Hurt or injury calculated to interfere with the health or comfort of the victim
c) Loss of consciousness
d) All of the above

K4 Which of the following elements are shared by both ss 18 and 20 of the Offences Against the Person Act 1861?

a) Intent to do some grievous bodily harm
b) Unlawfully and maliciously by any means whatsoever, wound a person
c) Wound or cause grievous bodily harm with intent to resist the lawful apprehension or detainer of any person
d) Wound or cause grievous bodily harm with intent to prevent the lawful apprehension or detainer of any person

K5 Which of the following statements is not true in relation to s 3(1) of the Public Order Act 1986 (affray)?

a) The person who is threatened or subject to violence has to be physically present
b) The use or threat of violence must be directed towards a person and not property
c) A person of reasonable firmness needs to be actually or likely to be present at the scene
d) A threat can be made by words alone

K6 Which of the following statements is not true in relation to s 2(1) of the Public Order Act 1986 (violent disorder)?

a) A person of reasonable firmness needs to be actually or likely to be present at the scene
b) It can be committed in private as well as public places
c) It is immaterial whether or not the suspects committing the offence use or threaten unlawful violence simultaneously
d) A threat can be made by words alone

K 7 Which of the following elements are not shared by ss 18 and 20 of the Offences Against the Person Act 1861?

    a) Unlawfully
    b) Maliciously
    c) Cause
    d) Wound

K 8 Which of the following statements is false?

    a) Section 18 of the Offences Against the Person Act 1861 (GBH with intent) can be racially or religiously aggravated
    b) Section 20 of the Offences Against the Person Act 1861 (GBH) can be racially or religiously aggravated
    c) Section 20 of the Offences Against the Person Act 1861 (GBH) is an 'indictable offence'
    d) Section 18 of the Offences Against the Person Act 1861 (GBH with intent) is triable on indictment only and the penalty is life imprisonment

The Railway Scenario

It is Friday afternoon, during a scheduled briefing at 14.00 and the start of the late turn tour of duty, and Sgt Vokes informs his section that the Intelligence Unit has received some limited but reliable intelligence that two self-styled local 'gangs' are planning a confrontation—time and location unknown.

The 'gangs'—groups of youths, mainly male—are well known to the local police. The 'Beach Crew' regard the seafront area and the adjoining roads as their territory.

A seaside resort for some, but not much for young people to do.

The 'Archers' are based around the railway arches and the train station up towards the town centre. The two groups have been involved in various public order breaches and their activities often feature in local petty crime incidents. The Intelligence Unit has built up a file of the names of group members (including a network analysis), their seniority, and the locations they frequent; the Archers generally meet up in the Railway just off the High Street.

During the briefing the Intelligence Unit Research and Development team draw attention to their briefing pack, recently posted on the secure force intranet.

Q1 What sort of information is generally provided in an intelligence briefing event?

> Ps Vokes also reveals that the previous evening a Ben Gilden, one of the Beach Crew, was admitted to hospital, with severe facial and abdominal injuries. He had been found unconscious behind a skip and seemed to have been beaten up. Intelligence suggests that the Archers were involved in the attack.

Q2 On the information supplied here in relation to injuries, what offences might have been committed?

> Pc Oben has made time to take a quick look at the presentation contained in the self-briefing pack and he is already familiar with the photos of the group members on display in the police station briefing room.
>
> *. . . I wonder if we're using a CHIS to get some of this information?*
>
> Pc Oben is a student police officer, and has recently gained sufficient competence to undertake Supervised Patrol. He has been designated to undertake mobile patrol in an emergency response vehicle (ERV) with a more experienced colleague, Pc Murphy.
>
> It is 22.00 when, as they half-expected, a call is relayed to them from the force communication centre:
>
> *'Charlie Foxtrot 10—report of a large fight in the Railway, landlord reports two large groups, some with weapons, attacking each other and members of the public, some severe injuries. Other vehicles are on their way, ETA five to ten minutes.'*
>
> Pc Murphy glances in his rear view mirror and executes a swift U turn, and Pc Oben calls Control.
>
> *'We will attend—ETA of five minutes. We're only two here—assuming back-up is on its way also?'*
>
> Pc Oben observes dryly that the hospital could well be busy later; Pc Murphy nods in agreement. A typical Friday night—'fight night'—is underway, but given the earlier intelligence briefing, this one could be particularly busy. As they make their way towards the scene they decide to work out best how to proceed once they arrive.
>
> Pc Murphy parks up and turns off the engine.

Q3 What factors should they consider before going directly to the pub?

The pub is just around the corner, and they can already hear the commotion.

Turning into Station Road they hear shouts echoing from the pub's open doors, and the sound of crashing furniture—a major disturbance is underway. People are spilling out onto the pavement from the open doors; some are standing around while others walk away quickly, head down or glancing back, but no one approaches the officers. One man howls out from the pub—everyone turns to look and other voices are raised in alarm—someone, perhaps a woman, screams.

Q4 What should the two officers do before they consider going inside the pub?

As they approach the pub Pc Oben receives a call to say that four other officers have been called to the incident.

Pc Murphy says nothing but hopes they'll get there soon. He knows he will take the role of First Officer at the Scene (FOAS) and that there will be plenty to do, particularly in terms of managing the situation—but first he will have to judge whether it is safe for them to enter quite yet. He hears a car engine accelerate fiercely close by, although there is no sight of the vehicle. The sound of the engine gradually fades into the distance, and he cannot help but feel relieved that the pub is now quieter—the fighting seems to have stopped.

Q5 What is the role of the FOAS?

Q6 What factors determine which officer takes the role of the FOAS?

Pc Murphy and Pc Oben step towards the open door and the noise level drops yet another notch, if only momentarily. Glass crunches beneath their feet, and the air is suddenly warm with the familiar smell of beer, sweat, and cheap disinfectant. Broken chairs and other debris are strewn across the room, but only about ten people are left—not as many as they expected from the earlier noise. Pc Murphy recognizes one of the young men as a member of the Archers group.

A man lies collapsed on the wet floor, alone, his feet near the door. A red stain is spreading into the pool of spilt drink near his head. There is more blood on the floor over on the other side of the room, and a second man appears to be injured—he is leaning on the bar holding his hand over his face. Two women sit hunched over on one of the bench seats—one of them is sobbing and the other is trying to comfort her.

Heads turn towards the officers but suddenly everybody is talking and shouting again. The younger men seem to brace themselves for action and the sobbing woman cries out and starts screaming, her hands covering her head. Pc Murphy knows the possibility of further 'trouble' is very real—he will have to act fast.

Q7   What should each of the officers do now?

Pc Murphy aims to 'get a grip' of the situation at the earliest opportunity, and makes a quick visual assessment. He stays near the door—that way he can prevent anyone leaving. As soon as he speaks the tension eases.

Both Pc Murphy (one eye on the door) and Pc Oben then instruct the small groups of people left in the pub. They speak in a clear but assertive manner—they instinctively know that this is more likely to get results and also provides reassurance.

> *'Can I ask you all to move to the other bar, please. Take a seat and we will come and speak to you. Is anybody injured? Does anybody here know the lad on the floor? Can you wait for my colleagues? They're on their way and will be here in a couple of minutes.'*

Q8   What else could the officers say to the people in the pub?

Q9   What should be communicated to Control immediately?

Q10   Who can the officers call upon for immediate help and information?

Pc Oben takes a quick look behind the bar—no one's hiding there, but he spots the way to the back door. He places a stool over a bloody shoeprint on the tiled floor just outside the toilets, and points this out to Pc Murphy.

> *. . . look at that . . . great forensics there . . . lovely and clear . . .*
> *. . . yeah . . . just scan their shoes . . . easy-peasey . . .*
> *. . . and check them for blood . . .*

Pc Oben also agrees to keep an eye on the back door to make certain that no one leaves by this route.

Both officers ensure there are no potentially dangerous bystanders or items nearby, no broken glass to endanger their movements in the pub, and no weapons which could cause injury (knives, blades, guns, etc). They also try to avoid contact with the blood.

Still keeping an eye on the door, Pc Murphy puts on gloves and carefully crouches down so that he can see the man's head more clearly. He knows that preservation of forensic evidence will have to take second place as the man's injuries could be life-threatening. He ensures the man is breathing and places him in the recovery position. Fortunately he seems to have no obvious injuries other than the head wound—but that looks bad enough.

The landlord agrees to stand at the back of the pub to make sure no one tries to leave by the back door— and to stop anyone moving the stool protecting the bloody shoeprint.

Q11   Why does Pc Murphy avoid moving any furniture?

Q12   Should someone stay with the injured man?

Pc Murphy hears the ambulance in the distance and stands up and looks around. It briefly crosses his mind that there are quite a few pebbles on the floor—not quite what he expected in a pub. However, he is relieved that the scene has become calmer; small groups of people are watching the officers and discreetly exchanging the odd comment. Some of the young women present are still crying, but the young men watch every move the officers make, and some still seem on edge. Nobody steps forward to talk directly to the officers—perhaps they are frightened or just don't want to be seen to be talking to the police, perhaps fearing reprisal.

Pc Murphy mentally breathes a sigh of relief as the paramedics arrive.

Q13   What should the officers tell the paramedics when they arrive?

Q14   What useful information could the paramedics provide for the officers?

One of the paramedics is already attending to the man on the floor. Using equipment from her bag, she ensures his airway is clear, and keeps talking to him, asking questions and trying to reassure him. The other paramedic attends to the head wound and checks that the man does not have additional, perhaps hidden, injuries beneath his clothing. Pc Murphy also asks them to check that the man has no weapons concealed in his clothing. One of the paramedics stands up and goes to get the stretcher from the ambulance. On his way out he moves a table to prop open the door; Pc Murphy grimaces.

The injured man groans as he is lifted onto the stretcher, but it is not long before he is wheeled out and the stretcher slid into the ambulance.

Q15   What information does Pc Murphy need to obtain from them before they leave?

Q16   What additional information should Pc Murphy provide for the paramedics?

Q17   Why is Pc Murphy 'none too pleased' about the paramedic moving the table?

Pc Murphy now turns his attention to other people at the scene. He approaches a group of older men nursing half pints. One of the men stands up and explains that he and his friends were just having a quiet half when 'all hell broke loose'. Pc Murphy listens attentively, but is distracted by the whistling sound coming from the man's hearing aid.

☺

. . . looks a bit senile . . . how much longer? . . .

The man glances round and bites his lip, hesitating before briefly waving his hand towards the three younger men over on the other side of the pub. He furtively says:

'Ask them what it is all about—they can tell you.'

He then turns away, shaking his head, and is unwilling to say any more.

Q18   Clearly, Pc Murphy needs to ask these older men more about what they have seen, but not right now. What information should he obtain from the man and from the other people (all potential witnesses) before they leave, in addition to their contact details?

The follow-up paramedics attend to other 'walking wounded'. Some of them appear to be in shock. One man is bleeding from his mouth and appears to have several teeth missing. Others just want to get home to safety.

Pc Oben is keen to find out as much as he can about what happened in the pub before and during the fight, but the events seem confused. Some witnesses provide identical accounts but others are reluctant to provide any information at all.

Pc Oben	Did you see what happened?
Customer	No. I didn't see nothing.
Pc Oben	Can you tell me what occurred?
Customer	No idea, mate, you had better ask them.
Pc Oben	Do you know the man who was injured on the floor?
Customer	Nope.
Pc Oben	Do you know any of the other injured people?
Customer	Nope, none of them.
Pc Oben	Who are you with?
Customer	A few mates—dunno where they are.
Pc Oben	Did you see anyone hit the man who was on the floor?
Customer	Nope.
Pc Oben	Did you see any other assaults?
Customer	Assaults? . . . oh right . . . no . . . nope, I didn't see anything like that.

Q19 Should Pc Oben ask this customer any more questions?

Q20 Why would it be wrong for Pc Murphy and Pc Oben to allow apparently innocent bystanders to leave?

Pc Murphy stands by the front door of the pub where a small group has assembled, waiting to leave. One man is limping and claims he stumbled on something hard and round on the floor and hurt his knee; he doesn't want to wait to see a paramedic—he just wants to go.

Pc Murphy checks that each person has had his or her identity confirmed and contact details noted. He knows it may be necessary to arrest or interview some of the walking wounded later at the hospital—and that some of the presumed 'witnesses' may end up as suspects.

Two supporting officers arrive at the scene to assist the FOAS. One of them is Sgt Joiner, the late turn supervisor. She is familiar with the local youth culture as she has lived in the town for nearly five years.

Pc Oben and Pc Murphy provide Sgt Joiner and the other officer with a very quick briefing— that there has been a serious fight, apparently involving members of the Archers and Beach Crew groups, that some of the suspects are probably still in the pub, and that many of the people still present are potential witnesses. Sgt Joiner nods briskly and listens, but the briefing adds nothing to what she hasn't already surmised.

As the newly arrived officers set about questioning the people in the pub they are, of course, fully aware that some of the witnesses are likely to be hostile, uncooperative, or untruthful.

Q21 What else do Pc Oben and Pc Murphy need to cover with Sgt Joiner?

Sgt Joiner takes over 'control' from Pc Murphy, and introduces herself to the landlord. Her main priorities are identifying key witnesses, safeguarding crime scenes, recovering potential exhibits, and preventing further trouble.

Now that four officers are on the scene (and the wounded man who was on the floor has been taken to hospital) the questioning of the witnesses proceeds more rapidly. They focus on gaining details of the witnesses still present, and also ask them about any other potential witnesses who have already left, noting their names and addresses when provided.

From the initial accounts it emerges that four or five young men had burst through the door of the pub, probably after being dropped off by a driver (as several witnesses reported hearing screeching tyres or seeing the car make off). The assailants were armed; witnesses reported seeing a baseball bat, knives, and what looked like a sock filled with pebbles. Some of the men sitting at the bar (known to one of the older female witnesses as 'fighting types') looked surprised but still seemed ready to fight. One of the 'intruders' hit one of the men at the bar over the head with the baseball bat; he fell to the floor, bleeding profusely from the side of his face. Another of the assailants had something that looked like a long 'bean bag' according to one witness, which he swung at several people hitting them and obviously causing them extreme pain. Another person had been hit on the head with what he thought was a billiard cue or something similar, and another thought he had been hit in the eye with a small hard object—perhaps a marble or a stone. Two men had been fighting on the floor, 'wrestling', but one of them had suddenly let out a 'howling scream'. One of the witnesses said that part of the man's ear had been bitten off. All the witnesses agreed that the man who had howled had run out of the back of the pub.

One young woman had collapsed but had since come round and was being tended by her friend.

The witnesses in the pub report that a number of other young men had left through the back door of the pub as soon as they heard police sirens and hadn't come back.

Q22   Assuming the men who burst through the door were in possession of their weapons on the way to the pub, what offences, if any, have the suspects committed (in relation to the weapons), before they even arrived?

Q23   What offences can be considered if the onlookers in the pub were shown to be put in fear of their own personal safety because of the degree of violence the attackers used towards their intended vicitms?

Q24   Apart from attempted murder, what specific criminal offences might arise from the assaults and woundings described above?

Q25   How should the officers segregate witnesses and suspects in order to reduce the chances of further violence or threats?

Some of the witnesses are denying having seen anything that happened, many of them claiming to have been 'in the toilets' as the fracas broke out. Sgt Joiner comments to Pc Oben that, taken together, the various individual accounts seem to suggest that a total of five men happened to be in the toilets at this crucial moment! Pc Oben, feeling somewhat frustrated, makes a mental note to check the number of facilities in the gents.

Other witnesses, however, are trying to be helpful and provide fuller accounts. The officers are keen to record their details and a brief description of what may later prove to be vital evidence. One of the more excited witnesses overhears another witness telling a police officer he was 'in the toilets' and says to the officer:

'That's rubbish, he was standing next to me when it happened, he must have seen it all, he was jeering the bloke on who had a thing in his hand he was swinging.'

Now that the key aspects of the incident seem to be clearer, Sgt Joiner can decide on any fast track actions (FTAs).

Pc Murphy starts to move some of the chairs in order to segregate the witnesses. He knows that the Crime Scene Investigators (CSIs) will not be pleased that the bar area of the pub has been altered in this way, but he also knows that a compromise has to be made between preservation of evidence and other pressing issues, such as managing witnesses.

Sgt Joiner tasks the fourth officer (a student officer early in her training who seems not to know what to do) to collect all the cigarette butts from immediately outside the pub for forensic purposes.

Q26   Is it appropriate for the landlord to help Pc Murphy segregate presumed witnesses and suspects?

Q27   With respect to the cigarette butts, what forensic purpose might Sgt Joiner have in mind?

> The landlord suggests using the lobby at the bottom of the stairs as one area and helps shepherd the less hostile people in the right direction, but is unwilling to allow the upstairs rooms to be used (as his children are upstairs and are already very upset). He suggests letting some of the witnesses who want to smoke stand outside in the covered bar area at the back.

Q28   Why might it not be a good idea to allow the witnesses to go outside?

> Yet more officers arrive and are tasked by Sgt Joiner to concentrate on the witnesses and victims and to make sure further breaches of the peace do not occur. They are on their guard for further outbreaks of violence and observe body language, groupings, spoken language, and attitude. All could be precursors to another incident either immediately in the pub or in the street outside, or later in the town centre.
>
> Sgt Joiner then tasks Pc Oben to find out if any CCTV evidence is available. He goes out into the street for a quick look around to see if he can spot any cameras nearby.

Q29   How could Pc Oben find out more about the availability of CCTV footage, and what actions could he take?

> Pc Oben notes the presence of a CCTV camera on a pole just along the street. He makes a note in his PNB to mark it up on the handover sheet for the investigating officers in the morning. He knows that specialist technical teams might be required to recover the CCTV images.
>
> Meanwhile Pc Murphy is looking under the tables and benches for the part of the ear that had been bitten off (according to the witnesses). He spots a small dark dusty lump under a bench seat and gets out his torch. The object looks sticky with congealed blood and is inevitably coated with dust and other assorted small debris—he points it out to the other officers but leaves it where it is. He also finds a sock containing a few pebbles, and shrugging his shoulders, shows it to Sgt Joiner. She pauses, her lips tight, and tells him to fetch a paper evidence bag from the police vehicle.

Q30   What should Pc Murphy do about the piece of ear?

Q31   Why does the Sergeant ask for a paper bag (and not a plastic bag)?

Q32   What potential evidence could be gathered from the sock?

Q33   What must Pc Murphy write on the label of the paper bag that will be used to secure the sock?

Q34   List some other key FTAs that might apply in this scenario in order to preserve the crime scene.

> At the same time as the incidents at the Railway, Pc Waite and Pc Chan are on mobile patrol, driving slowly around the beach area of the town. At their briefing they had also heard about the potential for an incident between the groups and so they are not entirely surprised to hear the communications about the incident and to be asked to attend a rendezvous point (RVP) near the Railway. On the main road into the town centre, Pc Chan recognizes a car moving in the other direction as one of the Beach Crew's vehicles. Pc Waite keeps an eye on the car while reporting the situation to Control, and luckily the road is wide enough for Pc Chan to turn around easily. She accelerates hard. Pc Waite switches on the light and Pc Chan switches on the two-tone horn.
>
> Fortunately the road is not too busy and they have clear views of oncoming traffic. They are able to stop the suspect's car in a bus-stop layby without obstructing the road for other road users.

Q35   What powers under the Road Traffic Act 1988 can Pc Waite and Pc Chan use to stop the vehicle in order to question the driver?

Q36   What should be the officers' priority actions once the vehicle is stopped?

> The two officers get out of their vehicle and approach the car. Pc Chan recognizes all three of the car's occupants as members of the Beach Crew. The driver picks her nails, and the male passenger in the front seems to be trying to get a CD out of the CD player. None of them speak or even look up. Pc Waite suppresses a wave of irritation.
>
> Taking control of the situation, Pc Waite asks for the car keys and tells them to keep their hands in view at all times.
>
> *. . . I'll be better off to keep this lot in the car—not having them running off!*
>
> The front seat passenger keeps rubbing his mouth, but fails to remove the dried blood encrusted on his cheek. Pc Chan notices an item of clothing on the back seat, half concealing what looks like a baseball bat.

For a baseball bat to be an offensive weapon it has to be shown that the person who had it in their possession intended to use it to cause injury to a person in a public place.

The driver provides her name in response to Pc Waite's first question, but is then less forthcoming.

Pc Waite   Okay . . . Kirsty, can I ask you where you're going and where you've just come from?

Driver   Nowhere really.

Pc Waite   Is this your car?

Driver   Yeah.

Pc Waite   Have you been in the town area at all in the last 20 minutes, Kirsty?

Driver   No.

Pc Waite   Have you been parked up or away from your vehicle—your car—in the past 20 minutes or so?

Driver   Nope.

Pc Waite   Okay, Kirsty, have you been near the Railway this evening at all?

The female driver pauses and then turns suddenly to look at a passing car, but Pc Waite is not distracted by this, and repeats his final question impassively. She remains silent.

Q37   Should Pc Waite have cautioned the occupants of the car before he began any questioning?

Q38   Should the officers have a closer look at the baseball bat?

> Meanwhile, Pc Chan contacts Control to obtain more details about the incident at the Railway, and particularly whether the vehicle they have stopped or its occupants had been seen leaving the pub. The officers receive information from Control that gives them reasonable grounds to believe that the vehicle and its occupants may well have been involved in the incident at the Railway.

Q39   Can Pc Chan arrest any of the people from the car merely because she has received certain information from Control?

Q40   For what reasons might Pc Chan believe it is necessary to arrest the occupants of the car?

Q41   Is there any reason why Pc Chan should make the arrests rather than Pc Waite?

Q42   What will happen to the car after it has been seized?

Q43   Should Pc Chan and Pc Waite call for the officers at the Railway to provide assistance in transporting the arrested suspects to the police station?

> Pc Waite arrests all three occupants from the car, and while he is busy cautioning them, Pc Chan calls Control again, this time to arrange transport for the suspects, and for the car to be seized.
>
> Meanwhile, Pc Goodey is on foot patrol, about 15 minutes quick walk from the Railway. He has heard radio traffic about the fighting and the calls for back-up and ambulances, and heard the police cars. He can picture the scene, but all is quiet down at his end of the High Street—apart from a group of giggling girls who keep looking his way. Suddenly, further along on the other side of the road, he sees one of the Beach Crew, a certain Frankie Ming, striding along, head down and looking determined. Immediately suspicious, Pc Goodey notes that there are no side turnings between Ming and himself, and recalls that Ming lives in the next street—could Ming be on his way home from the Railway? Pc Goodey maintains a steady pace—what will Ming do, what will he say?
>
> Pc Goodey crosses the road. Ming suddenly glances in the direction of Pc Goodey and then quickly looks away. Then, staring rather too intently at the plate glass of the shop windows, his pace accelerates. Just as he draws close to Pc Goodey, Ming raises his hand as if to scratch his forehead; he smiles but seems to be trying to hide his face.
>
> Pc Goodey greets him and asks where he is going. He's not sure why, but he's always quite liked Ming. However, he suspects Ming may be in possession of a weapon, and that he needs to be searched.

Q44   What are the probable grounds for Pc Goodey's suspicion?

Q45   Under what legislation can he stop and search Frankie Ming?

But before Pc Goodey gets a chance to say any more, Ming blurts out:

'Look, it wasn't me, I don't know nothing about that bat, you can't go accusing me of killing 'im or nothing . . . I just wanted to hurt them like— nothing really—just warn them off a bit like.'

Pc Goodey is surprised; he has not even mentioned the pub fight.

. . . hey ho . . . how does he know that someone's been badly hurt . . . or even about the fight at all?

Q46   What should Pc Goodey do when he hears this 'defence' from Ming?

Ming's words have immediately raised Pc Goodey's level of suspicion that Ming was at least present at the incidents in the Railway, possibly even taking an active part. Pc Goodey arrests and cautions Ming and then conducts a search, noting in passing his surprisingly white bare left ankle. Ming just shrugs when Pc Goodey asks him why he is only wearing one sock.

Q47   Under what legislation does Goodey conduct this search?

Q48   How might the sock(s) contribute to this investigation?

Q49   Ming has not answered Pc Goodey's question about why he is wearing only one sock. Does this amount to a 'significant silence'? And should Pc Goodey have even asked Ming about the missing sock?

Q50   Should Ming be conveyed to the same police station as the three people who were in the car?

Pc Goodey carefully applies handcuffs to Ming—a proportionate restraint method in these circumstances—and calls for transport back to the local station.

A police officer has to be able to justify the use of handcuffs. Unjustified use of handcuffs could be regarded as assault.

On arrival at the police station Pc Goodey presents Ming to the Custody Officer and, in Ming's presence, informs the Custody Officer of the justification and the necessity for the arrest. Ming is also photographed and informed of his rights as an arrested person. The custody suite video camera records the whole process. As Pc Goodey leaves he is relieved that the custody procedures have gone smoothly. He takes the car round the back to be searched.

Q51   What are Ming's rights as an arrested person?

Q52   How might the video recording be used in the subsequent investigation?

Q53   Why is the police car searched immediately after Ming has been transported to the police station?

Q54   Who will take the 'samples' from Ming?

Q55   What samples should be taken?

Later that night, Pc Murphy and Pc Oben 'stand down' from the crime scene at the Railway and tell Control that they are returning to the police station. Pc Waite and Pc Chan are already back at the station.

Q56   At the police station, what tasks should Pc Murphy and Pc Oben now complete in relation to the incidents in the Railway earlier that evening?

Q57   Should each officer preferably complete his or her own PNB entries without discussing the events with the other officers?

Outcome

> Subsequently, DNA was sampled from the sock and pebbles on the pub floor and both provided a match with Frankie Ming. However, Ming was not sufficiently identified as swinging the sock and causing bodily harm so he could not be charged with any assault.
>
> The baseball bat samples matched the DNA from one of the men in the car (Drake) but, as with Ming, he too could not be positively identified by witnesses as having used the baseball bat to inflict injuries.

Crime scene investigators are not usually drawn from the ranks of uniformed officers. They are police staff specially trained by police forces, often in conjunction with the National Police Improvement Agency (NPIA).

> The Crown Prosecution Service (CPS) eventually authorized charges of violent disorder against Ming, one of the male occupants of the car (Drake), and another man from the pub (Trimble). All three defendants pleaded not guilty—admitting their presence but not their involvement. Thus, the other forensic evidence at the scene had limited value. On conviction by jury (a majority verdict) they received custodial sentences and the judge set a tariff in an attempt to ensure a deterrent value.
>
> The other man from the car was later identified by witnesses for the ear-biting incident and charged with the offence of unlawful wounding under s 20 of the Offences Against the Persons Act 1861. Blood distribution and forensic odontology were conclusive, although the defendant claimed in interview that he was only acting in self-defence. He was found guilty and sentenced to a short term in prison.

The ID procedures were inconclusive for many of the others suspected of being involved in the fracas. The female driver was not charged with any offences but made a witness statement claiming that she only 'agreed to drive the boys to the pub and wait for them' and did not know of their intentions.

Unfortunately, surgery to try and re-attach the piece of ear did not succeed; the fragment was too ragged and torn. The victim has a permanent disfigurement to remind him of his evening in the Railway.

The Railway Answers

A1   Intelligence briefings often include information concerning stolen vehicles, hot spots for burglaries, and street crime. There is also normally a review of the active criminals in the area, involving sensitive and confidential information concerning the criminals' associates, MO, activities, and sightings. This information includes addresses, vehicle numbers, premises they frequent, known offences they commit, and weapons and warnings as to violence and more. Officers are also made aware of persons in the area who are wanted for various crimes and who, if seen, can be arrested. (This presumes the officers can justify a 'reasonable suspicion' to arrest or that a warrant has been issued by a court for his/her arrest.)

A2   Note that at this stage of the scenario, there are no indications of the severity of the injuries. However, you may wish to consider the following:

- common assault, but if the victim is barely conscious then the injuries are likely to be more serious;

- assault occasioning actual bodily harm (ABH) because the injuries have obviously interfered with the health or comfort of the victim in more than a trivial way because he was admitted to hospital;

- wounding or inflicting grievous bodily harm, if the injuries are consistent with really serious bodily harm;

- wounding or inflicting grievous bodily harm with intent, if the injuries are consistent with really serious bodily harm and the assailants intended such injuries to be sustained.

See Unlawful Personal Violence and Serious Offences of Personal Violence,
BSPOH 2010, 10.15 and 10.16

A3   These are difficult decisions and the priority for the officers must be to protect themselves and others from harm or further harm but also to recognize that delay in responding could mean that innocent members of the public could be seriously hurt. It is not acceptable to do nothing and at the least Pc Murphy and Pc Oben should provide as much information as they can to Control, including a recommended route into the town, and the selection of a rendezvous point which is in a safe environment for those who are not familiar with the location to attend. They should try and ascertain from a relatively safe position the scale of the problem and advise on the needs for further support and medical aid.

A4   One of the officers should report the fact that they have arrived at the scene and intend to enter the premises. The time will be recorded on their behalf at the control room, so there is no need for either of them to note it down in their PNB. A situation report (Sitrep) of any incident outside the premises is also sent to Control as this will assist other attending officers who may themselves meet with immediate confrontation (driving into a hostile crowd, for example).

A5   The FAOS should consider, as a priority, the following actions.

- Preservation of life is of the utmost importance. First aid and resuscitation must be attempted when necessary.

- Liaison and transfer to other emergency services is key to providing ongoing support and paramedics take primacy in this situation.

- Monitoring the activities of the paramedics.

- Endeavour to take control of the incident.

- Make an immediate assessment and report back to Control.

- Protection and preservation of the scene is a priority shared by all attending officers.

- Be alert, what is seen, heard, and smelled is vital and should be recorded as soon as possible. It may be essential evidence later.

- Call upon a supervisor to advise and guide at the earliest opportunity.

A6   If two officers arrive at the same time, there is no set protocol for a specific designated officer to take the lead, but the more experienced officer is likely to do so.

A7   Pc Murphy needs to take overall control. The environment needs to be made safe and this involves both of them working together. He must also provide basic first aid for the injured man because the paramedics have not yet arrived on scene. Pc Oben will concentrate on preservation of evidence and managing witnesses.

A8   The officers should reassure them that medical assistance is on its way, offering a generally positive message. They should also say that each person will be spoken with individually.

A9   Pc Oben should transmit an immediate situation report to Control advising them of the nature and extent of the incident and calling for, or confirming, the attendance of other emergency services, in this case paramedics and an ambulance. In addition, supervisors should be called to the scene for what might prove to be the initial stages of a major crime (murder or manslaughter).

A10   They should seek the support of the landlord or other staff to help to deal with customers and potential witnesses. For example, the staff can usher the customers to a part of the premises away from the area to be contained and perhaps they can be seated and positively supported while the police treat the injured and begin to control the events.

A11   The dynamics of the fight are recorded in the layout of the pub after the fight, so the positions of chairs and damaged articles, as well as the patterns of blood to be found later on floors, walls, and clothing are valuable forensic evidence.

A12   Yes, Pc Murphy will stay with him but also speak with any people who try to enter or leave the pub.

A13   Pc Oben should direct the paramedics to the injured man and tell them as much as he knows about what has happened and how the man has been since he received his injuries. This will enable the paramedics to make swift judgments about immediate medical aid, specialist services, and which hospital he should be taken to.

The officers should also tell the paramedics where there may be valuable evidence, such as blood spatter, so that they can avoid contamination where possible.

A14   Pc Murphy should note any clothing the paramedics remove from the man. Blood spatters on clothing, fibre, and DNA evidence may be available on outer clothing and in an attempt at first aid this clothing is the first to be discarded.

Any account given by the injured persons in answer to questions put by paramedics, (eg names of friends or associates), confirmation of the victims' identities, should also be noted. The police would also want to ascertain if this is 'life at risk'.

A15   He must ensure he finds out the name of the hospital the injured person is going to be taken to.

A16   He should tell them that the injuries occurred in the course of a dispute and that there is a risk of the fracas re-igniting if individuals from the opposing groups end up side-by-side in the same A&E department. If this is likely then the paramedics can communicate the situation to security personnel or require police attendance.

A17   He knows that the Crime Scene Investigators (CSIs) may bemoan the fact the evidence has been destroyed or taken out of context, and regrets not having reminded the paramedics once again about avoiding unnecessary interference with the wider crime scene.

Later, Pc Murphy will record the original positions of the furniture in his PNB, and list which items have been moved. This information must be communicated to the CSIs as soon as is reasonably possible.

A18   They should make notes of the 'first account' given by any witness as this will have significance later in the criminal investigation. Care should be taken in recording descriptions of various parties involved, and persons who are pointed out as possible offenders or key witnesses 'pointed to' should be identified as soon as possible. If at a later stage, when a full witness statement is taken, the description then given varies in any way from the first account, this has a potential detrimental effect on the weight of evidence this witness offers. At identification procedures the first account of the description is an integral part of the process of formal identification. Variances in account can lead to 'disclosure' (MG 6E) to the defence that a witness is unsure of the identity of any person identified—and this might undermine his/her value as a witness and assist the accused. (It is important that the officers note whether the witness is making an identification of facial characteristics and not just a description of clothing and stature. Many arrested persons are aware that they can be identified by clothing so switching external clothing between associates is common, to confuse the picture of who was responsible. Ill-fitting clothing should signal the possibility that switching attire has already occurred. If clothing is used to identify individuals then 'identification procedures' do not necessarily apply.)

At this stage, and given the issues they are confronted with, the officers also need to be thinking in terms of witness interviews and statement taking, and arranging Achieving Best Evidence (ABE) interviews away from the incident. Such an interview will take place at a time and in an environment where the witness feels safe and able to give a potentially comprehensive account of what he or she has seen.

A19   Yes. Pc Oben must obtain the customer's name and contact details. Even though this witness does not seem to offer any real 'evidence' of the incident—in what might be called a 'negative account'—the witness must be identified and this exchange recorded if at all possible, as the customer may later come forward and offer evidence for the victim or the offender, quite contrary to his initial account.

If this incident leads to a court case, the prosecution might want to contact this reluctant witness, and even issue a witness summons to require the customer to give evidence in court. If the police have not kept the contact details of the customer then a case may be lost.

A20   All those present were potential witnesses and hence may have important information. If the case goes to court the defence may argue that the case is 'unfair' if it emerges that the two officers did not make every effort to obtain evidence from all witnesses (see s 78 of the PACE Act 1984). If no effort is made to identify witnesses, then it is possible that a potential witness for the defence is lost, one who may point to a suspect's innocence. In the past the courts have taken the view that in these circumstances (*R v Linda Heggart, R v William Patrick Heggart* 2000

WL 1881358) witnesses identified but not interviewed by the police:

- should be disclosed to the defence;
- and in the absence of disclosure will be regarded as—
  - potentially undermining the prosecution case
  - assisting the defence case.

A21 Pc Murphy and Pc Oben should also tell Sgt Joiner their opinion on what immediate actions are required.

A22 Possession of an offensive weapon in a public place might have been committed. The suspects appear to be intending to cause injury with the baseball bat, the object described as a long bean bag, and with knives. Therefore these articles might be considered as offensive weapons (intended or made) under s 1(1) of the Prevention of Crime Act 1953.

See Offensive Weapons in a Public Place, *BSPOH 2010*, 9.19.1

Should the knives be anything other than a folding pocket knife, then an offence of possessing a bladed article in a public place under s 139(1) of the Criminal Justice Act 1988 may have been committed.

See Bladed and Sharply Pointed Articles in a Public Place, *BSPOH 2010*, 9.19.2

A23 These offences might include riot, violent disorder, and affray. Riot would require twelve or more people involved and it is not clear from the circumstances described thus far that this condition has been met. Violent disorder is a distinct possibility, as it would appear that three or more people were involved in the fighting, unlawful violence was used, and it caused at least one person present in the pub to fear for his or her safety (eg, the woman seen crying). Affray could also be considered as the violence involved two or more people and the conduct was beyond the use of words and was threatening and directed towards a person or persons. Although the offence of affray technically involves only one person using violence, the CPS recommends that affray should be considered when two or more people are involved in the violence.

In terms of the events portrayed so far in the scenario, the offence of violent disorder is the most likely to be considered.

See Serious Public Order Offences, *BSPOH 2010*, 9.7.4

A24 Common assault, unlawful wounding/inflicting grievous bodily harm, or wounding/causing grievous bodily harm with intent.

See Unlawful Personal Violence, *BSPOH 2010*, 10.15

A25 This will not be easy. The groups should be separated by barriers or by distance. Physical barriers are very useful for control purposes, and the officers here could use a row of chairs, even though moving furniture represents contamination (the scene state has been altered). The reality is that, by the time the police arrived, the scene would probably have been changed by the witnesses and victims anyway. Pc Murphy and Pc Oben, Sgt Joiner, and the fourth officer are in an invidious position, since they must attempt to control witnesses whilst also preserving evidence from further contamination.

A26 The landlord can certainly provide assistance, for instance by suggesting other rooms on the premises that could be used, helping cordon off the area of the bar where the fracas occurred, or by moving witnesses and suspects away from the focal area of the attacks.

A27 If a suspect is interviewed and claims never to have been in the vicinity of the pub, such cigarette ends may prove him/her to be lying—a fact, no doubt, that would be brought to the attention of the jury.

A28   At present there are not enough officers to supervise a separate group of witnesses in the covered area at the back of the pub. If the witnesses were unsupervised some of them might leave the scene before officers had had a chance to speak with them and record the necessary details.

A29   Pc Oben could ask the landlord if there are any CCTV cameras inside the pub or in the vicinity outside the pub. He should note the positions of any cameras and make a sketch plan, noting the camera angle if possible.

A30   Potentially, this piece of ear is forensically very important as possible evidence. In this case, it could almost be legitimately argued that the piece of the ear should remain in place for its proper recording in relation to other exhibits, but this might be regarded as over-preservation of the crime scene.

However, it is also important to remember that if the ear part can be protected and kept in a cold or chilled environment, it is possible it could be re-attached to the victim and thus reduce disfigurement. It needs to be taken to the hospital as soon as possible.

The ear should be wrapped in clean tissue or cloth (not toilet paper) and stored on ice—but not embedded within a quantity of ice. The ear must not itself become frozen. (A bag of frozen peas or beans can be used as a surface to chill a wrapped body part, as long as the body part does not freeze at all.)

The body part should not be immersed in fresh water or a brine solution made up on the spot. (A specially formulated saline solution can be used for storage, but this cannot be replicated with salt and water by a non-expert.)

A31   The bag needs to be paper and not plastic, otherwise the sweaty sock will start to rot and DNA will be destroyed—as will the sock if it is made of natural fibres.

A32   Quite apart from the fact that the officers may locate a person with only one sock and thereby possibly link that person to the pub, DNA could be recovered from the sock by a forensic scientist. This profile could be searched on the National DNA Database (NDNAD) or directly compared to the DNA of a suspect.

There are also opportunities in comparing the fibres within the sock to those within both shoes of the suspect, in the event that he has disposed of the second sock at a later time.

A33   The details required are:

- police force;
- exhibit number (the bag asks for an 'Identification Ref No');
- description;
- time and date of seizure; and
- where it was seized and by whom.

Certain information (such as suspect name, incident number, and court exhibit number) should not be added until later.

A34   1. Seize and package the pebbles securely. Fingerprints are unlikely to be recovered from a beach pebble, but there is a possibility of recovering Low Copy Number DNA from fingerprint residue which may identify a person who handled it, the owner of the sock, and who handled the pebbles from the beach. (Remember this does not prove who actually used the sock as a weapon, though the information might assist the investigation.)

2. Preserve blood spatters and smears for DNA or blood distribution analysis. Pools of wet blood on the floor are often of little value. However, fine patterns of blood sprayed on walls and fixtures may be of use, and trails of blood can be used to establish an offender's movements,

particularly the route whereby he/she left the scene. The clothing worn by people who were in the vicinity of an incident may also be spattered with blood.

3. Preserve broken bottles and glasses for blood and fingerprints, again offering potential evidence of who had been present at the scene, but not necessarily their role in the events. There may be viable DNA on the rims of glasses but, again, such evidence may only prove a person was drinking in the pub at some time, not that they were present or active in the fight.

4. Preserve items of clothing if discarded or bloodied. It is not possible or practical to seize all clothing of all victims or suspects at such an early stage. Any persons arrested will have clothing removed at the police station and where possible the clothing belonging to people who have been taken to hospital will be obtained by officers attending the hospital, and packaged and labelled accordingly. It is important to remember that the advice of a CSI should be sought—if clothing is soaked in blood there is a danger of confusing the patterns of blood distribution by folding the fabric. The CSI will have access to secure drying facilities. Any discarded material in the pub or its vicinity can be collected by the attending CSI. It is critical in the early stages to describe clothing fully when removed from a suspect, since many statements will describe age, race, sex, and the clothing worn by individuals.

A35　Under s 163 of the Road Traffic Act 1988 a constable in uniform can require any person driving a mechanically propelled vehicle on a road to stop. (There is no need for the constable to have any suspicion or belief that offences have been committed.)

See Powers to Stop a Vehicle, *BSPOH 2010*, 11.3

A36　On approach to the vehicle the officers should be aware that they may be at risk from the occupants or the vehicle. They should try and 'read the situation', approaching cautiously, and watching carefully for any movement in the vehicle. It is not uncommon for a vehicle to suddenly accelerate away, for the officer to be confronted and overwhelmed, or for physical exhibits and items to be discarded or hidden in the vehicle. In addition, they recall that weapons were mentioned in the earlier briefing.

A37　At this stage Pc Waite has no real cause for suspicion and hence no caution is required. If at a later stage Pc Waite suspects an individual of involvement or suspected involvement in a criminal offence then he must use the caution. Often, the answer to preliminary or opening questions can lead to the development of suspicion of involvement, but this does not apply here. However, if in any doubt the caution should be applied at an early stage.

See Cautions, *BSPOH 2010*, 8.4

A38　No, they should leave the baseball bat on the seat so that the photographs of the vehicle will show it in context. (See answer 42, below.)

A39　Yes, but she must form her own suspicions. Pc Chan alone will determine at what point her suspicions are aroused; it is not by surmise or conjecture, it is an objective assessment of the facts, intelligence, or information known to her. It does not matter if this is based on information provided by others as long as she believes the information to be reliable.

Here, Pc Chan suspects that the occupants of the car have been involved in offences at the pub. She has formed her own reasonable suspicion, even though she does not know the specific details. She must use the caution as described under PACE Code of Practice C para 11.1A as any questioning will now be regarded as an interview which, under para 10.1, must be carried out under caution.

See Involvement in the Commission of a Criminal Offence, *BSPOH 2010*, 8.7.3

A40　She must believe it is necessary to arrest the person in question. Here Pc Chan would probably believe the arrest is necessary in order to allow the prompt and effective investigation of the offence or of the conduct of the person in question, and to interview the suspects under caution in a formal interview setting.

See Reasons that Make an Arrest Necessary, *BSPOH 2010,* 8.7.4

A41   No, it makes no difference as long as the arresting officer has formed a sufficient suspicion and has a reason for the arrest.

A42   The car will be taken to a secure facility and later examined. The CSI will almost certainly photograph it (particularly as a witness may describe it) and examine it for fingerprints, DNA sources, and any material which might link it to the offence in question. The officers should inform the CSI who was sitting in which seat in the vehicle. Considerable intelligence may be derived from the vehicle: eg pay and display tickets and shop receipts can reveal various locations of the vehicle over time, and DNA and fingerprints may be used to identify further people who may turn out to be other, as yet unknown, group members.

A43   No. If more police officers are needed to support Pc Waite and Pc Chan then, if at all possible, none of these should come from the scene at the Railway. This is because officers who have attended the vicinity of witnesses and the injured people at the pub could directly transfer blood, fibre, and body fluids to the suspects whom Pc Waite and Pc Chan have arrested.

A44   Pc Goodey has heard about the fight in the Railway and is also aware that there are strong suspicions that members of the Archers and the Beach Crew groups were involved, that weapons were used, and that people were injured as a result of the fighting. He also knows Ming to be a member of one of the groups, so it is reasonable to assume that Ming might be carrying a 'prohibited article'.

Reasonable suspicion can be formed on the basis of the behaviour of a person, without specific information or intelligence.

See Reasonable Grounds for Suspicion, *BSPOH 2010,* 8.7.2

A45   Section 1 of the PACE Act 1984.

A46   Pc Goodey must record in his pocket note book exactly what Frankie Ming said about the fight and the resulting injuries, and request Ming to sign that the record is correct. As this comment falls outside the context of an interview it is an 'unsolicited comment'.

If Ming should make similar comments after he has been cautioned, but not during the course of an interview, this would be a 'significant statement'. For example, en route to the police station he might say something that is adverse to him, a verbal statement that could be used as evidence against him if he is charged with any offence arising from the fight at the Railway. It is particularly important to record accurately what has been said in such a significant statement, and offer it at some point to Ming to agree its accuracy in line with PACE Code of Practice C paras 11.4.and 11.4A.

See Unsolicited Comments by Suspects, *BSPOH 2010,* 8.5.1

A47   Under s 32 of the PACE Act 1984—search of an arrested person.

See Searching a Suspect after Arrest, *BSPOH 2010,* 8.9.4

A48   If Ming's single sock is of the same design and size as the sock recovered from the scene at the Railway then the jury in any trial may be easily convinced of his guilt. However, the investigator would need to be cautious about the value of evidence from the sock at the scene unless DNA analysis suggests it really does belong to Ming. In this case, the rarity of the type of sock and the possibility that it was taken from Ming's washing line should also be considered. Unlikely though this may seem, it would not be the most unusual defence offered in a British court.

A49 This may amount to a significant silence—a failure or refusal to answer questions or answer satisfactorily when under caution, which might (allowing for the restrictions on drawing adverse inference from silence) give rise to an inference under the Criminal Justice and Public Order Act 1994 Part III (PACE Code of Practice C para 11.4A).

However, the question and the answer could later be challenged (by the defence) on the basis that Pc Goodey was questioning Ming regarding his 'involvement or suspected involvement in a criminal offence' and that such an interview should be conducted at a police station. It is such an obvious question to ask, and as yet Pc Goodey may not have any information that links this missing sock with the sock found at the Railway, the sock that had been used as a 'made' offensive weapon. In such situations, no one can predict a court's interpretation of law, codes, and good practice. Therefore it is always safer to record everything exactly as it happens and justify why certain actions were taken. The lawyers can then examine the issues (with the benefit of hindsight) in the courtroom. Here, providing Pc Goodey is acting in good faith, he has little to fear from the courts, even where a decision is made to edit out certain parts of his evidence.

A50 Preferably, no, but the distances they may need to travel should be borne in mind. The standard advice is that suspects from the same offence should be conveyed to different police stations to ensure their forensic integrity. Each force will have their own policies on this.

A51 He has the right to have someone informed of his arrest; to consult privately with a solicitor or legal representative; and the right to consult the PACE Codes of Practice.

See The Detainee's Rights After Arrest, *BSPOH 2010,* 8.11.4

A52 The recording might be useful later in the investigation if Ming's clothing and physical features are relevant, for example to a witness who did not see his face.

A53 Any vehicle required to transport suspects to custody or between locations should be searched immediately after the suspect has been removed from the vehicle and before the vehicle is used again. Weapons, drugs, or other 'evidence' may have been hidden in the vehicle by the suspects.

A54 Bearing in mind that CSIs are a finite resource, the arresting officers or another police officer may be tasked with the process.

A55 A custody photograph, DNA, and fingerprints (probably taken using Livescan) are mandatory.

Other samples are required to 'prove or disprove' his involvement in the offence and are taken under PACE Code of Practice D. The objective is to link them to the various facets of the offence in question. This is a list of the minimum samples that are likely to be required:

- any head covering such as a cap;
- head hair combings;
- head hair pulled with the root;
- swabs of any blood on exposed skin;
- shoes, bagged separately;
- trousers;
- upper outer clothing;
- any injuries; and
- urine and/or blood.

Ming's single sock **must** be taken and it must be noted that one is 'missing'.

Ming's urine or blood samples may be used to calculate the level of alcohol or drugs in the blood since this may explain his behaviour. (However, alcohol and drugs are unlikely to be accepted as mitigation.)

Your force may have a policy or guidance on a second DNA swab to be used for comparison to the crime scene. It is common for the NDNAD swabs to fall into an 'automatic' system of dispatch. However, DNA swabs are now considered as 'evidence' rather than 'intelligence' so this may not be required.

If Ming has any bite injuries, a forensic odontologist may be required (not immediately) to match the bite marks to a suspect's teeth.

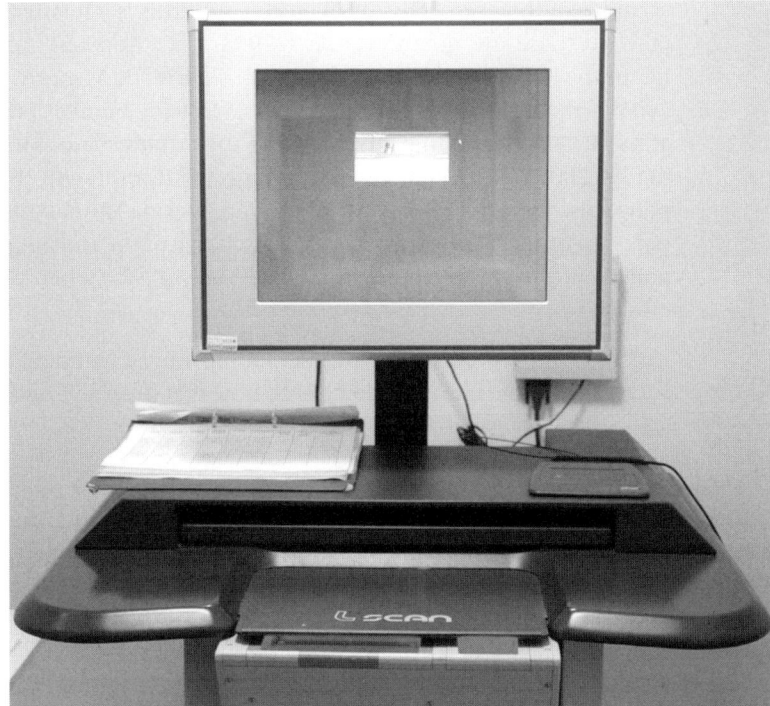

Fingerprints can be digitally captured using Livescan equipment, now in use at all main police custody suites (units). The prints can then be compared with the national fingerprint database, Ident1. If a suspect's prints are already on the database, a subsequent comparison and identification can be completed within a few minutes.

A56 At the conclusion of the incident and on arriving back at the police station, Pc Murphy and Pc Oben may be required to complete some or all of the following tasks depending on local procedures:

- complete the crime reports arising from crime complaints received from victims, applying the Home Office counting rules and the national standards;

- finalize any activity or incident management databases recording their actions and updating the details of the police response;

- complete any handover packages (which in some forces typically involves a 'Single Source Document') to inform the Investigating Officer (IO) of all evidence and intelligence available;

- inform the IO or the DO (Disclosure Officer), if not one and the same, of any issues relating to revelation and disclosure, in particular applying the 'disclosure test' (evidence pointing away from any accused or pointing towards another person's involvement);

- package, label, and store any exhibits they obtained in the course of the investigation so far (eg the sock, pebbles, etc) and liaise with the exhibits officer if one has been appointed;

- complete a duty statement (MG 11);

- complete an MG 5 (relevant to fast track management of the case, a recently revised form for outlining the facts of the case to assist the prosecutor).

See Duty Statements, see *BSPOH 2010,* 8.14
See Handover Procedures, *BSPOH 2010,* 8.16
See Disclosure, *BSPOH 2010,* 12.6

A57 The four officers are legally entitled to confer with each other in order to check on the factual accuracy of their respective PNB entries, and this is a relatively common occurrence in police practice. (Case law, notably *R v Bass* (1953) 17 Cr App R 51, allows for this.) However, the coroner in the inquest into the death of Jean-Charles de Menezes (shot by MPS firearms officers in 2005 in the mistaken belief that he was a 'suicide bomber') criticized the practice of MPS firearms officers 'conferring' when writing their notes some thirty-six hours after the fatal shooting. In 2008, ACPO changed its guidance to recommend that, in investigations concerning police discharge of firearms, officers should normally not confer with each other when making notes. In other cases (other than the discharge of firearms) it is also probably good practice for police officers to record in writing (eg in their PNBs) when they have conferred with another officer.

In conclusion, it is acceptable practice (at the time of writing) for Pc Goodey and his colleagues to confer in this case but they should each note that they have done so.

Test Yourself

And finally, solve the anagrams in the sentence below to complete the definition of s 2(1) of the Public Order Act 1986 (violent disorder).

Where three or more persons who are SERPENT together use or RANTEETH FAWNLULU violence and the conduct of them (taken together) is such as would cause a person of LASNOBEARE firmness present at the scene to fear for his LAPSOREN safety, each of the persons using or TARGETHEINN unlawful violence is guilty of violent REDDORIS.

Answers to Knowledge Check Questions

K1 b   K2 a   K3 d   K4 b   K5 d   K6 a   K7 c   K8 a

Answers to Test Yourself

SERPENT—Present

RANTEETH—Threaten

FAWNLULU—Unlawful

LASNOBEARE—Reasonable

LAPSOREN—Personal

TARGETHEINN—Threatening

REDDORIS—Disorder

7 | Beckett's Fishing Lakes

👣   forensic awareness required

✓   assessment opportunity

☺   diversity issues

💧   health and safety

▽   questionable practice

✏   a pen or pencil is required

Introduction

The chief responsibility of the First Officer at the Scene (FOAS) is for health and safety, first his or her own and, secondly, the health and safety of colleagues and the public. Why put the FOAS first? Simply because an injured police officer is unlikely to be of any help to the victim, and may be a burden to colleagues. Whilst some health and safety decisions are portrayed as over-cautious in the media, nothing is to be gained by recklessness or omission; such behaviour may result in further injury.

After safety (and possibly the saving of life) has been addressed, the crime scene must be managed in order to preserve as much physical evidence as possible, such as physical material (eg fingerprints and weapons), and the original position of items (eg furniture or vehicles). The relative position of items (one to the other) frequently produces valuable evidence.

Ensuring health and safety and scene management are both dynamic processes, as situations can change, for example as:

- a calm witness suddenly becomes agitated;
- the victim's medical condition suddenly deteriorates;
- a peaceful rural location is overrun by ramblers;
- an ordinary, quiet man unexpectedly 'kicks off';
- a routine search for a child who regularly runs away suddenly becomes a murder enquiry.

Judgements have to be made 'on the hoof', particularly about the potential dangers which may be present at the time or which may arise as circumstances develop.

At any scene of a sudden death, every police officer should 'think murder'; however routine an incident may appear to be, there is always the possibility that the incident is one of murder. If a police officer does this, he or she will at least have secured the scene and other evidence, and if the cause of death is later established to be an accident, then nothing has been lost.

Here we will examine the role of officers at major crime scenes and how to manage resources in the 'Golden Hour', particularly in relation to crime scene forensics. If you are a student police officer, then your in-force trainer in these matters is almost certainly a CSI with some experience and you should capitalize on their knowledge. In particular, your force may have geographic or legal limitations which may make some hard and fast 'preservation' rules seem difficult to apply, and after all, it is very easy for trainers to instruct their trainees that 'crime scenes must be preserved at **all costs**'. In this Workbook, we also attempt to be realistic.

Knowledge Check

Before you attempt this scenario, check your understanding of the underpinning legislation involved by undertaking the following knowledge check.

For the multiple choice questions K1 to K5 write down **one** of the letters a, b, c, or d as the answer to the question. Check your answers at the end of this chapter before beginning the scenario.

K1 Is there ever a case where you have 'enough evidence' and can sacrifice, say, tyre marks at a murder scene?

    a) Yes, a few tyre marks can comfortably be sacrificed if there are about 2 metres' worth

    b) Yes, most tyre marks are of limited use to the investigation anyway

    c) No, one can never have too much evidence

    d) Yes, if there is more than one tyre tread pattern at the scene, there is no forensic value

K2 Which legislation or case law relates to arresting a person for crossing a police cordon in a criminal investigation?

    a) *R v Knowlton* (1973)—an officer can refuse entry to, and subsequently arrest, a person who attempts to pass through a police cordon

    b) Section 34 of the Terrorism Act 2000—a superintendent or above can designate an area as cordoned (a constable can also do so if he or she makes a written record and later informs a superintendent) and can arrest a person who fails to leave the cordoned area or who does not comply with an order controlling access to that area

    c) *DPP v Morrison* (2003)—Morrison repeatedly attempted to enter a cordoned area and was arrested

    d) No one can ever be arrested for crossing a police cordon in a criminal investigation

K3 A wet jacket is seized as part of an investigation into a serious assault and may need to be sampled for blood. How should it be packaged as an exhibit?

    a) In a plastic bag as it is, but make a note on the label that the item is damp

    b) It should be dried before packaging it

    c) In a plastic box lined with absorbent paper

    d) Folded in such a way that the damp surfaces face inwards and placed in a perforated paper bag

K4 Which of the following is an 'intimate sample' from a living person, according to PACE Code of Practice D?

    a) A blood sample

    b) Saliva

    c) Scrapings from finger nails

    d) A skin print from the upper part of the arm

K5 'A police officer may seize any item he/she believes is evidence of a crime.' This is a paraphrased version of which case?

    a) *R v Lushington*

    b) *R v Turnbull*

    c) *R v Stone and Dobinson*

    d) *R v Ghosh*

Beckett's Fishing Lakes Scenario

Late at night the 999 service transfers a call to the ambulance service. The call is from a Mr Parker who is out night fishing with a couple of friends.

Mr Parker	I'm out at the old quarry lakes and I've just found a girl, I think she's dead by the way she's lying all still but awkward like—she's in some bushes and I can't get to her properly. I heard a car drive off and there's some footprints in the mud.
Ambulance control	Okay, Mr Parker, can you tell me exactly where you are please?
Mr Parker	I'm at the old pump house at Beckett's fishing lakes, up a dirt track off Watling Street outside Maidbury. I think she's been raped and murdered. I heard a car drive off really fast, so I came to check what was going on—but I never expected this sort of thing . . .

An ambulance is dispatched and the ambulance service coordinator also contacts the police with the information supplied by Mr Parker. The police control centre pass a message to the Maidbury resourcer, and the information is sent out:

'Can I have patrols, please, for a suspicious death. Caller states it's a murder, at the pump house on Beckett's lakes off Watling Street.'

The responses are immediate:

'Six-one, single crewed, I'm on Watling Street at a break.'

'Six-four, we're ten minutes away.'

'An ambulance is on its way and will meet you there, any other patrols to assist, please?'

'Four, duty inspector, I'm in Old Street village, 15 minutes away. Contact CID and SOCO please.'

Ten minutes later patrol six-one, Pc Aiken, turns off Watling Street onto the dirt track. He has to drive slowly—the track is slippery—and the mile of track to the pumping station seems endless. As well as concentrating on the road, Pc Aiken is thinking about what he will have to do—he knows he's going to be first officer at the scene.

. . . why did I ever give my scene control log to Liam yesterday . . . should have told him I needed it. I'll have to do it all in my PNB now . . . I guess I'm supposed to do CPR if she's still alive, I've never done it for real . . . and evidence . . . and all that 2G2.1 stuff I did a couple of years back when I was training.

But within a few minutes the old brick building looms into sight and he sees Mr Parker waving to him; now he'll need to do more than just think about what to do. As he parks up he calls Control.

Q1   What factors does Pc Aiken need to consider in this situation?

Q2   He was thinking about 2G2.1 from his previous initial training, but what is it?

Q3   Why does Pc Aiken call Control?

Mr Parker confirms his name and briefly explains what he had seen:

> *'A car came down the track about 15 minutes ago, stopped for five minutes, then drove off really fast. I came over and, well, you can see, over there in those brambles. It looks like she's been raped and then murdered.'*

Pc Aiken goes over to have a look. A young woman is lying awkwardly on some bushes, quite still, but partly clothed. Pc Aiken decides not to mention this or to ask why Mr Parker had said he thought the victim had been raped. Pc Aiken thought Mr Parker seemed a decent sort of bloke . . .

. . . what was it old Tallis used to say . . . there are only three types of witness: right ones, wrong ones, and liars? . . . and that many a truth is spoke in jest?

He had often wondered if Tallis would have liked the world of modern policing.

Q4   Sergeant Tallis's old adage about the three types of witness is making a serious point. Suggest what could be meant here, about 'three types of witness'.

Q5   Why should Pc Aiken avoid asking Mr Parker any further questions at this point?

Pc Aiken pushes some nettles aside and eases his way into the thicket to get a closer look. He is pretty certain she is dead and makes a mental note of her appearance for his PNB notes—very pale face, bare feet—clean feet—no cuts or scratches, hands and face also unscratched.

Q6   What immediate conclusions could be drawn from Pc Aiken's observations?

Q7   What should Pc Aiken do now?

Before he can take any further action, Pc Aiken hears another vehicle approaching. He makes his way out of the thicket and turns to see a police vehicle bumping along the mud track about half a mile away. Pc Aiken calls the officers, Pc Jones and Pc Roget, over the radio and asks them to stop.

Q8   What is Pc Aiken's likely reason for telling them not to come any further?

> At that moment Pc Aiken realizes he is standing—and that his patrol car is parked—on the very spot where somebody who may have dumped the body would have probably parked up. He calls Pc Jones and Pc Roget again and asks that one of them gets out of the vehicle and waits there, and for the other officer to go back up the track, to control access and to prevent further damage to the scene; a search of the area will have to wait until other patrols arrive.
>
> Pc Aiken knows that Mr Parker is a witness and therefore needs to be questioned further and will have to make a formal statement—and that this should be done soon, while the events are still fresh in his mind. He needs to be held nearby until an officer is available to take him back to the station.

Q9   Where should Mr Parker be held, and should he be escorted there on foot or in a vehicle?

Q10   If Mr Parker were to be held temporarily as a witness in a police patrol vehicle, suggest what precautions should be taken.

> So Pc Jones waits half way along the track and Pc Roget returns to Watling Street and blocks the track with her vehicle at the turning onto the dirt track. This junction is then designated as the rendezvous point (RVP).

Q11   What aspects of the junction might make it suitable as an RVP?

> An inspector arrives at the RVP and strides over to Pc Roget who is busy making notes in her PNB.
>
> | Insp Jarvis | So what exactly has been happening here? All the details so far please, right away, please. |
> |---|---|
> | Pc Roget | All we know is that it's been reported that a car drove up the track, stayed a couple of minutes and then left. An angler, Parker, I think, went to see what they had been up to and found a woman dumped in the bushes, and he thought she was dead. Six-one, Pc Aiken, is up at the end of the track with the fisherman, and my partner, Pc Jones, is half way along keeping an eye, and I came here to seal off the road. |
> | Insp Jarvis | So we're no further on than that? We don't even know if we're dealing with a fatality . . .? |
> | Pc Roget | No but . . . Pc Aiken says that . . . |
> | Insp Jarvis | I repeat, we don't know. We don't know much, do we? |
>
> Pc Roget says nothing. The inspector stamps his feet in the cold and Pc Roget suggests they could wait in one of the vehicles and make sure the scene control log is up to date. But he dismisses this suggestion and decides instead to drive down to the pumping station, ignoring what Pc Roget tries to tell him about the tyre marks Pc Aiken had mentioned; Inspector Jarvis wants to see the victim for himself, and to confirm Pc Aiken's view that the victim is dead and that the body has been dumped.

Q12 What problems could be caused by the inspector's actions?

Finally the ambulance arrives at the RVP and the driver speaks to Pc Roget. She tells them to drive down the track, avoiding any obvious tyre tracks where possible. Clearly, the safety of the victim is the first priority so the ambulance staff must be allowed access—Pc Aiken's view that the victim is dead has to be verified by medical personnel.

Pc Roget goes back to sit in her patrol car and thinks back to the forensics training course she completed a couple of months ago. At least the ambulance staff seem to be on the ball, but overall she is concerned about the way the investigation is proceeding.

Q13 In these particular circumstances, why should the ambulance crew drive rather than walk to attend to the victim?

Q14 Who should accompany the ambulance crew from the ambulance to the body, and why?

Q15 In what ways are the initial stages of this investigation failing to follow best practice in terms of forensic investigation?

Q16 What should be done with respect to questioning possible witnesses?

Inspector Jarvis waits with Mr Parker while Pc Aiken escorts the ambulance staff over to the body. It doesn't take long; the ambulance staff leave, having confirmed that the woman is dead. No one covers the body.

Q17 Why is the body left uncovered?

Q18 Why should one of the officers record the identities of all the ambulance crew?

Q19 Should Pc Aiken search the body for any means of identification?

Mr Parker is looking very tired and cold, and Pc Aiken also feels weary, wondering how much longer they'll have to wait. So when they hear the distant clatter of a helicopter, it is a relief; a bit of action at last! Mr Parker speculates that it might be a helicopter taking photos for the news . . . Pc Aiken cannot resist commenting that he thinks this isn't very likely . . . particularly at this very early stage of the investigation.

The force helicopter swings into view and carries out an area search, taking video images of the scene. The pilot requests that Pc Aiken indicates the precise position of the woman's body so that he can hover down low at 100 feet to ensure he gets high-quality images. Pc Aiken turns away from Mr Parker as he politely suggests to the pilot that this might not be a good idea.

Q20 How might the helicopter's low hovering affect any forensic evidence at the scene?

A CSI arrives and parks up at the RVP on Watling Street. She has already been advised about the incident but knows a short cut to the pump house, and thinks that it will be quicker and easier to take that route, especially because it would completely avoid the dirt track. She makes a couple of sketch plans, one of the whole site and the other showing more detail of the area around the deceased.

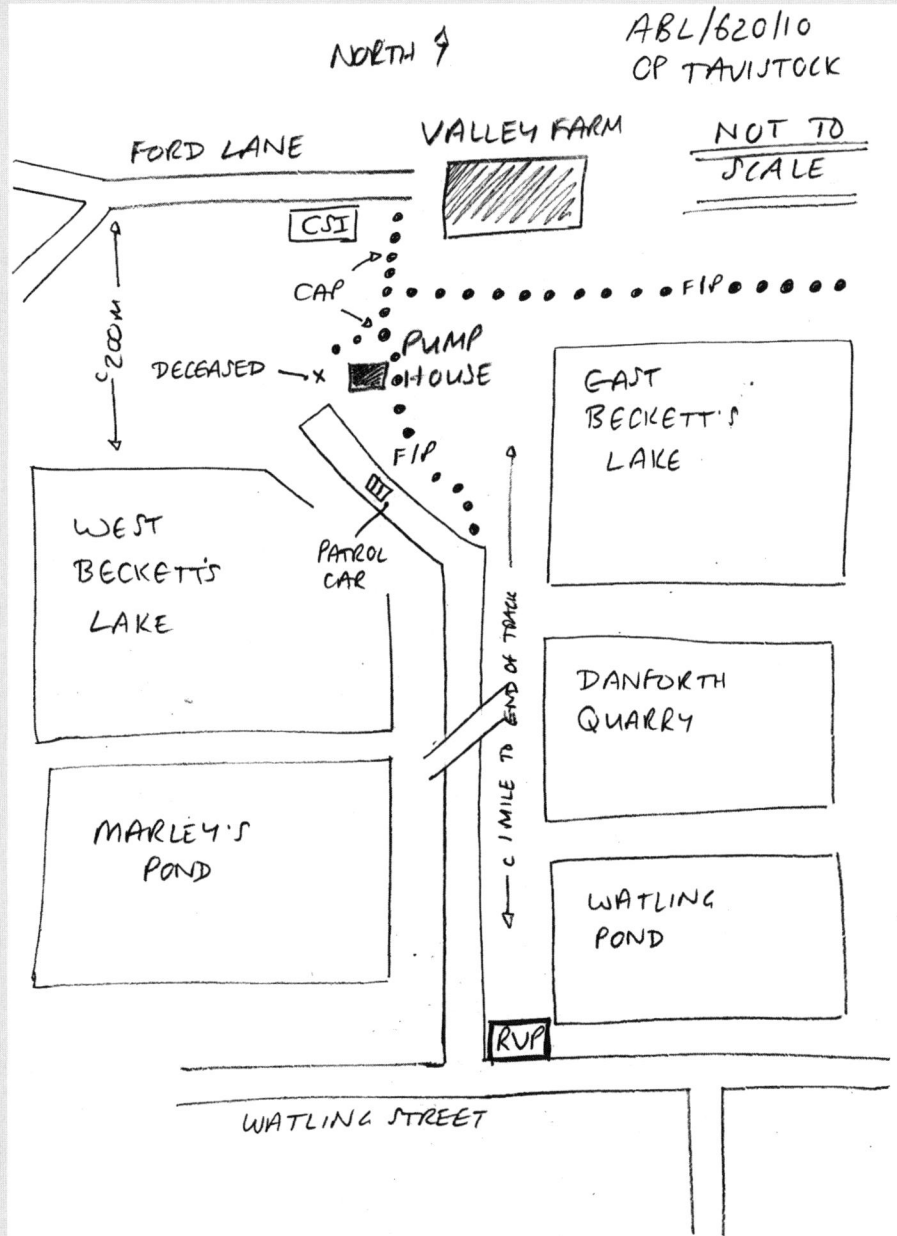

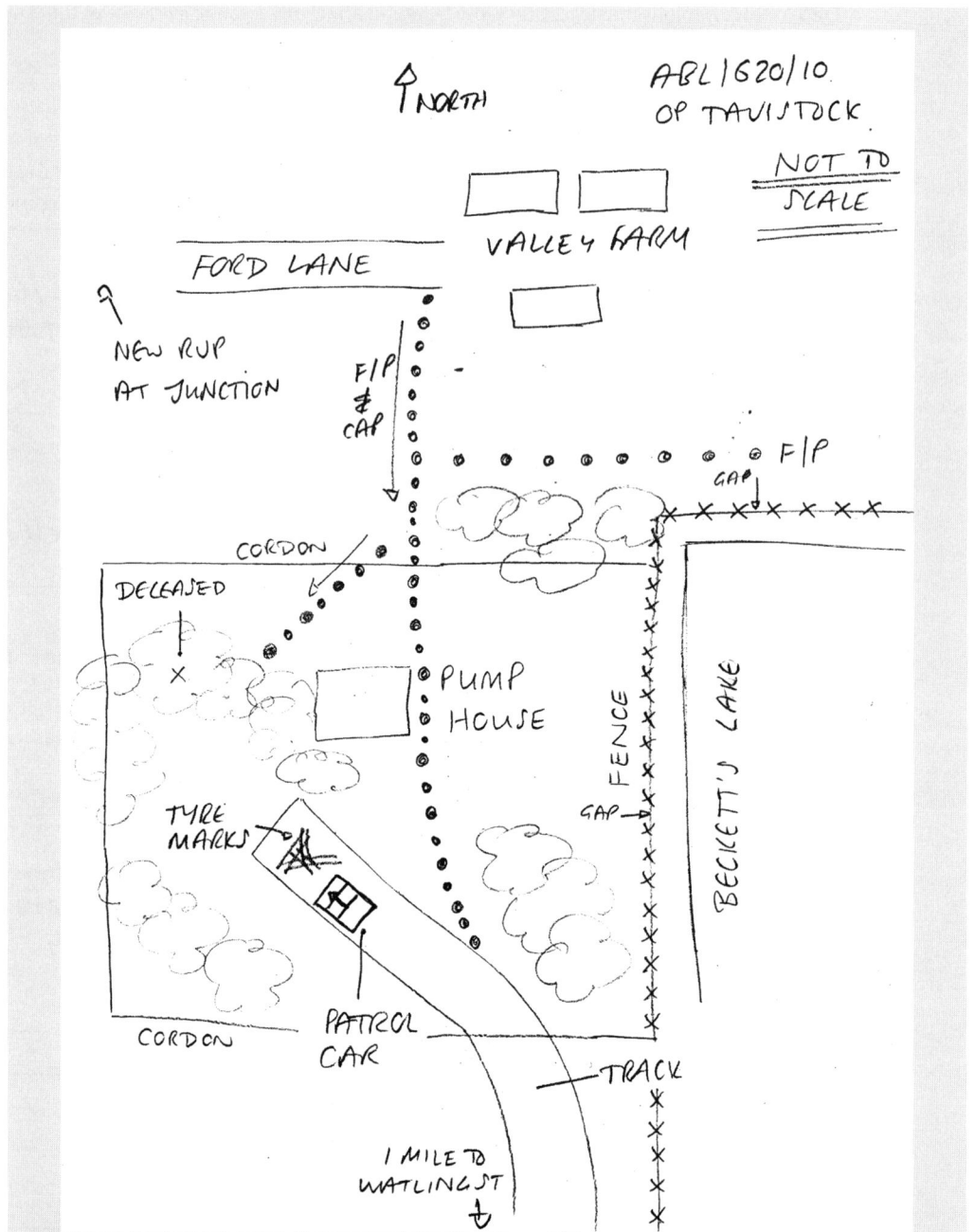

She calls Pc Aiken on the radio:

'Where are you now?'

'I'm with the witness, Mr Parker, next to the ponds, about 50 metres from the pumping station at a fork in the footpath. I think we should stay here or walk out.'

'I'll come round via the lane to Valley Farm and down the hill. I need you to hang on to brief me and tell me where you've put the Common Approach Path. Have you cordoned the scene?'

'No chance. The tape's stuck in the car. With my lunch box . . .'

Shortly afterwards the CSI cautiously picks her way through the scrub along towards Pc Aiken, moving parallel to the footpath which heads south from Valley Farm. She calls out to ask how Pc Aiken got from the deceased to where he is now. Pc Aiken explains that he walked towards the pump house where he met the witness and looked at the body. Then they both walked back alongside the footpath, north (away from his vehicle), avoiding walking on the dirt track. Their route was then designated as the Common Approach Path (CAP).

Q21 Does it matter if the CAP is circuitous, and takes the long way round to the crime scene?

Q22 What is the best type of surface for a CAP?

The CSI checks and photographs the CAP. She finds nothing of any apparent significance on this route (next to the footpath) except some old cans and debris—probably left by anglers. All of it is dusty, damp, and sun-bleached—been there for a while she presumes—and there are no shoe marks on the CAP or the footpath.

Finally she reaches Pc Aiken and Mr Parker. A newly arrived officer approaches and takes Mr Parker back along the CAP. Mr Parker is reassured that his fishing gear will be protected; the officer explains that the CSI is installing a cordon that will cover quite a wide area, at least 200 metres by 200 metres, to encompass all the routes in and out of the focal point.

Unfortunately, on the third side of her square she runs out of cordon tape.

Q23 As there is insufficient tape, suggest how any member of the public could be prevented from crossing the proposed line until more tape is brought to the scene.

Q24 Later, with further assistance, the CSI will install another cordon closer to the body. What will the CSI hope to find within the innermost cordon?

Q25 On a road that is open to the public (such as this dirt track), the majority of evidence found will not be very useful in terms of forensics (although it must still be protected). But how might the wide array of natural and man-made material present on the track be used to great effect in the subsequent investigation?

A bald man walking a large dog approaches the RVP and walks right past and onto the dirt track. Pc Roget calls out to him that a crime has probably been committed and the area is being cordoned so he cannot carry on along the track. He ignores her. She hurries over to him to emphasize the point but the man insists that he will walk on through.

'It's a bloody right of way!'

An officer is actually in the process of placing cordon tape across the track when the man lifts it to pass under.

Pc Roget reaches out to stop him and warns him that he should go no further, but the man dodges out of reach, moving sideways before calling his dog to him.

Q26   Can the officers arrest the man?

> The RVP become quite busy as more officers arrive. Pc Roget explains the situation to one of her colleagues.
>
> ☺ *'I knew he'd be trouble as soon as I saw that tattoo.'*
>
> The number of officers standing by the entrance to the dirt track seems to persuade the man—he finally agrees to turn around and go back the way he came.
>
> The officers breath a sigh of relief—there's enough going on already.

Q27   Should some of these officers start searching the area?

> The CSI and her colleagues photograph the area around the victim and call for the assistance of a forensic pathologist.
>
> Fortunately it is only about half an hour before the pathologist arrives. Pc Aiken watches them prepare the body for removal. After removing some obvious fibres adhering to the victim's clothes, they place protective bags over her head, hands, and feet. They are treating this suspicious death as a murder, but must keep an open mind for other possibilities. One of the new CSIs is speculating about what has happened.
>
> *'So . . . my hypothesis is . . . she's a drug addict who was here to shoot up around the old pump house. She injected something and it killed her. Then someone stole her trainers.'*

Q28   What information do the officers already have that does not fit with the CSI's hypothesis?

> They roll the body over and notice some white squares imprinted in the skin of her back. There are two and they measure approximately 14.25 centimetres by 12.5 centimetres. Along one side about one centimetre in from the edge is a red line.

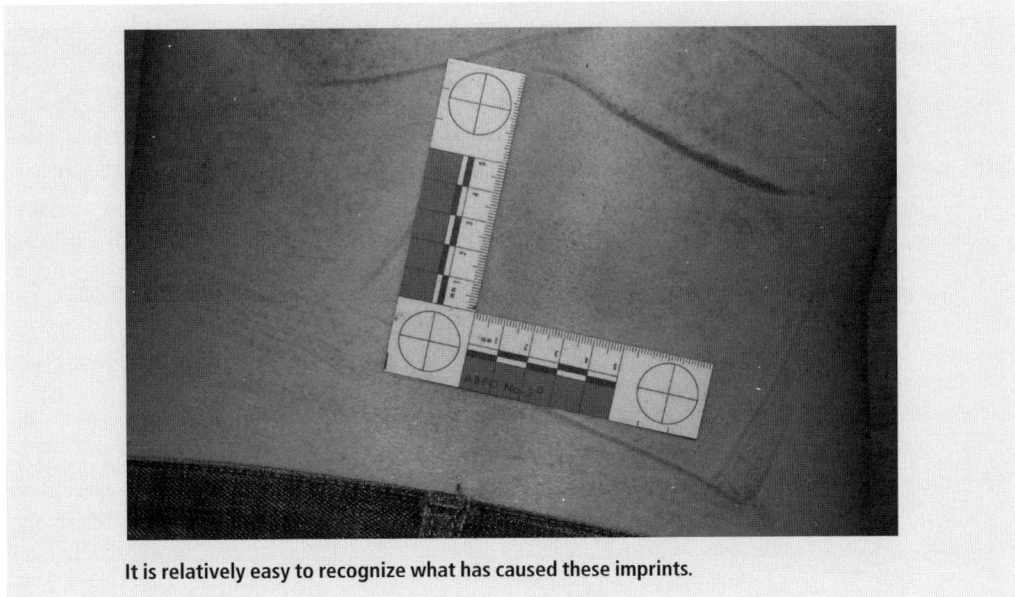

It is relatively easy to recognize what has caused these imprints.

Q29   Think carefully about the dimensions of these imprints—what everyday object could cause such imprints?

The body is later taken for a post mortem (PM) at the nearest facility. Not much happens at the crime scene but it is still guarded.

At the PM the pathologist is assisted by a mortuary technician, and a number of other people also attend.

A CSI (the 'dirty' CSI) collects the evidence from the pathologist. The 'clean CSI' packages the evidence and takes notes. The senior CSI takes photographs (with special attention paid to bruises and cuts) and acts as a forensic strategist.

'I'll pop back in a couple of days to photograph any new marks which have developed—we might get a few here—poor lass. You know we need to keep her out of the deep freeze for a couple of days until I come back . . .'

The coroner's officer also attends and takes notes for the coroner (who has agreed to the PM). A Senior Investigating Officer (SIO)—as 'owner' of the investigation—and her deputy are also present.

The samples taken include clothing, samples for the sexual offences kit, blood for DNA and toxicology, urine, stomach contents, nail scrapings, and any extra material which may assist the investigation, such as fibres (as standard for all Home Office PMs).

Q30   How can the victim be identified?

The victim is identified as a certain Mandy Gerrant. Relatives and friends are contacted and Gerrant's last movements are established—leading quickly to a certain Mark Smith's front door.

The officers find Smith's flat in a state of chaos—beer cans, takeaway pizza boxes, clothes, dirty cups and plates, CDs and magazines—all strewn across the floor. They start to search.

. . . wow, there's loads of evidence here . . . but what could show that he supplied the drugs that killed her? . . . not much here that I can see would help with that . . .

However, one of Gerrant's shoes was found in the lounge, and the other one from the pair was found in the boot of Smith's car.

Q31   How can these shoes assist the enquiry?

The CSIs are very interested in the car. The back seats are covered in assorted items such as takeaway food packaging and items of clothing, but the boot is relatively empty.

Q32   How might it be established that the body had been transported in the boot of the car?

Q33   What feature found on the body supports the idea that the victim had died before being placed in the car?

Regarding the deceased, as a result of the efficient management of the geographically large crime scene, coupled with good forensic results and detective work, Smith and his friend Blain were arrested the next day and the following story unfolded.

Smith was a small-time dealer in skunk and heroin. To facilitate the sale of drugs he was quite happy for his customers to smoke or inject in his house. He had a code of never assisting them because if they died he thought it would probably be murder.

His friend Jezza Blain had come round to the house and bought some cannabis. He had rolled a joint and sat on the sofa and the pair had talked for a while before Blain fell asleep. Whilst he was asleep, Mandy Gerrant had turned up and bought some heroin and skunk from Smith. She had smoked the skunk and injected the heroin inside the premises.

Blain eventually awoke around 6 pm and saw Gerrant on the floor next to the sofa. He had given her a gentle kick—just a nudge—and asked her if she wanted a cup of tea. She did not reply, so he got up and moved closer to see if she was okay—he noticed that she was cool, and that a needle was on the floor next to her. Blain had then alerted Smith who came into the lounge. He had looked at her pupils and shouted at Blain to turn on the light—but the pupils remained dilated. He sat her up, pulled up her top, and ripped her bra off and listened to her heart but could not hear it beating.

Smith and Blain had started to panic and laid out the 'logical' arguments regarding their options. As far as they could see, there were two such options: call an ambulance or dispose of the body.

Q34   Why would their first option have almost certainly led to police involvement?

Smith then persuaded Blain that they should drop the body off near the lakes. That evening at 7 pm Blain took Smith's car out for the nightly pizza run and, when he returned, he reversed the car onto the drive. He and Smith then ate the pizzas and pulled Gerrant up from the floor. Two CD cases were stuck to her naked back and Smith peeled them off and threw them on the floor. They manhandled the body to the car with difficulty (as they were under the influence of cannabis). As they grappled with the body, Gerrant's jeans slipped down from her hips, pulling her panties, and her shoes fell off, one in the house and one in the boot of the car.

Smith drove out of town to an area he knew quite well: it was a fishing lake in a quarry, about a mile down a dirt track. The quarry was suitably quiet upon arrival so the two men carried the body (more easily now as it was wrapped in a blanket from the car boot) into the trees. They dumped her in a bramble thicket and left, throwing the blanket into a ditch, climbed back into the car and drove off fast.

Outcome

The investigation of the crime required detailed analysis of:

1. the dump site at Beckett's fishing lakes;

2. the victim;

3. the house where she bought the drugs and injected herself;

4. the car that transported the victim;

5. the route the car took;

6. Smith;

7. Blain.

The forensic objective was to check for possible links between all six crime scenes. This involved using a wide variety of physical evidence and other supporting evidence such as that gained from witnesses and the suspects through interview.

What initially was believed to be a case of murder was, quite quickly, established by the SIO to be an unfortunate death due to drug abuse. It is important to note that while Smith and Blain have clearly broken a number of laws, neither actually *injected* the victim with the drugs that killed her. Whilst most people will be repelled by their actions, scenarios like this are not unusual.

Smith was charged with supplying a controlled drug (under s 4(3) of the Misuse of Drugs Act 1971) and knowingly permitting or suffering the production, supply, preparation, or smoking of drugs (s 8) as this took place on his premises. These charges related to Blain as well as to Gerrant. Smith and Blain were both charged with the offence of the disposal of a corpse with intent to obstruct a coroner's inquest, contrary to common law. The judge took into account the seriousness of the offence, but also that Smith and Blain had acted more out of their drug-induced panic than for any other motive. They were sentenced to a relatively short custodial term, and Smith was further sentenced for the supply of drugs to Blain as well as to the deceased.

The advantage of physical evidence is that it cannot be wrong and cannot lie; but mistakes can be made by the people who collect the evidence (without following proper procedures) or interpret the evidence (often without the full facts). Because physical evidence has the potential to be so powerful in providing leads and helping to drive an investigation forward, it is vital that it is protected in situ by the first officer at the scene.

Beckett's Fishing Lakes Answers

A1   He needs to consider his own security; a single-crewed car going into the unknown in a remote area should be a major concern particularly as from the information provided so far it seems that a violent crime has taken place. The offender may be present; Mr Parker could be the offender—it is quite common for an offender to pose as an innocent person coming across a crime scene. Pc Aiken could justifiably await the arrival of the second (double-crewed) patrol, but he knows another crew is just a few minutes behind him.

He will also be thinking about how to cordon the scene. If he knows the area well he can start planning his scene management, but there is a danger that he will have preconceptions and fail to keep an open mind regarding the cordoning. He needs to be guided by what he sees, not what he thinks he knows. He should have kept his scene log! A piece of paper, even the back of a printed form, will do in the interim.

He should conduct life-saving attempts if safe to do so.

A2   Element 2G2.1 is from the National Occupational Standards (NOS) used in initial police training, and the relevant knowledge is:

- how to maximize useful evidence and minimize loss of potential evidence;

- how to prevent the cross-contamination of evidence.

A3   Pc Aiken contacts Control to give his time of arrival.

A4   The witnesses who are 'right' are high-quality witnesses who are observant and deliver their evidence with clarity. The witnesses who are 'wrong' are trying honestly to speak the truth, but may be mistaken. This may be because they saw only part of an incident, they may have made assumptions which they consider to be correct conclusions as to what they saw or believe, or perhaps their eyesight is not as good as it could be. The third type, liars, attempt to deceive. This is often seen when the informant is the offender and attempts to steer the investigation or to remain close to it by offering information and generally 'helping' the enquiry. Examples of these include Tracie Andrews, who murdered her fiancé Lee Harvey in a fake road-rage incident, and Karen Matthews, who allegedly faked the kidnap of her daughter.

A5   Pc Aiken should not question Mr Parker about finding the body or any injuries to the body as if there is any suspicion that Mr Parker was involved in the incident, then the questioning would amount to an interview and would need to be conducted under caution back at the station.

A6   She would have dirty feet if she had walked there and then collapsed for some reason, and clean feet if she had collapsed elsewhere and then been dumped.

Also, if she had been walking around in the thicket in a heightened emotional state (or was drunk or on drugs), then it would be expected that she would have scratches on her hands, face, and exposed skin.

A7   Pc Aiken should cautiously approach the body and check for vital signs. If he believes the victim to be alive then he should attempt resuscitation or assist her. If he believes the victim to be dead then he should withdraw. Either way, he should update Control with his opinion as soon as practicable and be mindful of damaging potential evidence.

See Preserving the Scene, *BSPOH 2010*, 13.3.2

A8   This is a procedural matter to some extent which depends exactly on local conditions and local knowledge. Any extra traffic approaching along the dirt track will destroy potential evidence. The vehicle Mr Parker heard leaving the scene may have been used to dump the body, and even if it had left hundreds of metres of tyre marks, **none** of the tyre marks should be sacrificed at this stage except in an emergency. One can never have too much evidence.

As the angler appears to be no threat, then it is better to ask colleagues to keep their distance.

A9   The best policy is to abandon the vehicle and guide the angler away, towards a suitable RVP or holding area. It is obviously preferable that they do not walk on any tyre tracks or shoe marks, so it may be better to travel cross-country. This activity now leaves the body unguarded, and there is a remote possibility that somebody may tamper with it, so Pc Aiken should ideally return to the vicinity. We should bear in mind that a patrol car is a useful 'holding facility' where witnesses can sit. In this case, the car is within the crime scene so this is ill-advised.

A10   When placing somebody who is believed to be a victim or witness in a patrol car for a short period, the officer should:

- remove the ignition keys;
- switch off the radio;
- search the vehicle first (just in case) and afterwards;
- remove potential weapons.

Your police colleagues will be only too pleased, on long night duties, to tell you about an officer who left his keys in the car, only to watch it being driven off into the sunset. Likewise, witnesses may listen to the radio and glean information regarding the incident, they may conceal weapons within, or they may use the officer's torch, briefcase, or other article as a weapon. It is impossible to judge accurately somebody's mental state. An outwardly calm individual could be dangerous and looking for an opportunity to attack.

A11   It was well away from the scene, and was suitable for parking and turning.

A12   Unless the inspector has specialist medical equipment and skills, there is absolutely no reason for him to verify what the first officer has seen. Every officer viewing the victim will add material to the crime scene and take other material away. Locard's principle works against the police as well as for them. The best course of action is to remain at the RVP and await a CSI who will—eventually—clear the route to the scene. This could take several hours to achieve.

See Attendance at Crime Scenes, *BSPOH 2010*, 13.3

A13   This is extremely difficult to answer for certain. If Pc Aiken was satisfied that the victim was dead, based upon condition of the body (such as a missing head, a skeleton, or dismembered remains) then it is unlikely that the ambulance crew will feel the need to rush to the victim and risk damaging evidence.

But none of this applies here, and a waxy, pale complexion (indicative of death) could actually be a symptom of a heart attack in a living (but critically ill) patient. So there is an outside chance that the victim is still alive and, if in doubt, they should drive.

If they were to walk to the victim, walking through the bushes would cause less damage to forensic evidence than walking along the track, although they should, of course, try and use the same route as that used by Pc Aiken—this would become the CAP.

A14   The ambulance crew should be accompanied by the FOAS, who has the best current knowledge about the location and condition of the deceased. Allowing a different officer to do this will introduce unnecessary extra contamination. The FOAS must warn the ambulance crew of any evidence previously spotted, such as tyre tracks, shoe marks, discarded material, as well as dangers such as ditches. By doing this, the victim is attended to and the evidence will, hopefully, remain untainted. It must be borne in mind that, even though ambulance crews attend many crime scenes, their role is fundamentally to preserve life and this may be at the expense of evidence.

The ambulance crew will ask the police officers present to assist with treating the victim, should this be necessary. In any case, it is advisable to 'listen in' to the activity and discussions that take place for any information of significance.

A15 On reflection, the logistics of the crime scene and its preservation should have been considered a little earlier:

- two patrols and an inspector are tied up—and are now contaminated with potential evidence from the scene and therefore cannot take part in the rest of the investigation, such as the arrest of any early suspects; and

- nobody has started a scene control log.

Police activity within the 'Golden Hour' has been confusing and fast paced, and this has led to problems. The scene log should have been started already—it is part of good scene management to start a log as quickly as possible, in order that the future contamination of other—linked—crime scenes can be prevented. In addition, nobody has yet cordoned the scene so there is a danger that people in the vicinity will stumble across the crime scene.

A16 Nobody has spoken to any of the other anglers and taken a decent early account. The police investigators will need to speak to them to gain evidence or to eliminate them (and their shoes or tyres) from the enquiry. Some of the anglers may have already left at first sight of a patrol car.

However, here there are many potential witnesses who should be identified and questioned. Their assistance may be pivotal in quickly solving this crime. Remember, too, that each angler might describe others by their clothing and general description. CID will want to identify every person described in every statement.

A17 In nearly every instance, the deceased should be left uncovered. This is because the covering material, particularly if not brand new, may contaminate the victim with material such as hair and dried blood from the police or from people previously conveyed in the police vehicle which carried the cover. If necessary, the CSI can erect a small tent. The cordon should be of sufficient size that the public cannot see the deceased.

A18 If possible, officers should take details of the crew and warn them that their outer clothing and footwear may be needed for elimination purposes by the CSIs investigating the case. Quite apart from this, the crew are witnesses. However, the officers also need to bear in mind that the ambulance crew may be needed elsewhere.

A19 No. The body should not be searched for identification unless the CSI does it with the sanction of the SIO. Such a search may be deemed an investigative priority—a fast-track action—but the decision is one which is based on an assessment of the potential loss of evidence compared to the perceived intelligence value of finding identification.

A20 Categorically, helicopters should avoid proximity to crime scenes unless their presence facilitates the capture of a suspect or the saving of life. The downdraught from a helicopter at this altitude is sufficient to blow away small or light items which could be useful as evidence, such as fibres, paperwork, and clothing. At the very least, these items could subsequently be taken out of context by being moved.

A21 The CAP should be the route which the offender and victim probably would **not** have taken. If necessary, a circuitous route, deliberately avoiding obvious or constructed paths, should be used. The CSI will check and clear this CAP early in the investigation. In this case, the CAP is tortuous and leads out to a remote farm, even more remote than the junction with Watling Street, but it is a sound choice. It merely lacks convenience.

A22 Putting a CAP on a soft surface such as grass or soil means that small items of evidence which are missed early on may be pushed into the ground and therefore lost to the investigation. It is always preferable to use a hard surface if one is available (but not if it is thought to be the route taken by the offender).

A23 In the absence of sufficient tape, experience shows that a force helicopter makes a useful 'guard dog' and that a small number of officers can guard a large area as long as they can see each other. In very large crime scenes the cordoned area can be massively extended to make use of natural and man-made barriers such as rivers, hedges, ditches, fences, and even train tracks.

A24 The focal point immediately surrounding the deceased is likely to yield large amounts of evidence such as the body, shoe marks, cigarette ends, fibres, and discarded material used by the offenders. The outer cordon will cover a very wide area, at least one square mile, which will later be reduced in size. Most of the outer area probably has no significance, apart from tyre marks and other material the offender might have left along the track.

A25 Naturally occurring materials (such as soil, pollen, and roadstone) present in a particular locality can be used to link the offenders and the vehicle to the location. This material will adhere to the underside of the car and the tyres. It is the combination of the differing materials and their relative rarity which makes this very powerful evidence of association. Most pollens do not travel very far from the parent plant, and most roadstone is sourced from as close as possible to the road where it will be used. Couple this with fishing line and a scientist could describe the source of debris found in the wheel arches of a car. The investigator's job is to find the location!

A26 Yes (although it is acknowledged that there is debate concerning this). Pc Roget has cajoled or encouraged him twice to stop and he has not taken heed, so she could arrest him for obstruction. The relevant case law for an arrest in these circumstances is *DPP v Morrison* [2003] EWHC 683. The crime scene was cordoned in order to preserve evidence: 'Under common law, police have a power to erect a cordon in order to preserve the scene of a crime.'

Other case law relates to crossing cordons that have been set up for security purposes. *Knowlton* is a Canadian case about preventing a man crossing a cordon which was erected to afford protection to a visiting dignitary. Using the Terrorism Act 2006 in this circumstance is inappropriate since the police are dealing with a suspicious death which appears to be a murder rather than a terrorist act.

A27 Even at this stage, an area search for suspects may be beneficial, but officers need to balance this against the potential contamination they may cause by arresting people nearby, should the need arise. In a perfect world, other 'clean' officers would do this work.

There is no need to hurry a search. A 'walk through' can often wait, but the SIO may decide that a search is required. He or she will do this after consulting a police search adviser and ensuring the right resources are in place.

A28 Although rather bald and horrible, it is not bad as a working theory. The objective is to support or refute the hypothesis with evidence from a variety of sources, such as witnesses, physical evidence, and forensic examination. However, this hypothesis does not account for the vehicle heard by Mr Parker—an important feature. What happens now is critical: the owner of this hypothesis may ignore the possibility that the car is involved: 'The car is of no significance, it was just a couple of lads out for a spin.'

We would then have a death due to misadventure and a minor theft from a corpse. We will see that this is not the case.

A29 Regular, perfect rectangles of this size almost certainly do not occur naturally, so this must be a 'man-made' feature. The marks were left by CD boxes which prevented blood pooling in her skin when her heart stopped. Any part of the body which is in contact with a surface will take on an image of that surface as the blood settles. This is hypostasis. Areas that are not compressed will be reddened by the blood.

The presence of these marks on her skin, and the absence of CD boxes at the scene, implies she died elsewhere. Therefore, the hypothesis raised above must be modified or abandoned.

See Changes to the Body after Death, *BSPOH 2010*, 13.4.3

A30   She should be identified as quickly as possible, and this can be done in a number of ways. The most common, and fastest, is to take fingerprints from her after the PM and run these through the national fingerprint database, Ident1, which could identify her very rapidly. It is likely, but not certain, that she has a criminal record if she is a drug addict.

Failing this, a trawl through the missing person files may provide the police with a 'suspect' in order to make a comparison by DNA or dental records (if the body has been severely disfigured) or by visual confirmation by a close relative or partner. Tattoos, marks, and scars coupled with a good knowledge of local addicts can assist the police in focusing their enquiries.

A31   The shoes can be used to show Mandy was almost certainly in contact with the house and car at some stage, and can be tested for DNA to show that Mandy had worn them. Fibres inside them may match her socks, either those worn at the time of death or on other days. Test marks of the soles may match marks found in her house.

A32   Mandy's clothing was covered with fibres. If her body had been transported in the boot then the interior of the boot will contain the same mix of fibres. Note that it would be difficult for just one person to move such a body.

A search of the crime scene or the suspect's property may produce a blanket or piece of cloth that could have been used to wrap and help move the body. Anyone involved in moving the body would have the same fibre mix on their clothes, but this will have limited forensic value if the cloth or blanket had been in the possession of one of the suspects previous to the evening's activities. If no fibres matching those found on Mandy's clothes are subsequently found inside the passenger cabin of the car, it strengthens the notion that Mandy was placed in the boot. Additionally, Mandy's body may have leaked a variety of fluids, especially saliva, into the car.

A33   The CD boxes on the floor of the flat had marked her back during hypostasis. Clearly, she must have been dead for hypostasis to occur. There are no CD boxes in the car and none where the body was found. Hypostasis fixes in the skin after a while, and so moving or 'posing' a victim after this fixing has occurred shows that the body has been moved after death has occurred.

A34   Every UK ambulance service has a policy of informing the police of suspicious serious injuries and deaths, and these events fit neatly into this category. There can be no doubt that a swift police response would have followed the medics' call and the incident would have been treated as murder until shown otherwise.

The ambulance service would also have considered that she may actually still have been alive: it is difficult to be sure death has occurred when somebody has taken heroin unless the right training has been undertaken.

Test Yourself

And a final review of some key facts relating to forensic investigation.

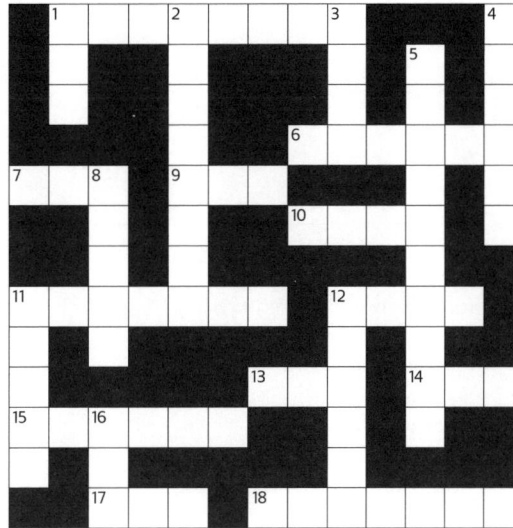

Across

1 Powder left after explosion.
6 Dead body.
7 DNA, a tiny amount.
9 Guidance for investigating some violent deaths.
10 In the beginning, possibly the only one at the scene.
11 Major Incident mnemonic.
12 For taking DNA samples from the mouth.
13 Alternative for 10 across.
14 Made fingerprinting messy.
15 His principle works both ways in forensics.
17 Doubles the DNA, again and again.
18 Seized item to be used as evidence?

Down

1 Meeting place at a crime scene.
2 Type of sample, Code D, bite here.
3 Old CSI.
4 Print, invisible until treated.
5 Gravity acting on dead blood.
8 Mass record of genetic differences.
11 Location of DNA in the body.
12 A good surface for fingerprints.
16 Shared route in and out.

Answers to Knowledge Check Questions

K1 c   K2 c   K3 b   K4 a   K5 a

Answers to Test Yourself

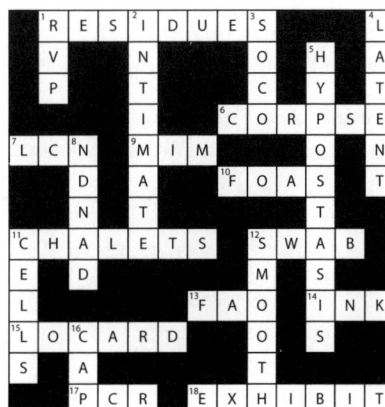

8 | Mortesbury's

   👣   forensic awareness required

   ✓   assessment opportunity

   ☺   diversity issues

   🌢   health and safety

   ▽?   questionable practice

   ✎   a pen or pencil is required

Introduction

This scenario involves an incident of alleged shoplifting from a supermarket, a common crime. In the UK, customer theft during 2008 is thought to have led to an overall loss of £1,595 million to the commercial sector (Bamfield, 2007). Despite its prevalence, investigations into shop theft present both technical and legal difficulties, particularly when multiple offenders engage in a number of offences at different locations in what might be termed a 'shoplifting spree'.

The interviewing of suspects is tightly regulated by the PACE Codes of Practice. Here, we present the reality; and not as it is sometimes depicted by the media. Constraints on questioning styles and techniques, and the presence of an active legal adviser oblige the police officer to exercise significant skill and employ knowledge of the relevant legislation and associated codes.

Knowledge Check

✎ Before you look at this scenario, check your understanding of the underpinning legislation involved by attempting the following knowledge check.

For the multiple choice questions K1 to K5 write down **one** of the letters a, b, c, or d as the answer to the question. Check your answers at the end of this chapter before beginning the scenario.

K1 Under s 24A of the PACE Act 1984, for certain categories of offence a person other than a police officer can arrest a suspect without warrant. For what categories of offence does this **not** apply?

    a) Indictable only offence
    b) Any indictable offence
    c) Summary only offence
    d) Either way offence

K2 Under s 24 of the PACE Act 1984, which of the following is **not** a reason for making an arrest necessary?

      a) To protect a child or other vulnerable person from the person in question

      b) To allow the prompt and effective investigation of an offence

      c) To prevent any prosecution for the offence from being hindered by the disappearance of the person in question

      d) To detain a person to enable a search under s 1 of the PACE Act 1984 to take place

K3 The case *R v Ghosh* (1982) 2 All ER 689 is an important piece of case law for the offence of theft (s 1 of the Theft Act 1968) as it helps to define certain terms used within the legislation. To which term does it relate?

      a) Dishonestly

      b) Appropriate

      c) Property

      d) Belonging to another

K4 At what point of an investigation can an utterance made by a suspect be classed as a 'significant statement' as described in PACE Code of Practice C para 11.4A?

      a) Before caution only

      b) After caution only

      c) Any time before the start of the interview

      d) After arrest only

K5 What does the C in PEACE stand for?

      a) Check

      b) Confirm

      c) Closure

      d) Clarify

Mortesbury's Scenario

It is Monday and Pc Dunn, a student police officer, is on Supervised Patrol with his tutor constable, Pc Owen when they receive a call at 10.45 to attend a large Mortesbury's supermarket on the outskirts of town. Three alleged shoplifters have been detained, two men and a woman. By 11.00 Pc Dunn and Pc Owen arrive at the manager's office, where they find the supermarket duty manager at his desk, and a number of other people sitting in the lobby area outside the office.

The officers begin by introducing themselves to the manager who in turn names himself and his colleagues; two security staff (both men) and one other staff member, the checkout supervisor. The manager proudly explains that both his staff and the three suspects had remained calm throughout; the suspects had been stopped and simply invited to the manager's office, and had come along quietly with no manhandling required. A number of items including spirits and electronic goods from the shop are stacked on the table in the manager's office—he explains that these are the goods that were recovered from the suspects.

Pc Owen then asks the manager:

'Can you tell me exactly what you think has happened here?'

Q1   Why is it important that Pc Owen ensures that the manager's account is given in the presence and hearing of the suspects?

Q2   Is it right for the manager to speak on behalf of the other witnesses and staff present, if he so chooses?

> The manager provides a description of the incident, indicating which members of staff were directly involved and who actually witnessed the alleged theft of goods. He points to the goods which have been recovered and invites the officers to examine the items, but they decline the offer for the time being.

Q3   How should Pc Owen record this information?

> Pc Owen then asks the three suspects to give their name, address, and date of birth. They comply, but the two men are sullen, and one of them has a strong accent and has to repeat himself before the officer can understand properly. One of the security staff sighs impatiently. The female suspect looks close to tears.

Q4   What should Pc Owen do with the details provided by the three suspects?

Q5   Should the two officers speak with any of the other supermarket and security staff present?

Q6   How might these initial accounts be used subsequently?

> Pc Owen knows that other people (such as customers) may have witnessed the suspects in the alleged act of stealing or concealing the goods and that their direct oral evidence could be used to either corroborate or contradict other accounts, including accounts from the suspects. Pc Owen is also aware that this information might provide a basis for challenging the suspects' accounts in any subsequent interview, by pointing to inconsistency and untruths.
>
> Pc Dunn is sent down to the shop floor. A small group of customers are waiting by the customer services desk with the shop floor manager. He takes details and brief accounts from some of the customers and also checks if anyone witnessed the detention of the suspects by the store detective and the other staff. Some of the customers stated that they had not seen anything unusual occur. Pc Dunn records these observations too, and takes their contact details.

Q7   Why is it important that the officers take all reasonable steps to identify witnesses and record this information, including those witnesses who say they saw nothing unusual?

Q8   Why don't the officers simply ask the suspects about the alleged theft at this point?

> After a few minutes of brief questioning Pc Dunn has two additional witnesses. He takes them to one side and notes their details before going back up to the office. In all, there are now six potential witnesses (one security man who detained the suspects, one store manager, one

checkout supervisor, a female member of the checkout staff who raised the alarm, and the two customers) and three alleged suspects. The staff need to get back to work and Pc Owen knows that careful questioning and obtaining accurate statements takes time. The officers also know they may soon be busy with the suspects if they decide to arrest them; conducting searches and then arranging transportation to the designated custody suite. Further questioning of the witnesses will have to wait until later.

Pc Owen also realizes that CCTV footage from inside and outside the store could provide vital information. He thinks that it might be impracticable (and unnecessary) to view the master tapes right now, but wants to ensure the footage will be made available to him soon. Pc Owen is also aware of some occasional technical difficulties in arranging copies of the hard drive recording (the master copy) and he has to conform to local police practice for the recovery of CCTV footage from private systems.

Q9   What should Pc Owen ask about the CCTV recording system?

Satisfied that copy recordings can be made available to him soon, Pc Owen advises the manager to ensure the recordings remain secure, and warns the manager that the investigation and prosecution of the shoplifters would probably fail if the recordings were lost. The manager nods earnestly and looks impressed. Pc Owen also explains that once he has received a copy of the CCTV footage he will take a statement from the manager about the type of recording equipment, and to confirm that the copy is a de facto copy of the original—without any alteration or adjustment. However, Pc Owen also explains to the manager that this may not happen immediately but in the near future.

Q10   If when viewed the CCTV does not appear to show any crime occurring, why might it still be considered relevant under the Criminal Procedure and Investigations Act 1996 (CPIA)?

Back in the manager's office, Lisa Sharp, the female member of the checkout staff, says (within earshot of all the witnesses and suspects) that she became suspicious when the three suspects joined the queue at her checkout, all holding large shopping bags but only buying a few small, low-price items. She wondered why they had not gone in the 'baskets only' queue, and why they were wearing bulky coats on such a warm day. She told her supervisor who then alerted security staff.

Pc Owen confirms with her that she will be available later to make a written statement.

The security man then explains that he had been alerted on the basis of Lisa Sharp's observations and stopped the group after they had left the shop. He questioned the suspects and asked them to return to the store with him. He then discovered (after they voluntarily agreed to be searched) that they each had items concealed within their clothes and in their shopping bags—Mortesbury's branded store goods for which they could produce no sales receipts. He points out to Pc Dunn exactly what was retrieved from each of the three suspects. They simply look blank and say nothing. One of the men is looking around impatiently but the woman is staring at her hands, blinking back tears.

The store manager adds that the total cost of the goods is approximately £240 and that the store has a policy of always prosecuting for theft—he seems impatient for Pc Dunn or Pc Owen to arrest the suspects. Instead, Pc Owen asks the security man about where exactly he had detained the three suspects.

Q11   Why is it important for Pc Owen to establish exactly where the security man claims to have detained them? Will the answer determine whether he arrests the suspects?

> The security man is adamant that he detained the suspects outside the supermarket, clearly beyond the exit, and Pc Owen knows that the two customers already identified will confirm this. The manager tells Pc Owen that other staff members also saw the actual detention outside the store entrance. Pc Owen writes these details down in his PNB—he might need to interview the additional staff members later, if the exact location is in dispute.
>
> By now Pc Dunn is thinking that Pc Owen already has enough prima facie evidence to arrest the suspects on suspicion of theft under s 24 of the PACE Act 1984.

Q12   Is Pc Dunn right in thinking that Pc Owen now has grounds for having 'reasonable suspicion' that the suspects have committed theft?

> Pc Owen asks the security man if he found receipts on the suspects for the goods that are now on the manager's desk. There is a brief pause and, before the security man can answer, the female suspect gulps and answers instead that they don't have receipts, but that the reason is that they were offered one at the till but didn't bother picking it up.
>
> Pc Owen gets out his PNB again.
>
> *... not a significant statement, but still ... better note it all down and get her to sign ... need to ask her more about it at the start of the interview ...*
>
> Pc Owen notes down her comments, noting the precise words she used, and she signs the entry as a true record of what she said. He doesn't ask any more questions; he believes he has reasonable grounds for suspecting they have committed an offence, and that an arrest is necessary.

Q13   From Pc Owen's point of view, what is the most likely reason for the arrests being necessary?

Q14   Which part of the PACE Codes of Practice covers the reasons why an arrest might be necessary?

> He arrests all of the suspects and cautions each of them in turn.
>
> *... they might have something else on them ... best check ... s 32 search ...*
>
> Pc Owen then searches the suspects but he doesn't find anything else of any apparent significance. He then asks the suspects if they drove to the store. The female suspect describes her car hesitantly, and manages to recall the first few letters of the registration plate. She mumbles that it is parked in the supermarket car park a few lanes from the entrance and hands over the keys, head bowed. Pc Owen asks Pc Dunn to search the car and then calls Control.
>
> *'Transport required to take three, no two, repeat two suspects from Mortesbury's front entrance to the station, please.'*

Q15   Do these questions about the vehicle amount to an 'interview'?

Q16   Where should an interview with an arrested suspect be conducted?

Q17   Does Pc Dunn have the power to search and seize the female suspect's vehicle and its contents?

Meanwhile Pc Dunn searches the car used by the suspects and under a blanket in the boot he finds some new, still-packaged electronic goods from Electromart, a high-street discount store for household goods. It is now 12.00 and Pc Owen asks Pc Dunn to accompany the suspects to the police station whilst he attends to further tasks at the supermarket.

Q18   What will happen to the suspects' car, in terms of any forensic analysis?

The back-up car arrives and the two male suspects (who are by now becoming restive) are quickly put into the car and taken to the police station. Pc Dunn follows with the female suspect.

. . . prefer it not to be just me and her . . . but . . . well, we have searched her . . . she seems a bit happier now she's away from the other two . . .

On the way back to the station, he is careful not to initiate any conversation with her, as he knows he must not question her in any way. However, she begins to talk about the events of the last hour or so, including implicating the other two suspects in organized thefts from other stores across the town over the last month.

Once he has parked up inside the secure yard at the back of the station, Pc Dunn explains that he needs to make a note of what she has said in his PNB and check it with her.

A secure yard reduces the chance of a suspect escaping custody during the transfer from a police vehicle to the custody area. Many older custody suites are not so well equipped.

She does not reply and suddenly seems nervous and close to tears again. He hands her a tissue before getting out his PNB to note down what she has said. He then asks her to read the entry and to write a short declaration on how much she agrees or disagrees with the content, and to sign it. She shakes her head angrily and refuses to even look at the entry. He makes a note of this in his PNB.

. . . note 11E . . . I do believe . . .

They get out of the car and go over to the holding pen—the custody officer has just taken the two male suspects into the custody suite.

The holding area for detainess while they wait to be seen by the custody officer.

Pc Dunn leaves her to the custody officer and makes his way into the office to write up the remainder of his PNB.

Q19   Why was Pc Dunn right to avoid engaging her in conversation on the way to the police station?

Q20   Why was it vital for Pc Dunn to note down what she had said in his PNB, even though she had already said she would not read or sign the entry?

Q21   Under what part of the PACE Codes of Practice must she be asked to sign the record of what she has said?

Q22   She has refused to sign; does this affect whether the statement can be used as evidence?

By 12.30 the custody officer has accepted all three suspects and has authorized their detention.

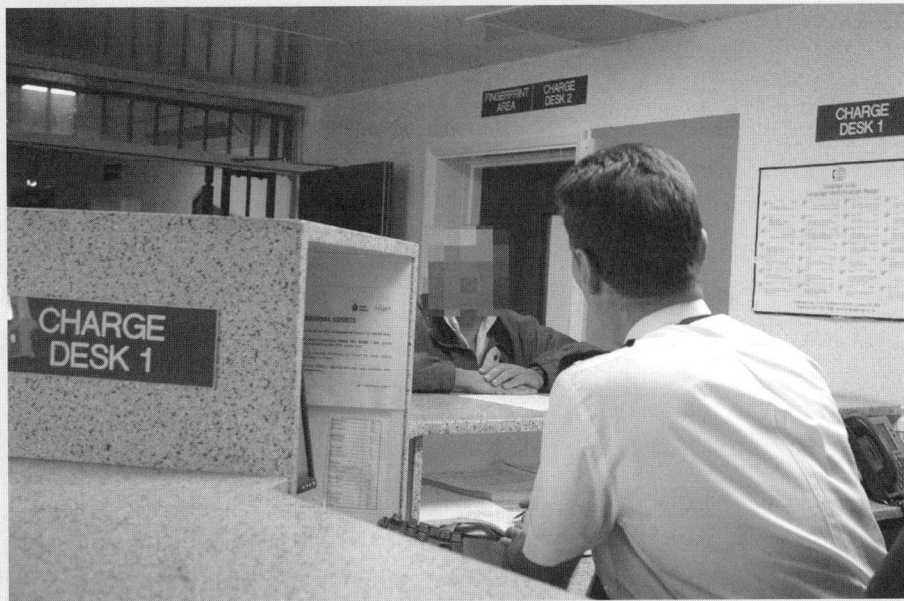

The desk in the custody suite is especially high to discourage suspects from trying to jump over or assault the custody officer.

The usual procedures are followed for all three suspects, including confirming identities, fingerprinting, photographing, and taking DNA samples.

When checking the personal property of three suspects it is clear to the custody officer that none of them had sufficient money, or means (such as a credit or debit card) to pay for the goods found in their possession, individually or as a group.

... they could say they just forgot to pay ... but not very likely ...

A little later, after dealing with his remaining responsibilities at Mortesbury's supermarket (eg, seizing the goods that were allegedly stolen from the supermarket), Pc Owen returns to the police station.

Q23   What should Pc Owen do in relation to the property which appears to have been stolen from Electromart and which Pc Dunn found in the boot of the suspects' car?

Q24   How would Pc Owen or a colleague be able to ascertain if the property in the car was stolen from the other stores?

Pc Dunn approaches Pc Owen to explain that one of the suspects, who he now knows to be a certain Nicola Kayes, began to volunteer statements about the crime and her two associates on the way to the police station in his car. They agree together that it would probably be a good idea to interview her first. Pc Owen says he will suggest it to the interviewing officer as part of the handover package.

Pc Owen and Pc Dunn begin work on the handover package for the next stage of the investigation into the alleged shoplifting. In the meantime the legal advisers for the three suspects are contacted and begin to arrive during the course of the afternoon.

Q25   What is likely to be in the handover package?

Q26   What fast-track actions may be taken at this stage?

At 15.00 two experienced officers, Pc Alison Wyatt and Pc Jon Singh, are delegated to carry out the interview of the female suspect, Nicola Kayes, after receiving the handover package from Pc Dunn and Pc Owen.

Pc Wyatt knows Kayes' age—she is 28—and the custody officer has determined (after an assessment of Kayes' educational background and intellectual ability) that an appropriate adult is not required.

Kayes has accepted initial legal advice from the duty solicitor, Mr Williams. He has explained to her that he will talk with her privately after being briefed by the police officers, and that he will also be present during her interview.

Pc Alison Wyatt and Pc Jon Singh then carry out a pre-interview disclosure with Mr Williams.

They briefly outline the circumstances of Kayes' arrest and detention with the two other suspects. They have decided in their planning process that they will relate all the facts to the solicitor about the incident at Mortesbury's, including the significant statements made by his client in the police car, and explaining that his client declined to sign the attributed statements. Mr Williams also requests to see the stolen goods.

Pc Wyatt decides not to reveal the property recovered from the car to Kayes or to Mr Williams at this stage.

Mr Williams then consults privately with Kayes while Pc Wyatt finishes preparing for the interview.

The rooms for meetings between solicitors and their clients do not have police recording facilities as such consultations are confidential. However, a solicitor may choose to bring his or her own equipment to record discussions with police officers or with clients.

Q27   Apart from her normal preparation (she is PEACE-trained), does Pc Wyatt need to find out more about Kayes before interviewing her?

Q28   What is the risk of not mentioning at this stage (to Kayes or her solicitor) that further items (apparently stolen) have been found in the car?

Nicola Kayes is brought from her cell to the interview room.

All interview rooms have recording facilities as all interviews with suspects at police stations must be recorded.

Pc Wyatt signs the custody record to indicate she is present with the suspect for 'interview purposes' and also notes the time.

Pc Wyatt	Good afternoon, I'm Pc Alison Wyatt and this is Pc Jon Singh. What would you like us to call you?
Kayes	(Faintly) I'm . . . you can, um, call me Nic.
Pc Wyatt	That's short for Nicola, isn't it?
Kayes	Yes, Nicola Kayes.
Pc Wyatt	OK, Nic. Have you had a cuppa? Would you like a drink of tea or a glass of water or something?
Kayes	(Gratefully) Oh, a cup of tea would be great, thanks.
Pc Wyatt	How do you take it? Milk? Sugar? I gave up milk once, but I couldn't hack it so I went back to milk.
Kayes	(Smiling shyly) Milk, no sugar, please.

Q29   Why does Pc Wyatt introduce herself and Pc Singh using their full names and ask Kayes how she wants to be addressed?

Q30   What is Pc Wyatt's probable motive for mentioning trying to give up milk?

Pc Wyatt	Now, Nic, I'm going to explain why you're here, what we will ask you about and the things which will happen afterwards. We'll take it slowly, and you must ask if you need anything explained more, is that okay?
Kayes	Yes.
Pc Wyatt	Now Nic, we are going to tape record this interview. You are entitled to have a solicitor or other legal adviser present when you are interviewed, and that is why Mr Williams is here. We'll explain to you later how you or Mr Williams will be able to obtain copies of the tape. Is this clear so far, Nic?
Kayes	Yes.

Pc Wyatt unwraps two new audio tapes and puts them into the recorder. She switches it on to record.

Pc Wyatt	The interview is now being recorded. I am Pc 10899 Alison Wyatt from Maidbury police station.

Pc Wyatt then gives the date and time and states that the interview is taking place in interview room 3.

Pc Singh	I am Pc 11267 Jon Singh from Maidbury police station.

Pc Wyatt now asks Kayes to confirm her name, address, and date of birth.

Pc Wyatt	Mr Williams, please can you identify yourself and explain your role here today?
Mr Williams	My name is David Evan Williams, of Raznovich and Waters Solicitors. I am duty solicitor for Nicola Kayes, and I am here to advise her.

Q31 For what reason (other than to be polite) does Pc Wyatt record the solicitor's presence on the tape and ask him to identify himself?

Pc Wyatt	Nic, you have been arrested on suspicion of theft from Mortesbury's super-market earlier today. This means that my colleague Jon and I will ask you to tell us what happened there this morning.
Kayes	Yes.
Pc Wyatt	Mr Williams will already have talked to you in private and will have advised you. Pc Jon Singh and I will ask you questions about this incident. Either Jon or I may take notes as well as having the tape on. We may show you things and ask you to identify them. These are called 'exhibits'. What we would like you to do is to tell us what happened and why. We need to know the truth about today's incident and hope that you will be able to fill in the details for us. We will stop for a break after about an hour, and you are free at any time to consult with Mr Williams. All we'd ask is that you tell us when you are going to do this, because we need to stop the tape. Your conversations with Mr Williams, as I'm sure he has told you, are confidential, which means that Jon Singh and I are not allowed to hear what is said. Do you understand what I've said so far?
Kayes	Yes.
Pc Wyatt	Thank you. My colleague and I must interview you under caution. Do you know what that means?
Kayes	Yes.
Pc Wyatt	Good. Nicola Marie Kayes, you do not have to say anything. But it may harm your defence if you do not mention when questioned something which you later rely on in court. Anything you do say may be given in evidence. Do you understand the caution, Nic?

Kayes	(Hesitantly) Um, I think . . . um . . . some of it . . .
Pc Wyatt	That's okay—so let me put it this way. Say this matter goes to court at a later date, and you tell the court something in your defence, for example an inno- cent explanation of what took place at Mortesbury's supermarket today, and they think that you could reasonably have given me that explanation here today, but you didn't explain. Then in court, they may not believe you, and that could harm your defence. Also, everything we are saying in this room is being recorded and we could use all of this conversation as evidence at court if required.
Kayes	Yeah, okay.
Pc Wyatt	Good, it's important to me that you do understand it, so I am going to ask some quick questions to make sure—is that okay?
Kayes	Yes.
Pc Wyatt	Nicola, do you have to speak to me in this interview?
Kayes	No, I don't.
Pc Wyatt	That's right. And what might happen, for example, if in court you gave an innocent explanation about what happened at Mortesbury's, but you hadn't mentioned it here in this interview, if it was reasonable to do so?
Kayes	Well, the court may not believe me, they may think I made it all up, and that could make anything what I say in court look . . . untrue.
Pc Wyatt	Okay, so could we use everything said in this interview as evidence if it went to court?
Kayes	Yes, you could.
Pc Wyatt	Thank you. Now Nic, I am going to ask you some questions about this morn- ing. Take your time and think about your answers, okay?
Kayes	(Nervously) Okay.

Q32 Why does Pc Wyatt tell Kayes so clearly about the reasons for her being in the police station and for being arrested?

Q33 Suggest some advantages of encouraging Kayes to tell her story in her own words.

Q34 Why is it so important to make every attempt to ensure that Kayes fully understands the caution?

Pc Wyatt then asks Kayes to confirm what she (Kayes) said about not picking up the receipt. Pc Wyatt reads Kayes' actual words from Pc Owen's PNB, and Kayes confirms that the account is correct.

Pc Wyatt then moves on to what Kayes said to Pc Dunn.

Pc Wyatt	Nic, in the police car on the way to this police station you were reported to have said to Pc Dunn that . . . (Pc Wyatt reads the following): 'It was the other two who wanted me to do it. I didn't like it but they said we had to go thieving, speak to Stacker, he was the one who came up with the idea. I knew we would be caught.' Pc Dunn made a note of what you said and asked you to read his note and sign it and to write whether you agreed or disagreed that you said this. You refused to read and sign it. Is that true?
Kayes	Yeah, I didn't want to read it. I don't want Stacker to know what I said.

Pc Wyatt	Okay, let's go back to the supermarket earlier; you were stopped by the security staff when you were leaving Mortesbury's this morning. The security staff have told me that you had things which you didn't pay for. Can you explain to me what happened this morning and what you did?
Kayes	Yes. I, um...I had to do what Alan said. He, uh...he said he'd bloody kill me if I didn't, um...go with him on this one and he's nearly done it before (crying) hitting me and stuff and and I was scared. I've never done anything like this before and I've never been in trouble with the police until now, but he made me do it. You don't know Alan—he seems so normal most of the time but for no reason he'll just go bloody mad and smash things up and if you're in the way you get smashed up too.
Pc Singh	Did you, or the other two, have sufficient money in your possession to pay for the rum and the other articles taken from you?
Kayes	No
Pc Wyatt	Who is Alan, Nic?
Kayes	Alan Stacker, the man who was with me at the shop and who got arrested too.
Pc Wyatt	Was anyone else involved, Nic?
Kayes	Yeah, that wanker Bolgomov.
Pc Wyatt	Who's he?
Kayes	Sergei Bolgomov. He follows me about. I don't like him. Alan said he'd be good to have along when we did the supermarket and he's been living in a squat down at Ledbury. I hate him. He's always, you know, um...looking at me like with his eyes, sort of thing, and watching me all the time. He's a bloody creep. I don't know why Alan wants him along. He can hardly speak any English and he's just a creepy pig.

Q35   Mr Williams has clearly advised Kayes to answer the interviewers' questions. When might the advice be to remain silent?

Q36   The solicitor has also not intervened up to this point. Under what circumstances might a solicitor choose to intervene?

Q37   Notice that Pc Wyatt did **not** say, 'Alan is Alan Stacker, isn't he?' Why is it better to avoid this style of question?

Q38   If what Kayes says is true—that Bolgomov has poor English and that he lives in a squat—what might this suggest, and what consequences might this have for managing the investigation?

Q39   Suggest what Pc Wyatt's next question might be.

Q40   As well as inviting Kayes to talk about the crime, Pc Wyatt will be keen to find out what was in Kayes' mind at the time (the *mens rea*; one of the points to prove). What questions could she ask to find out?

When Pc Wyatt asks Kayes about what happened in the supermarket, it seems that Kayes is now quite relieved to talk about what occurred.

Kayes	It was all Alan's idea. He'd met this bloke in a pub who'd said he was in the market, sort of thing, for anyone with booze and new cameras and the latest phones and all that kind of thing. And Alan said that nicking this sort of stuff was easy, especially if we went as a couple because we'd look as though we were shopping. I didn't want to do it and I've never been in trouble with the police before but Alan said that we wouldn't be caught if we were cool. He said that he and Sergei were going to do over Electromart's because they had good stuff there you could sell off and I didn't have to come but I have to go to the supermarket because two men shopping alone might be suspicious. I said again that I didn't want to and Alan went mad. He, um, he hit me and said that he'd fucking kill me if I didn't do it with him because there was no money coming in now I'd lost my poxy job and how could he get a drink if he didn't have any sodding cash. So I said yes, more to stop him hitting me again than because I wanted to. This morning, we drove there in Alan's car and just went in. Alan said go for the small spirits and razors and stuff and to push them inside my coat or in the bag. So I did. I was sort of hoping we'd get caught. I don't know. I just want to get away from him because he's mental. I don't want to get hit again. Look.
Pc Wyatt	Nicola Kayes is showing me a large bruise on her left breast and left collar bone. This will be photographed later.
Kayes	That's what he did last night, the bastard. I can't bear this any more. (Crying) Oh God, what have I done?

Q41 Kayes has described the *mens rea* and the *actus reus* of an offence. Which of her words describe the *actus reus*?

Q42 Has she confessed to a crime?

Pc Singh now ensures that everyone present, particularly Kayes, is in agreement about the 'account' she has just given. He does this by summarizing the key claims and points that Kayes has made. Immediately after Pc Singh's summary, Mr Williams intervenes.

Mr Williams	I think I should speak to my client privately.
Pc Wyatt	Of course. This interview is suspended. The time is 15.05.

Q43 What action must be taken in relation to the injuries Kayes has sustained?

Q44 Why do you think that the solicitor intervened at this point in Kayes' narrative, immediately after the agreed summary?

Q45 When the interview starts again after the recess, what must Pc Wyatt say first?

Pc Wyatt and Pc Singh share the subsequent questioning, and they question Kayes politely but robustly about the minimal part she claimed to play in the theft at the supermarket.

The police officers are mindful, as noted above, that Kayes could be transferring all the blame to the two men in an attempt to exonerate herself or to play down her part.

However, both officers are aware that her account may either be corroborated or contradicted by the CCTV evidence, hopefully to come later, and so directly challenging her account at this stage serves no real purpose as there is little or no contradictory evidence. In their experience, under these kinds of circumstances, the interview can quickly become a 'Yes you did'/'No I didn't' farcical event.

The officers then explore Kayes' allegations of violence against her by Stacker in more detail and ask her to make a witness statement later, after being formally released from police custody. She agrees.

It is time for closure. There is not much more now to be gained from continuing the interview with Nicola Kayes; she is getting tired and starting to repeat herself.

However, they may need to interview Kayes again, especially if any new evidence emerges or following Crown Prosecution Service (CPS) guidance (if the officers decide to seek 'early consultative advice'). New evidence could be derived, for instance, from the other interviews, from the CCTV footage that is being retrieved, or from further police enquiries.

Q46   What are the questions that any subsequent interviews with Kayes are likely to explore?

Pc Wyatt now explains to Kayes that she will be detained until Pc Wyatt consults with the custody officer, the CPS, and a supervisory officer about what further enquiries the police still have to make. However, Mr Williams has a final question:

'Will my client be released on bail, pending these further enquiries?'

Pc Wyatt replies:

'Bail, with or without conditions, is a matter for the custody officer in consultation with the CPS if necessary and is not a matter I can deal with. I will make representation to the custody officer that you have requested bail on behalf of your client.'

Q47   Why is Pc Wyatt's response to the request for bail so carefully and formally phrased?

Q48   What procedures must be followed at the end of an interview?

The interview concludes at 16.00 and Kayes is returned to the cells.

Pc Wyatt is pleased with how the interview went:

. . . she has admitted she's guilty . . . nice and clear . . . and gave us lots about the other two suspects . . .

However, both she and Pc Singh want now to evaluate the interview.

Q49   What is the importance of the evaluation stage of the PEACE model?

Q50   Why do Pc Wyatt and Pc Singh also need to keep an eye on the time in relation to the PACE Act 1984?

Pc Singh points out that Kayes has admitted she played a part but this is not the same as a confession of guilt. He also admits that he is unfamiliar with all the law concerning coercion and duress and needs to find out more about it for the subsequent interviews.

. . . look it up online . . . one of those databases . . . much quicker . . .

Pc Wyatt and Pc Singh now turn their attention to interviewing the second suspect arrested earlier that day. At 16.30 Stacker is brought from his cell to the interview room. Pc Singh notes the time and signs the custody record as for 'interview purposes' and follows the usual procedures before starting the interview proper.

Pc Singh	This is an interview with—please give your name, age, and date of birth . . .
Stacker	Alan Maurice Stacker, 39, 16 April 1968.
Pc Singh	At Maidbury Police station in interview room 1. Present with Mr Stacker is Mr Stacker's solicitor . . . please announce yourself . . .
Ms O'Connor	Michaela Mary O'Connor, Duty Solicitor.
Pc Singh	And Pc 11267 Jon Singh and Pc 10899 Alison Wyatt as interviewing officers. The time is 16.25. Mr Stacker, what would you like us to call you?
Stacker	No comment.
Pc Singh	Okay, we'll just stay with Mr Stacker then. . .

Pc Singh then administers the caution and explains it. He repeats the three-stage process as used by Pc Wyatt earlier and asks Stacker to answer the three questions posed to check comprehension. Stacker continues to answer, 'No comment'.

Pc Singh	Mr Stacker, you were detained this morning outside Mortesbury's supermarket in Pound Lane Estate. You had in your possession supermarket goods for which you had no receipts or proof of payment. How do you account for that?
Stacker	On the advice of my solicitor . . . I'll make no comment.
Pc Singh	I am showing Mr Stacker some of the goods alleged to have been taken by him without payment. Mr Stacker, can you account for your possession of these two bottles of rum?
Stacker	No comment.
PC Singh	Did you, or the other two, have sufficient money in your possession to pay for the rum and the other articles taken from you?
Stacker	No comment.

Pc Singh	Mr Stacker, I have witnesses who are prepared to testify that these bottles were recovered from an inside pocket of your jacket where you had concealed them. Can you account for this?
Stacker	No comment.
Ms O'Connor	Pc Singh, my client will insist on not answering questions and replying 'no comment'.
Pc Singh	I have put an allegation of theft to your client, Ms O'Connor, and have invited him to account for his possession of bottles of spirit. This is not an unreasonable line of questioning.
Stacker	I'm saying nothing.

Q51 If true, why might Ms O'Connor have advised Stacker to remain silent, and will this necessarily help him?

Q52 Why is it important for Pc Singh to persist, despite Stacker's lack of cooperation?

Pc Singh continues to question Stacker but makes no progress against Stacker's stonewalling. The interview is brought to an end at 16.30 and the usual protocols followed.

A few minutes later in a corridor near the interview room Pc Singh encounters Mr Jones, one of the duty solicitors.

The numbering of the interview rooms enables the precise location of an interview to be recorded on the tape.

Mr Jones	You are Pc Singh?
Pc Singh	I am.
Mr Jones	I am Peter Jones of Jones, Gateweigh and Bord, Solicitors. You have arrested my client, Sergei Bolgomov?

Pc Singh	Mr Jones, I do recognize you. Yes, we are preparing to interview Mr Bolgomov in connection with an alleged theft.
Mr Jones	Yes, I would presume as much . . .
Pc Singh	We'll meet later for a pre-interview disclosure. I'll see you in about half an hour?

Q53 What form could the pre-interview disclosure take?

When they meet up later, Pc Singh finds Mr Jones to be more forthright than he had expected. The following exchange takes place.

Mr Jones	What evidence do you have to justify the detention of my client?
Pc Singh	I am sure you have had the chance to read the custody record and have been supplied with a copy. As you will see, your client was detained at Mortesbury's supermarket this morning in possession of items for which he had not paid and could . . .
Mr Jones	How do you know he hadn't paid?
Pc Singh	. . . could not account for. Because he had no receipts for the goods in his possession.
Mr Jones	What if someone else had the receipts?
Pc Singh	Our enquiries have not confirmed that.
Mr Jones	So it is possible that others have the necessary receipts?
Pc Singh	I intend to explore with him his account of what happened this morning.
Mr Jones	You realize that he cannot speak much English?
Pc Singh	Yes, we have arranged for an interpreter.
Mr Jones	What is the evidence that he did not intend to pay?
Pc Singh	That is something I intend to ask him.
Mr Jones	Who else was involved?
Pc Singh	Other suspects are in detention, Mr Jones, but I am not prepared at this stage to outline all the facts to you until I've heard Mr Bolgomov's account.
Mr Jones	One of them is Alan Stacker, isn't it?
Pc Singh	I am not prepared to reveal all the facts of the case at this stage.
Mr Jones	You're deliberately holding some evidence back, aren't you?
Pc Singh	Some of the facts are being withheld at this stage and I am not prepared to discuss it with you. I fully accept that you will want to advise your client at the time this evidence is disclosed, but I have given you enough in my disclosure briefing for you to advise your client for the purpose of the forthcoming interview.

Pc Singh shakes Mr Jones' hand as he leaves the room, but his smile is forced.

. . . great . . . just what I need . . . this is going to be a difficult one . . . I hope I've done the right thing not telling him about the other property . . .

Bolgomov is interviewed later, at 17.15, by Pc Singh and Pc Wyatt. The interpreter is sitting next to Bolgomov, but they appear to be avoiding eye contact and right at the outset of the interview Mr Jones insists that he will answers questions on Bolgomov's behalf because 'his client has difficulties with the interpreter'.

Q54   How might Pc Singh respond to Mr Jones' insistence?

After discussion, Mr Jones agrees that Bolgomov will respond himself through the interpreter. However, Bolgomov provides only 'no comment' responses and the interview soon comes to an end.

It is now 18.00 and the three suspects have been in custody since 12.00. Pc Singh calculates that there will not be a problem with the time here:

. . . they've only been in six hours and we're nearly done . . . I think.

Q55   Consideration needs to be given to how much longer they will need to be detained. Why is this?

Pc Wyatt and Pc Singh consult with the custody officer, an investigative adviser, and CPS representative on the appropriate next steps in terms of the suspects. By 18.30 it is decided that all three suspects will be released on 'conditional bail' to return to the police station at a later date for further interviews or charge after the case has been referred to the CPS.

After the usual procedures have been followed the three suspects leave the police station separately. Bolgomov leaves last, at 19.30, with the interpreter.

Q56   What conditions was the custody officer likely to have attached to the suspects' bail?

Officers Owen, Dunn, Wyatt, and Singh know of course that this is not the end of the matter, although they hope that it is at least the end of the beginning.

Investigation frequently involves managing large amounts of information and careful sifting to identify the information that is relevant to a particular case.

Finally, before going off duty, Pc Wyatt and Pc Singh check that:

- the handover package for the appointed investigating officer is complete;

- all crime reports have been completed according to the Home Office counting rules;

- all live 'action logs' have been updated on the computer;

- the PNC has been updated; and

- forensic and medical examinations have been arranged for Nicola Kayes and that she has an appointment for an interview as a witness (possibly as an 'intimidated witness' and hence requiring an Achieving Best Evidence (ABE) interview on completion of an MG 2) and that arrangements are in place to take her to a safe haven or family members if she so requires.

✓

Pc Dunn, the student police officer, remains at the police station to 'capture' the events earlier in the day in his Student Officer Learning and Assessment Portfolio (SOLAP). He also considers whether he might have claim to some evidence towards completion of his Police Action Checklist (PAC).

Q57   What potential evidence has Pc Dunn been able to collect towards completing his SOLAP and his PAC?

Outcome

The officers all know an investigating officer will be appointed to take the investigation further, and that enquiries are likely to continue for some time before a decision is made on whether to charge the suspects with the offences of theft and (in Stacker's case) other offences which might include actual bodily harm.

Subsequently, after further police investigation, Kayes agreed to accept a caution. However, she withdrew her allegation of assault against Stacker and continues to co-habit with him. No charges of assault were brought against Stacker.

Later the CPS decided to charge Stacker and Bolgomov under s 1 of the Theft Act 1968 and to proceed with a prosecution. At the magistrates' court both pleaded guilty and each received a 12-month community order, including 150 hours of community service. They were also ordered to pay prosecution costs.

Mortesbury's Answers

A1   Pc Dunn does so in an attempt to avoid any potential complications that may otherwise arise later if the suspects were to be prosecuted. If the accounts from the manager (and other staff) were not given in the presence of the three suspects then the potential evidence that may result could be challenged. It is not mandatory for the witnesses to present an account in the presence of the suspects but in these circumstances it is practical and offers certain advantages to the prosecution and the defendants. The prosecution might benefit should the suspects make unsolicited comments or significant statements whilst the manager outlines his account. Later (if this goes to court) everybody including the police officers will be able to give evidence of what they heard the manager say during the account. On the other hand, such circumstances may present advantages to the suspects as Pc Dunn is providing them with the opportunity to challenge anything said by the manager. (Remember that the suspects have not yet been cautioned by the officers.) Similarly, the defendants may also be advantaged by hearing what evidence has or has not been gathered by witnesses to prove or disprove the accusation made against them.

A2   Yes, the manager can tell the officers about accounts given to him by other staff. During this phase it is not necessary for Pc Dunn to limit the manager to events he himself witnessed, Pc Dunn can allow the manager to provide a comprehensive account gathered from his staff.

(However, if the manager later gives an account that is to be formally recorded evidence in a witness statement then it will be necessary to restrict his account to his own personal experience of what he saw, heard, smelled, and touched.)

See Witness Statements, *BSPOH 2010*, 8.13

In practice it is difficult to stop the manager from introducing other people's accounts and recollections into his own version of events—if in doubt Pc Dunn should record it all and only later with the CPS or counsel 'edit' the witness statement and restrict any answers given in evidence at court to that deemed to be 'admissible evidence'. Note that on occasions 'hearsay evidence' (eg evidence which is not direct oral evidence given in court) may in fact be 'admissible'. The law surrounding hearsay evidence has changed significantly in recent years and there are now many exceptions to the 'rule against heasay'.

A3 He should note it down in his pocket note book.

A4 Pc Owen should conduct a PNC (Police National Computer) check on the three suspects. The PNC might flag up particular information that will assist the two officers—such as warnings for drugs or violence, and whether any of the suspects are currently wanted by police elsewhere. However, the identity of the three suspects will also need to be rechecked if they are subsequently arrested and taken to the police station—normally by using the Livescan fingerprint system.

A5 It would be sufficient at this stage for the two officers to note the names of all the staff present and make brief notes describing their involvement in the alleged events. It would be impracticable to question each member of staff in any detail there and then. No doubt one or two members of staff witnessed the alleged offences and the part played by individual suspects but others would have been involved only in terms of responding as 'security' or 'support', possibly in answer to a pre-arranged coded signal over the public address system. The officers should therefore identify the key witnesses and ensure the witnesses agree with the brief account of the events as recorded in the officers' PNBs. Any contradictions between the accounts from the key witnesses, and any additional information the other staff members think might be important, should also be recorded.

A6 These initial accounts from staff and witnesses may provide the information the officers will need to give the custody officer as justification and necessity for arrest, plan an interview later with the suspects, or to construct a 'handover pack' for other officers to conduct the interviews and finally to consult with the CPS.

In any subsequent prosecution the initial accounts will also need to be revealed to the CPS and if necessary disclosed to the defence (using forms MG 6C and MG 6E).

A7 Under CPIA the officers are required to undertake all reasonable lines of enquiry (an objective test, bound by proportionality) to ascertain if any other witness can be identified. If there is any possibility that a witness can be traced, then it falls to the officers to trace them, even if the likely outcome is that no new or pertinent information will be forthcoming.

Information that does not support an existing line of enquiry (sometimes termed 'negative information') can sometimes be as significant to an investigation as information that does support the present line of enquiry ('positive information'). Examples of negative information in this scenario might include:

- a CCTV camera that does not record the crime/location/suspect in a manner which is consistent with the prosecution case (the fact that a CCTV camera did not function or have videotape loaded will not usually be considered relevant negative information);
- people present near the till where the offence is alleged to have taken place state they saw nothing unusual.

It is impossible to define precisely when negative information may be significant, as every case is different. However, it will include the result of any enquiry that differs from what might have been expected, given the prevailing circumstances. Any information or material that casts doubt on the suspect's guilt, or implicates another person must be retained, just as material or information that would support a prosecution case will be retained.

It is important to record promptly any information from any source, which might be considered relevant to the investigation. A record should be made at the time the information is obtained, or as soon as practicable after that time.

A8 The suspects' accounts will be given later at interview at the police station, under caution.

A9 He should ask the manager about the CCTV recording format—hard drive, VCR, or DVD—and the time delay before the content is overwritten.

> See CCTV Evidence, *BSPOH 2010*, 13.5.13.1

A10 The CPIA imposes a duty on the police to retain and reveal the existence of all 'relevant material'. The tape might provide evidence that implicates or exonerates each or any of the suspects, but in either eventuality it is still relevant material.

> See Record, Retain, Reveal, and Disclosure, *BSPOH 2010*, 12.6

A11 Pc Owen needs to establish whether the suspects were detained outside the store. If they were outside there would be no possibility that the suspects could plead that they were trying to get to a pay point inside the store. In this case, the fact that the suspects had left the store may provide stronger evidence of an attempt to avoid payment. The exact route they were witnessed to take (or admitted taking) could be vital, and floor plans of the store may be necessary to emphasize the point that they were deliberately avoiding pay points.

Note, however, that in general terms arrests that occur inside a store are no less justified than those conducted when suspects leave a store. In the former case, an arrest may be justified on the grounds of an attempt to commit a crime even if the 'full' theft has not occurred.

A12 Yes. In cases of alleged shoplifting such as this, reasonable suspicion can be formed as a result of listening to presumably reliable witnesses such as the staff working at the store.

A13 The necessity for the arrests in this case might be to allow the prompt and effective investigation of the offence by the interviewing of the suspects on tape at the police station.

A14 PACE Code of Practice G para 2.4 provides the reasons why an arrest could be 'necessary'.

> See Reasons that Make an Arrest Necessary, *BSPOH 2010*, 8.7.4

A15 Probably not. The suspects' vehicle does not appear to be associated with the alleged occurrence of shoplifting. If the exchange with the female suspect develops and borders on asking questions about the alleged acts of theft, this would be part of an interview, and should not be pursued at this stage.

A16 An interview with a suspect has to be conducted at a police station (designated or non-designated).

> See Interviews with Suspects, *BSPOH 2010*, 12.5.5

A17 Pc Dunn has the power under the PACE Act 1984 to search the suspects' vehicle. Section 32(2) states that a constable has the power to search any premises in which the suspect was present before the (indictable) offence for which he/she was arrested, and to seize and retain anything found (s 32(9)). This would cover any vehicle used by the suspects to travel to the store.

Furthermore, if the presence of the person at a place (other than a police station) is necessary for the effective investigation of the offence, a search of the vehicle could be made under s 18(5) of the PACE Act 1984. For example, it would make sense for the suspects to be present while the officers search the car as this would help the officers establish which items found in the car are in fact stolen property. Any items that are suspected to have been stolen or used in relation to any indictable offence connected with or similar to that offence can be seized and retained (s 18(1) and (2)).

A moveable vehicle may be seized as the vehicle itself amounts to 'premises', and 'anything' has been established by case law to mean 'everything'. An officer of the rank of inspector or a deputed sergeant must be informed of the search as soon as practicable after it has been made (PACE Code of Practice B para 4).

See Search of Premises After Arrest, *BSPOH 2010*, 7.7

A18 It is possible that a crime scene investigator (CSI) will examine the suspects' vehicle after it is seized and removed to a 'forensic' holding location. However, it is more likely that a CSI will be called (if available) to the vehicle to simply photograph the goods as found, hidden under the blanket, but little other than this. Since the suspects appear to acknowledge an association with the vehicle it can be assumed that their fingerprints and fibres from their clothes would be found in the vehicle, and hence there would be little investigatory value in using forensic science to establish such a link.

A19 Questioning suspects about the offences after they have been arrested and before arrival at the police station would be a blatant breach of the PACE Codes of Practice. It could render Pc Dunn's evidence inadmissible and put at risk any potential prosecution. Pc Dunn could also be subjected to disciplinary procedures.

See Unsolicited Comments by Suspects, *BSPOH 2010*, 8.5

A20 The suspect has voluntarily made a statement outside the context of an interview, but which might be relevant to the offence. When the suspect is first formally interviewed on tape the interviewing officer must first put any 'significant statement' (a statement which could be used in evidence against the suspect) to the suspect and ask if she agrees about the accuracy and content of what has been recorded.

See Unsolicited Comments by Suspects, *BSPOH 2010*, 8.5

A21 PACE Code of Practice C Note 11E advises that the suspect should be asked to endorse the PNB with the words 'I agree that this is a correct record of what was said'. (See also PACE Code of Practice C para 11.13, for more details.)

See Unsolicited Comments by Suspects, *BSPOH 2010*, 8.5

A22 If a suspect refuses to sign a significant statement recorded in a PNB, it is no less valid; the suspect is still questioned about it at interview in precisely the same way.

A23 If the property is identified as having been possibly stolen, Pc Owen (or another officer tasked with the investigation) should try and obtain additional evidence. The store could confirm whether they had the relevant items on sale, and any stock accounting system could confirm a sale of the items during the relevant period—of course, no such sale would be shown if the items had been stolen. The store might also be able to provide descriptions of any possible suspects seen in store during the relevant time, or additional CCTV footage for the relevant period. Any CCTV footage should at least be secured for the time being.

A24 It is often very difficult to determine conclusively whether property has been stolen from a particular store at a certain time. Brand names appear in many stores and shops and are not exclusive to a particular store. The onus is on the police to establish that a theft has occurred, not on the accused to prove they did not steal the property. It is sometimes possible to show stock movement and indicate that no reported sales have been made from the store or a particular pay point of such items over a fixed (short) period of time or on capture from CCTV at those stores.

A25   Procedures for handover packages (sometimes referred to as a 'Single Source Document' or SSD) vary from force to force but the officers are likely to include the following:

Handover package entry	Examples/notes
Alleged offender(s)	• DoBs and custody numbers; • PNC/force intelligence database checks; • statements made at the scene and arrest.
Pc Owen and Pc Dunn's account of the circumstances leading up to the arrests	They should avoid offering opinion in this section.
Investigation checklist	• arrest (including a copy of their PNB entries); • searches; • exhibits, eg the copy of the CCTV hard disc to be collected; • scene and forensic evidence.
Custody checklist	• prisoner and custody consideration, eg free, independent, legal advice, any need for an 'appropriate adult', interpreter, medication needed, etc; • custody 'time clock' list.
Witness details and statements	• names, addresses, and contact numbers of witnesses; • a summary of witness statements.
Other officers involved	Details of those who also attended, including copies of their PNB entries and statements.

A26   During the afternoon the following police actions may have occurred:

- Searches of the suspects' home addresses (under s 18 of the PACE Act 1984) and items removed suspected to be evidence of an offence (s 19 of the PACE Act 1984).

- The suspects' vehicle left outside Mortesbury's supermarket has probably been recovered, the suspected stolen goods photographed in situ as 'hidden' or witnessed by officers and then seized and stored.

- The Intelligence Unit may have been informed of the detention of the three suspects for consideration of potential 'cell intervention'. For example, there might be significant intelligence on Stacker and there may be opportunities to seek intelligence from his associates. Kayes might well be prepared to talk of Stacker's offending activities, and may require Covert Human Intelligence Source (CHIS) status in due course. However, cell intervention has to be carefully considered and it must not be linked with the crime under investigation or give rise to an impression of inducement or advantage for assisting the police in this way.

- CCTV evidence has been collected from the manager at Mortesbury's, other relevant locations.

- If there was intelligence on Stacker and his violence towards women then this would need to be revealed to the CPS using MG 6E as this may support Kayes' contention that she was exposed to his violence (ie, material deemed capable of undermining the prosecution's case). This intelligence might include previous allegations of assault, reports of violence not pursued by the victim, and third-hand accounts of Stacker's violence. In some instances the information may be deemed 'sensitive material' and identities not revealed. This would require a skillful approach and probably the completion of MG 6D (the Schedule of Sensitive Material will not be disclosed to the defence because it is not in the public interest to do so. The officer must state the reason why the item should not be disclosed to the defence.)

- Enquiries made with Electromart concerning the goods found in the suspects' car at Mortesbury's supermarket.

- A meeting with the reviewing lawyer of the CPS to seek early guidance on two issues: the defence raised by Kayes in her interview (that she was acting under duress) and the question of whether the accused were acting together in concert or independently.

A27   Pc Wyatt will be familiar with the planning process and how the interview might proceed. For example, she will be prepared for the possibility of a 'no comment' interview, the use of prepared statements, and so on.

In terms of the suspect, prior to opening the proposed interview, she will also need to:

- find out about Kayes' personal circumstances;

- establish, if possible, how Kayes knows the other two suspects;

- conduct background checks about Kayes' previous history; and

- establish whether Kayes has previously been involved with the police, particularly in relation to evidence of bad character.

See Evidence of Bad Character, *BSPOH 2010*, 12.8
See Planning Interviews, *BSPOH 2010*, 12.5.3.1

A28   There are risks here. If Pc Wyatt subsequently opens up this line of questioning (about the apparently stolen property in the car) in the interview with Kayes, the adviser may challenge Pc Wyatt's actions as amounting to an 'ambush' in the interview. Remember that the role of the suspect's legal adviser is to give the best advice in the circumstances, and how can that advice be given if the solicitor is not party to all the facts? If this line of questioning were to occur then the solicitor would probably seek time out for private consultation, to which they are perfectly entitled.

See Briefing the Solicitor, *BSPOH 2010*, 12.5.5.3 and 12.5.5.4

A29   This is to try and avoid intimidating Kayes any further—she is already feeling nervous. Note how Pc Wyatt picks up on Kayes' offer of a shortened form of her name—Nic— and how she makes it into a friendly gesture, followed by concern for Kayes' comfort. Had Pc Wyatt been overbearingly formal or pompous or 'standoffish', Kayes may well have clammed up completely.

See Engaging the Interviewee, *BSPOH 2010*, 12.5.3.2

A30   Again this 'ice-breaker' is to try and build a rapport with Kayes, trying to suggest that the interview is not likely to be oppressive or threatening (and may even be more like a conversation). It gives a touch of humanity to the interviewer, who comes across as more of a real person, and in this case it seems to work, because the suspect is smiling as she replies. These gambits may seem trivial matters, but research suggests that they do work.

A31   All persons present at the interview have to be accounted for. It also helps to make the tape clear and comprehensible when it is replayed (especially in court), and helps underline that Pc Wyatt is in control of the interview process.

A32   Apart from being generally reassuring by explaining the situation, under the PACE Act 1984 all suspects must be informed of these facts.

A33   We are currently in the 'account phase' of the interview and a freely delivered account without interruption or assistance adds to the weight of the evidence gained from the suspect. The defence solicitor will not be able to claim that Kayes was led into making certain statements that distort the truth.

See PEACE—Account, Clarifications, and Challenge, *BSPOH 2010*, 12.5.3.3

A34   Apart from the duty of care to Kayes, there is a danger otherwise that the defence in any prosecution might try to suggest (later in court) that Kayes did not fully understand the meaning of the caution, particularly the second phase touching on 'failing to mention' and 'rely on'.

It should be remembered that a legal adviser is not likely to intervene to attempt to remedy a 'defective' caution (either badly administered or wrongly explained), in order to aid their client's understanding. Instead, the adviser will quietly observe and note the situation, recognizing that opportunities may arise later in court to have the interview ruled inadmissible through the misleading or inaccurate explanation of the caution.

A35   Note that what follows is drawn in part from Shepherd (1996, 2007) and Cape (2006).

A legal adviser might advise their client to remain silent if the adviser thinks that:

- the police have not disclosed a case to answer at this stage and hence the suspect need not incriminate him/herself;

- the case is based on inadmissible evidence;

- the police have failed to disclose adequate information;

- it is unreasonable to expect an immediate answer to complex or complicated matters that require further thought;

- a suspect is emotionally overwhelmed or otherwise disorientated; or

- a suspect is vulnerable (in the sense that they cannot present themselves well in interview, in which case a prepared statement could be offered followed by a 'no comment' interview).

A36   Note that what follows is drawn in part from Shepherd (1996, 2007) and Cape (2006).

The solicitor may choose to intervene in one or more of four circumstances:

- if he considers that Kayes is struggling to deal with the interview, perhaps through confusion or being emotionally affected;

- to challenge what he believes to be inappropriate questioning of Kayes—for example, Pc Wyatt asserting guilt, generalizing without foundation, making false assumptions, misrepresenting the facts or the law, using ambiguous or otherwise confusing words and phrases, hypothetical questions, or leading questions;

- if he believes the actions of the interviewer are becoming 'oppressive'—for example, Pc Wyatt talking over Kayes, or raising her voice;

- in order to have a private consultation with Kayes (perhaps to reconsider the 'tactics' and to revert to 'no comment' or the use of a prepared statement), or to seek further disclosure from Pc Wyatt on previously undeclared evidence or information.

A37   This would have been a leading question and might be seen as an attempt to 'put words into Kayes' mouth'. Instead, Pc Wyatt quietly asked who 'Alan' was, and let Kayes implicate the man in the incident. Notice too that Kayes alleged that Stacker is capable of violence and that she has been the victim of his anger.

A38   This might suggest that he is not in the UK legally or that he is 'of no fixed abode', which may make full identification difficult. In addition, an interpreter might be required for the interview with Bolgomov and this needs to be arranged. Remember the custody 'time clock' is already running.

A39   The next question would probably be, 'Tell me about the supermarket business, Nic.' Remember to avoid the temptation to ask leading questions. The solicitor would no doubt have intervened if Pc Wyatt had said, 'So you're admitting you went to Mortesbury's with the intention of stealing?' because it is a leading question which invites Kayes to incriminate herself. It is far better to let Kayes say things in her own words.

A40   To establish *mens rea* she could ask:

- 'What were you feeling when you went into the supermarket?';

- 'What were you thinking when you were inside Mortesbury's?';

- 'How did you feel when you went to the checkout?'; or

- 'What were you intending as you passed by the checkout?'.

A41   The words used to describe the *actus reus* are, 'This morning, we drove there in Alan's car and just went in. Alan said go for the small spirits and razors and stuff and to push them inside my coat or in the bag. So I did.'

A42   What she said fits the legal definition of a confession as 'any statement wholly or partly adverse to the person who made it, whether made to a person in authority or not and whether made in words or otherwise' (paraphrased from s 82 of the PACE Act 1984). However, this is an equivocal admission—an admission to a crime that is normally followed with a 'but'.

Hence Kayes only partly accepts her role in the crime and will probably discuss with her solicitor whether she has a strong case for a defence of coercion and duress. Her solicitor will be mindful that if Kayes does not have a sustainable defence and does not make a full admission to the offence (fully admitting her own part, without equivocation), then certain penalties, for example a caution, may not be available.

If she is a first-time offender with no prior history, the solicitor is likely to make sure she explains to the police (and the CPS) that she is mitigating her part in the crime, not denying it. The CCTV has not yet been seen and this may influence both the solicitor and the CPS as to their future course of action.

A43   Pc Wyatt would be considering how this evidence might be visually recorded, such as arranging for the bruise to be photographed (as she suggested earlier in the interview), and whether Kayes needs to be examined by the custody nurse, or to attend hospital for X-rays.

A44   Kayes has perhaps realized the implications of all she has said to the police officers (her comment, 'Oh God, what have I done?') both in partially admitting her guilt and in implicating Stacker. The solicitor may want to reassure her.

Kayes has partially admitted her part in the theft and the solicitor appreciates that it is likely that the CPS will authorize charges against her, believing that her defence is untenable and the case could proceed to conviction (applying the Full Code test). However, if convicted she could receive a 'light' sentence because of the intimidation by Stacker (mitigation) and for an early indication of guilt.

The solicitor may also be thinking that Kayes could avoid prosecution and accept a caution or a conditional caution if offered, but she would have to abandon any defence of coercion or duress. He will want to follow this up in private with her.

Notice also that Pc Wyatt made no attempt to interrupt Kayes at any point. She let the suspect talk about what had happened in her own way and did not seek to lead, guide, or otherwise influence her. This demonstrates good listening skills.

See Effective Communication, *BSPOH 2010*, 6.18

A45   After such a break PACE Code of Practice C para 10.8 requires the person being questioned to be reminded that he/she is still under caution and, if there is any doubt, for the caution to be repeated.

Certainly, Kayes' solicitor will be expecting Pc Wyatt to do exactly that; failure to do so will breach the Codes of Practice, and the solicitor will be keeping a close eye on this.

Opening the second phase of the interview also provides an opportunity to re-summarize what Kayes has said and to invite Kayes to comment on the accuracy of the summary.

See Re-starting an Interview after a Break, *BSPOH 2010*, 12.5.5.5

A46   There are a number of reasons why further interviews with Kayes might be arranged.

- To ask questions concerning the items found in the car at the supermarket. It makes sense if this interview occurs after enquiries at Electromart's have been made and any potential evidence discovered. For example, CCTV might show Kayes herself placing the items in the car.

- If Kayes was not acting independently in the alleged theft of items from Mortesbury's, then the allegation may well be that this was a 'joint enterprise' in which all three suspects were involved together in stealing the goods. This could change the outcome and influence the decisions made by the CPS. Kayes could be lying and it is possible that she was not only a participant but the initiator or leader, contrary to the picture she painted in earlier interviews.

- The CCTV evidence is vital in these circumstances. She may be shown the CCTV footage in subsequent interviews, and her initial account probed and compared with events shown in the footage.

A47 Apart from the fact that the decision is not hers to make, Pc Wyatt needs to ensure that any discussion of bail is not misconstrued as offering early release as an inducement.

A48 There are some legal requirements to be met before the interview tape machine is switched off. Kayes must be asked whether she wants to add to or clarify anything she has said. Pc Wyatt needs to tell her what will happen to the tapes, reinforcing this by providing a written explanation, and must state the time before switching off the machine. Pc Wyatt and Pc Singh need to sign the tape labels and seal the tapes in Kayes' presence, witnessed by Mr Williams, the solicitor. Finally, the officers must sign the custody record to note the time of completion of the interview.

A49 Part of the 'Evaluation' in the PEACE mnemonic is to determine whether emerging enquiries should be undertaken before the suspect's release or before others are alerted to the investigation. Rapid action might be required before the suspect has the opportunity to put other associates on alert who could, for example, dispose of stolen property held at their home address from previous thefts or otherwise interfere with the investigation. The police might also wish to question witnesses given as alibi before they can be approached by the suspect.

A50 The custody time clock is an important issue in dealing with suspects in custody.

All persons in custody must be dealt with expeditiously and released as soon as the need for detention no longer arises (PACE Code of Practice C para 1.1). The time spent in custody is subject to continual re-assessment and review by the custody officer and supervisory officers.

As part of the planning process for the interview the officers would have taken into account the 'time clock', review periods, and maximum periods of detention.

A51 A court or jury might draw an 'adverse inference' from Stacker's unwillingness to answer questions. Case law suggests (notably *R v Howell* [2005] 1 Cr App R 1 at [1], *R v Hoare and Pierce* [2004] EWCA Crim 784 at [28], [54], and *R v Beckles and Montague* [1999] Crim LR 148) that the court or jury can consider whether it was **reasonable** to expect Stacker to have relied on Ms O'Connor's advice not to mention a relevant fact or facts. The court or jury might conclude that it was not reasonable for Stacker to rely on that advice, or that Stacker relied on the advice because it suited his purpose in trying to evade the truth.

A defendant's reliance on legal advice not to put forward relevant facts could be seen as reasonable by a court. But this would apply only if there were 'soundly based objective' or 'good' reasons for that advice. The following could be considered 'good reasons':

- little or no disclosure of evidence by the police so that the solicitor cannot usefully advise the defendant;

- the case is so complex, or relates to matters so long ago, that no sensible immediate response is feasible;

- the suspect has substantial difficulty in responding as a result of factors such as ill-health, mental disability, confusion, intoxication, or shock.

A52 Interviewees can sometimes move from refusal to cooperation within the course of an interview and may begin to answer some or all questions. (Although if this change occurs, the solicitor is likely to either intervene or seek a private consultation to remind his or her client of the advice to remain silent during the interview.)

Here, Pc Singh is doing his job perfectly well; he is polite, logical, and relaxed. He should proceed with his questioning as planned. He probably picked up from the pre-briefing with Stacker's solicitor that she would advise him to make no comment to any of the points put to him. Pc Singh has quite properly drawn the attention of both Stacker and the solicitor to the implications of refusal to answer questions. Pc Singh seems calm and continues to be in control of the situation, and does not appear to be intimidated by the solicitor, despite the fact that Stacker is refusing to answer questions.

In relation to the other witnesses mentioned by Pc Singh, the solicitor might intervene and ask if written statements have already been taken from them (unlikely), and comment that the interviewing officer cannot presume to know the content of their statements if they have not yet been written. However, Pc Singh knows that the absence of a written formal statement from witnesses does not justify 'silence' on the part of the accused. Adverse inference from silence may still apply (see answer 51, above). It is entirely appropriate for Pc Singh to base his questions on the first accounts provided by the staff at the supermarket.

A53 Pc Singh could offer Mr Jones a prepared written disclosure outlining the key facts (and withholding information or evidence he chooses). However, Mr Jones is likely to enquire beyond the brief notes and explanation and so Pc Singh must plan how he will deal with additional questions from the solicitor—or decline to do so, with reasons.

Pc Singh could consider taping his planned pre-interview disclosure to Mr Jones (to be recommended in serious cases) to thwart any later attempt by the defence to use justification for silence based on lack of disclosed material. In any event, Mr Jones might himself decide to tape the pre-interview disclosure meeting.

A54 Pc Singh should explain to Mr Jones, the solicitor, that he appreciates the professional role of a solicitor or legal adviser, but that that role does not extend to answering the suspect's questions for him.

In exceptional circumstances a solicitor can be required to leave an interview if his or her conduct is such that an interview cannot be conducted properly. Where this occurs the interview should cease and the custody officer should be informed. A senior police officer will need to be informed (at least at inspector rank or above, but preferably at superintendent rank). A decision to require a solicitor to withdraw is a very unusual and serious event and the decision will need to be based on evidence that would satisfy a court that it was reasonable and proper (see PACE Code of Practice C para 6.11).

A55 The suspects have now been in custody for six hours. Although they may be kept for a further eighteen hours it is now 18.00 and they are entitled to eight hours of uninterrupted sleep, meals, and exercise periods. If there is a need for one or more of the suspects to be detained beyond 24 hours then plans need to be made now and a superintendent put on notice that a period of extended detention to thirty-six hours might be necessary. However, in the circumstances described in this scenario it is unlikely that such a request would be made or granted.

A56 The custody officer imposes the following conditions.

- None of the three suspects can, either directly or indirectly, contact a named person or persons, for example each other or known witnesses. This will probably mean no contact whatsoever, including by telephone, text, email, fax, or letter or through another person.

- The suspects must not go to a named place, for example the shopping areas involved in the alleged offence(s). This is usually given as a specific address, but may also be a street, a town, an area, or even a whole county. Sometimes the condition will state that the defendant must not go within a specified distance of a named place. Exceptions are made for legitimate reasons, for example health needs or to visit his or her solicitor.

- The suspect must reside at a named address, normally his or her home address.

- The suspect must report to a named police station on a given day (or days) at a stated time, for example every weekday morning at some time between 08.30 and 10.00.

The conditions the custody officer applies are proportionate and reasonable in the circumstances, and he is satisfied that 'bail' is appropriate; the 'threshold test' has been met.

A57   Pc Dunn might consider using his experiences as the basis for:

- an entry in his Learning Diary (eg under Phase 3, Supervised Patrol) contained within his SOLAP;

- as the basis for evidence towards completion of the Police Action Checklist, under the headings of patrol (demonstrate communication with control rooms), demonstrate correct handling of exhibits, demonstrate lawful search (vehicles), disposal (convey a suspect into custody), and custody officer procedures (present a suspect to custody in accordance with force procedures);

- discussion during his next Learning Development Review.

In addition, it is also possible that Pc Dunn will have accumulated evidence (eg through using copies of his PNB entries) towards at least some of the following NOS elements:

AB1.1   Develop and maintain communication with people.

BE2.1   Provide initial support to victims, survivors and witnesses.

CA1.1   Apply principles of reasonable suspicion or belief.

CA1.2   Use law enforcement actions proportionately.

CA1.3   Use law enforcement actions fairly.

CD1.2   Respond to incidents.

2K1.1   Escort detained persons.

2K2.1   Present detained persons for custody process.

Test Yourself

And finally, a quick look at the requirements for a lawful arrest.

According to PACE Code of Practice G para 2.1, a lawful arrest requires two elements. Solve the anagrams to fill in the gaps. Each group of words in capitals is one word when solved correctly.

A person's VEIN MEN VOLT or suspected involvement or DATE TEMPT involvement in the SEEN MELT of a criminal offence and A LEASE BORN grounds for believing that the person's arrest is SCARY SEEN.

Answers to Knowledge Check Questions

K1 c   K2 d   K3 a   K4 c   K5 c

Answers to Test Yourself

VEIN MEN VOLT—Involvement

DATE TEMPT—Attempted

SEEN MELT—Elements

A LEASE BORN—Reasonable

SCARY SEEN—Necessary

References

ACPO (2005a) *Guidance on the Management, Recording and Investigation of Missing Persons*
—— (2005b) *Major Incident Room Standard Administrative Procedures (MIRSAP)* (Wyboston: NCPE)
—— (2006) *Murder Investigation Manual* (Wyboston: NCPE)
—— (2008) *Guidance on investigating domestic abuse*, available at <http://www.acpo.police.uk/asp/policies/Data/Domestic_Abuse_2008.pdf> (last accessed 20 Sept 2009)
ASH (2009) *ASH Facts at a Glance*, available at <http://www.ash.org.uk/files/documents/ASH_93.pdf> (last accessed 18 Sept 2009)
Bamfield, J (2007) *Global Retail Theft Barometer*, available at <http://www.retailresearch.org/theft_barometer/index.php> (last accessed 16 Sept 2009)
Bryant, R and Bryant, S (eds) (2009) *Blackstone's Student Police Officer Handbook 2010* (Oxford: Oxford University Press)
Cape, E (2006) *Police Station Advice Advising on Silence*, Criminal Practitioners' Newsletter Special Edition, January 2006 No 63 (London: Law Society)
CEOP (2009) *Offenders exploit a converged environment*, available at <http://www.ceop.gov.uk/mediacentre/pressreleases/2009/ceop_07092009a.asp> (last accessed 18 Sept 2009)
CJS (2006) *Working with Intimidated Witnesses (CJS 2006)*, available at <http://frontline.cjsonline.gov.uk/_includes/downloads/guidance/victims-and-witnesses/06_November_20_Working_witness_manual.pdf> (last accessed 21 Sept 2009)
Cook, T and Tattersall, A (2008) *Blackstone's Senior Investigating Officer's Handbook* (Oxford: Oxford University Press)
Flanagan, R (2008) *The Review of Policing by Sir Ronnie Flanagan: Final Report* (London: Home Office)
Hodgkinson J et al (2009) *Reducing gang related crime: a systematic review of 'comprehensive' interventions*, available at <http://eppi.ioe.ac.uk/cms/Default.aspx?tabid=2444&language=en-US> (last accessed 18 Sept 2009)
Home Office (2001) *Diary of a Police Officer*, Home Office, Police Research Series Paper 149 (London: Home Office)
—— (2009a) *Crime in England and Wales 2008/09*, available at <http://www.homeoffice.gov.uk/rds/pdfs09/hosb1109vol1.pdf> (last accessed 18 Sept 2009)
—— (2009b) *Domestic Violence Mini-site*, online available at <http://www.crimereduction.homeoffice.gov.uk/violentcrime/dv01.htm> (last accessed 20 Sept 2009)
IAS (2009a) *Adolescents and Alcohol*, available at <http://www.ias.org.uk/resources/factsheets/adolescents.pdf> (last accessed 17 Sept 2009)
—— (2009b) *Drinking and Driving IAS Factsheet*, available at <http://www.ias.org.uk/resources/factsheets/drink_driving.pdf> (last accessed 16 Sept 2009)
Joseph Rowntree Foundation (2008) *Young people and territoriality in British cities*, available at <http://www.jrf.org.uk/publications/young-people-and-territoriality-british-cities> (last accessed 18 Sept 2009)
Scarman, Lord (1981) *Report into the Brixton Disorders* (Cmnd 8427)
Scottish Government (2007) *Drinking and Driving 2007: Prevalence, Decision Making and Attitudes*, available at <http://www.scotland.gov.uk/Publications/2008/03/04152525/0> (last accessed 18 Sept 2009)
Shepherd, E (1996) *Police Station Skills for Legal Advisers: Pocket Reference* (London: Law Society)
—— (2007) *Investigative Interviewing: The Conversation Management Approach* (Oxford: Oxford University Press)
Youth Justice Board (2003) *Groups, Gangs and Weapons*, available at <http://www.yjb.gov.uk/publications/Scripts/prodView.asp?idProduct=342&eP=> (last accessed 20 Sept 2009)
—— (2005) *MORI Five-Year Report: An analysis of Youth Survey Data*, available at <http://www.yjb.gov.uk/publications/Resources/Downloads/MORI5yr.pdf> (last accessed 21 Sept 2009)

Index

Index

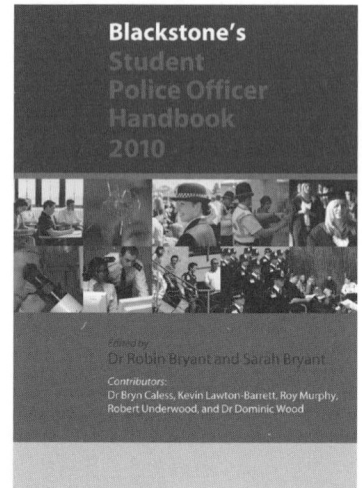